# THE BOOK OF ELDERS

# THE BOOK OF
# ELDERS

*The Life Stories of Great American Indians*

*as told to Sandy Johnson*

*Photographed by Dan Budnik*

HarperSanFrancisco

*A Division of HarperCollinsPublishers*

Text design by David Bullen

FIRST HARPERCOLLINS PAPERBACK EDITION PUBLISHED IN 1994

---

Library of Congress Cataloging-in-Publication Data

The book of elders : the life stories of great American Indians / as told to Sandy Johnson : photographed by Dan Budnik. —1st ed.

p.   cm.

ISBN 0-06-250837-7 (pbk. alk. paper)

1. Indians of North America—Biography.  2. Shamans—United States—Biography.  3. Indians of North America—Religion and mythology.  4. Indians of North America—Medicine.  I. Johnson, Sandy.

E89.B66  1994

970.004'97'0099—dc20                                            93-43639

CIP

---

94  95  96  97  98  ❖  RRD(H)  10  9  8  7  6  5  4  3  2  1

This edition is printed on acid-free paper that meets the American National Standards Institute Z39.48 Standard.

TO MY MOTHER

# CONTENTS

# ACKNOWLEDGMENTS

My profound thanks go not only to those who appear in this book, but to the many others who have encouraged, advised, and supported this project. Among them: Craig Carpenter and his wife, Sharon Laurence, Peter and Cindy Catches, Hildegarde Catches, Charlotte and Basil Brave Heart, Mildred and Emery Holmes, Tom Tarbet, Byron Pickett, Pat Fransceschini, Robin Young Bear, Jeanette Cypress, Lisa Snow, Glen Wassen, Cliff Gardner; Sandy Sacher, for the many hours of faithful transcribing; Glenn Schiffman; Joanne Baldinger and Catherine Butler for editorial assistance, Glen and Connie Tallio, Pat Locke, Peter Tadd, Janice Rouse, Jeffrey Reiss, D.B., Mark Robinson, for his patient technical support, and to my editor, Amy Hertz; her assistant, Rachel Lehmann-Haupt; and production editor Luann Rouff.

My thanks to those who on occasion made the journey with me: Ingrid Nelson, Neale Ward, Marsha Downey. And to those whose countless kindnesses kept me on the path: Frank Hladkey, Bill Johnson, Anthony Johnson, Elly Paulus, Carylon Stone, Melinda Morrison, and Servando Trujillo.

My deepest gratitude, in memorium, to Tish Hewitt, who cared so very much.

# INTRODUCTION

The red man is alone in his misery. We behold him now on the verge of extinction, standing on his last foothold . . . and soon he will be talked of as a noble race who once existed but have passed away.

GEORGE ARMSTRONG CUSTER,
in his term paper for his ethics class at West Point

Today, seven generations later, you turn to us as your own culture is failing. The land you took from us, tricked us out of, is becoming too poisoned to feed you. Your rivers and streams are dying. I wonder, why do you turn to us now? Is it because through it all we never stopped praying? Never stopped beating our drums, dancing and singing songs to the Creator? And that somehow, somehow, you couldn't silence us?

SIOUX ELDER, Rosebud reservation

My three-year journey through Indian country had its unlikely beginnings in the bedroom of my Manhattan apartment on what I thought must be the darkest night of my life. The two preceding years had been filled with loss. My father and brother had died within a year of each other, the novel I had been working on for more than two years had been shelved, putting me in financial difficulties, and I was holding myself to blame for the failure of yet another relationship.

And lately I had been having serious misgivings about the biography I was researching on Katharine Drexel, the "millionaire nun" who is a candidate for canonization for her life's work building schools for Indians a century ago. My knowledge of Indian history and culture was scant. I'd read little besides textbook versions written by non-Indians, and like most pre–*Dances-with-Wolves,* East Coast urbanites, what I knew of Indians I'd learned from Hollywood. Had these boarding schools succeeded in christianizing the Indians and bleaching them white? If so, did that make this woman a saint or a misguided zealot? It was indeed a dark night.

What happened next might be explained as a dream except that in my numbed state I know my eyes weren't closed. Suddenly, a bright, white light flashed like lightning across the darkened room. I turned to the window expecting to see a storm, but the night outside was clear. I could glimpse stars between the rooftops. The light was in my room. I turned back and stared wide-eyed, terrified, wondering what form of madness had seized me, when suddenly, in the very center of the light, a man's face appeared. It was unmistakably that of an Indian: gaunt, with deeply etched lines, high, strong cheekbones, an arched nose, and long, straggly hair. But what kept me from screaming out and reaching for the bedside lamp were his eyes. They gazed at me, wise and compassionate, and reminded me of my father's. His hands reached out to me as if to take my face, and then, just as suddenly, the light and the face were gone.

Oddly, the next day I did not think about what I had seen. A week later I was at the Clinique counter at Saks Fifth Avenue shopping for a skin moisturizer when a thought startled me: *I have to go find out for myself.*

My journey to Indian reservations across North America began in South Dakota in July of 1989, the time of the Sun Dances. I flew to Rapid City and rented a car. I looked at the map and saw that Route 44 would take me through the Badlands and past the monument at Wounded Knee.

A midsummer sun was just beginning to set, casting pink shadows on the oyster-gray cliffs and majestic sand carvings that rose from the clay floor of the Badlands. The land stretched before me for several miles, a pale moon rising full as the sun blazed into the horizon. Two horses stood motionless on top of a butte, their coats brilliant in the now coppery afterglow.

I drove out of the Badlands and into the high open plains. The first Indian community was Manderson, a village of trailers and tar-paper shacks with broken windows, the skeletons of cars and trucks in treeless front yards. In startling contrast, a clean, white clapboard church sat surrounded by a neatly clipped lawn. A few miles farther south on Route 28 was Porcupine Butte, where a sign read: Chief Big Foot Surrenders. I learned later this was where

Chief Big Foot's band of Minnecojous—more than two hundred men, women, and children—headed for sanctuary at Pine Ridge and was captured by the Seventh Cavalry and herded to Wounded Knee Creek. A few miles farther I came to another historic marker: Wounded Knee Massacre. One hundred years later, the small church on the knoll overlooking Wounded Knee had served as headquarters for members of the American Indian Movement (AIM) at Wounded Knee II, during the tragic, violent occupation following the Trail of Broken Treaties. Two Indians and one federal marshal were killed, and many Indians were seriously wounded during the siege.

Finally, I reached Highway 18 and a sign that pointed to the Rosebud Indian Reservation to the east and to the Pine Ridge Indian Reservation to the west. Katharine Drexel had built schools in both places; I decided my journey would begin at Rosebud.

I don't know what I expected an Indian reservation to look like, but I was not prepared for the ordinariness of the Housing and Urban Development (HUD) houses on treeless streets, for the discarded pickups and cars strewn everywhere like rusted beer cans. Nothing particularly "Indian," just poverty American-style.

Then I found a powwow in progress. The dancers, some of them tiny children, were in full regalia, swooping and whirling like exotic birds, their moccasin-clad feet padding the ground to the beat of drums and the loud, high-pitched songs. I looked at the people in the stands and saw for the first time the faces of Indian country.

"You look like someone who's woke up in the wrong dream."

Startled, I turned to see a tall, lanky Indian in blue jeans and buckskin vest, a cowboy hat over long braids.

"Where're you from?" he asked.

"New York," I answered.

"Come all the way out here to look at us wild Indians?" His smile teased, but his eyes were hidden behind mirrored sunglasses.

"I've come to talk to elders," I said, the words sounding somehow foolish to my ears.

"Well, count this your lucky day, lady, here comes my uncle. He's a real medicine man too, honest injun."

I shot him a wary glance then looked to see where he was pointing. A small, round-faced man in a checkered shirt and broad-brimmed hat was being helped to a seat by two young Japanese women. A moment later I was being tugged by the hand to where the old man sat.

"Hello, Uncle. This here lady's come all the way from New York City to meet a medicine man."

The old man looked up at me with eyes the color of blackberries and puffed his cigarette. "Never trust a medicine man who wears a watch or wants your money," he said.

The hand that was holding the cigarette wore a two-inch-thick, stainless steel watch that all but dwarfed his arm. The blackberry eyes laughed. "And look out for coyotes." I still didn't get it. "Coyotes," he repeated. "The trickster."

The Japanese women were smiling, yet somehow I was not certain they understood. "These girls came here to study with me," he said in a gravelly voice. "I doctored their parents when I went to Japan last year to work on people with bad scars from Hiroshima." The women nodded, still smiling. "Faces good now. All healed."

I spent a week in Rosebud. I visited Katharine Drexel's school, St. Francis, and spoke to priests and Indian elders, each telling their own very different versions of the effects of the boarding school system.

Robert Steed, the medicine man I first met, introduced me to my first sweat lodge ceremony, to my first Yuipi healing ceremony, and to the very special brand of Lakota humor. In answer to my question about whether he doctored people at the local hospital, he said, "Heck no. Too many moonwalkers around that place." *Moonwalkers?* A grandmother explained to me that Robert was referring to women in their "moontime" (menstruating), who are too powerful for a medicine man to be around.

I had planned to interview this very special man formally for this book; alas, I was too late. In the summer of 1992, just before Sun Dance, Robert Steed died.

From Rosebud I went to Pine Ridge, the first Indian reservation Katharine Drexel had visited exactly one hundred years ago, where she met Chief Red Cloud. The old chief, despairing for his people, told her he wished to establish a school for the children, and he wanted the Black Robes (priests) as teachers.

Pine Ridge, population sixteen thousand, covers fifteen miles—nearly two million acres of nameless roads, most of them unpaved and rutted. "Town" consists of the white-owned Sioux Nation Supermarket, a laundromat, a post office, a gas station, and a convenience store. There is no public transportation on the reservation, yet only a fifth of all households have a car. Unemployment is at 90 percent, and Shannon County leads the nation in poverty. Pine Ridge is America's Soweto.

It was growing dark; I drove across the Nebraska border to the nearest town and spent the night in a motel. Early the next morning I got back on the highway and headed north of town, past the Public Health Hospital to the Holy Rosary Mission, also known as Red Cloud Mission and School. I stopped and got out of my car. The stately stone and brick mission is set among quiet, tree-lined walks and serene gardens. I noticed the name above one of the doors, Drexel Hall, and wandered in and found an art gallery and gift shop that displayed the work of local Indian artists. I introduced myself to Brother Simon, a tall, bearded, black-robed man who runs the gallery, and explained the purpose of my visit. He eyed me carefully, puffing on a pipe, then took me to meet Robert Brave Heart, the principal of the school and a Lakota Sioux.

I was invited to midday meal in the dining hall and was seated next to a young Jesuit who asked me such provocative and intelligent questions about the biography that I found myself confiding my concerns about the "saintliness" of Katharine Drexel's life and the schools she founded. He expressed his opinion that my concerns were healthy ones and added, soto voce, "Go for it. The story needs to be told."

Indians are invisible to most of white society. They are not our bank tellers or grocery store clerks; they do not wait on us at restaurants. We don't stand in line with them at the check-out counters of supermarkets. I only realized this after living in Santa Fe, where Indians are so much a part of that city's culture, and then on a trip back to New York, where Indians are not part of America's great melting pot. Over lunch in a New York restaurant, a writer friend asked me what I was working on. When I said a book on Indian elders, the response was an amazed, "Are there still real Indians?" Real, meaning unacculturated, is what I suppose he meant. I admitted I had never given the question much thought either until this recent series of events had sent me on my own odyssey into Indian country.

Actually, there are more than 350 Indian reservations tucked away throughout North America. They lie hidden from the casual eye of the white traveler, on dusty, unmarked roads miles beyond the highways and shopping malls of modern America. Sometimes there is a sign marking the boundary of a reservation. More often the only indication that one has left the white world is the abrupt change of scenery: Post and rail fences surrounding white, frame farmhouses give way to flimsy trailers enclosed by trampled wire fencing. Instead of a Ford Escort in the driveway there is a pickup with its broken windows taped closed—an "Indian car."

On most of these reservations lives an elder. Not defined by age or gender, an elder is one who carries the knowledge of the tradition and wisdom of the heart, one who walks in truth and dignity no matter how poor, in humility no matter how revered. An elder serves the people, even when his or her own larder is down to the last sack of coffee, even when the body aches with fatigue. Even when there is nothing left to give, there is always an open door, an open heart. Some elders heal with a knowledge of natural medicine not yet known or recognized by the dominant culture. Some heal with a spirituality worlds beyond many of those who don black robes and preach on Sundays. Some heal with a song. Their places of work and worship are the sweat lodges, the mountains and streams, and by the tallest redwood and the smallest seedling. Their colleagues are the eagle, stones, corn, tobacco, and water. Their teacher is the fire.

*Unma'ciya'tan* is a Lakota Sioux word that means "from the other side, from the other world." Elders who are medicine men and women, through repeated fasts and vision quests, perceive and communicate with the "other side." In these meditations, they receive teachings and healing knowledge. Some are born into families of medicine people; others learn song and ceremony and the use of herbs from teachers who pass along medicine bundles to their apprentices.

Today, with white society's current fascination with shamans, a medicine man's demeanor is carefully observed by members of his tribe. He is harshly criticized if he leaves the reservation to charge money for ceremony, or if he engages in sexual misconduct with the white women who come seeking guidance, sometimes making him their guru. He would be similarly judged for attracting a side-show type of publicity.

Medicine women work primarily with herbs, roots, and hands-on healing. They treat psychological problems with their wisdom and compassion, and with their gift of "second sight."

Spiritual leaders, or holy men, are also healers. And they are the priests and prophets who heal illnesses of the soul. Not all medicine people are open to whites. One Sioux elder said, "First they took our land, now they want our pipe . . . all these wannabees, these New Agers, come with their crystals and want to buy a medicine bag to carry them around in. If you want to learn our ways, come walk the red road with us, but be silent and listen."

As young children, these elders witnessed their lands being taken away and saw their major food sources, buffalo and game, disappear. They watched their people die of disease and starvation. They saw railroad tracks cut through their homeland, destroying their hunting grounds. In silence they wept. The government banned the practice of their religion and ruled that all children from the age of six be taken from their homes and placed in government or religious boarding schools. These children were taught that Indians would always be second-class citizens until they left the reservations and moved into mainstream society. They were told that their own culture should die. In textbooks, they read that their parents and grandparents were savages—jobless, lawless, and Godless.

Misguided missionaries, confusing humiliation with humility, punished them for speaking their own language and mocked their "pagan superstitions," leaving in their wake seven generations of dysfunctional families. As a result, today's men and women in their thirties and forties—tomorrow's elders—have struggled with drugs and alchoholism.

To break the curse of this legacy, many of tomorrow's elders are teaching their children to take pride in their tradition. They encourage education, but education balanced with spirituality, which includes instruction about their own culture, traditions, and language.

The focus of this book is on the traditional elders, whose lives are dedicated to preserving and protecting their culture for the children of the Seventh Generation. They speak of the challenges that face today's youth, who, according to prophecy, will lead the people back to their traditions.

Many of the elders included in this book appear in print for the first time, and some speak of matters that until now have been considered too sacred to share. They speak out now in the name of Mother Earth, who, according to their prophecies and empirical evidence, verges on destruction. They share with us their knowledge of healing—ways to heal ourselves, each other, and the planet.

Many books have been written about the American Indian by non-Indians; this one is written by elders in their own words. They speak openly of their personal struggles to stay on the path against impossible odds. Their stories, of what they have lost and of what they have fought to save, are both tragic and heroic. They provide a deep and profound look into the lives and hearts of these extraordinary—often supernatural—men and women.

# SIOUX

## PETE CATCHES: THE SACRED DREAM

*While in Pine Ridge I met several Lakota elders. I kept hearing about Pete Catches, an Oglala holy man and medicine man, and was told I should go and talk to him. I was given directions: "Just over that rise there, at the second big tree turn left, then look for the rock on the right. Can't miss it."*

*I missed it repeatedly over the next few days. Then on the fourth day, as I was preparing to leave Pine Ridge, I decided to give it one more try. This time I noticed a tree I hadn't seen before and a rock I was certain hadn't been there either. A sand-covered road twisted and turned its way up a rather steep hill, too steep for the low undercarriage of my rental car. Its wheels spun, digging deeper ruts in the sand, and the bottom scraped the road. I might have given up had there been a place to turn around. But then at the top of the hill I spotted a trailer, an arbor of pine boughs beside it, and suddenly, mysteriously, the car rolled out of its ditch and made the rest of the way easily.*

*Two cinder blocks formed the steps to a flimsy aluminum door; I knocked timidly. From inside came a man's voice asking who was there. "My name is Sandy," I answered, not quite sure how else to identify myself. "Just a minute. I'll put on my shirt." I waited. The door opened, his tall, slender frame standing partly in shadow. As he stepped down, I said "Hello" and stopped. I gasped, staring at his face. It was the face that had appeared to me in my New York apartment. He was looking at me with those same wise, compassionate eyes. I felt my throat tighten as I fought to hold back tears.*

*I started to explain, but he held up his hand and nodded. "I know," he said softly. "Come let's talk."*

*We sat underneath the arbor overlooking a wide expanse of the reservation, silent for a time. He likes to sit here in summer, he told me, to watch the sun rise and set.*

*"The moon is often still hanging in the sky when the sun rises." This he takes as a special sign. "I'm in a natural place," he said, "where the soul constantly expands in the presence of beauty."*

*He talked of a time when there will be oneness in the land, a true spiritual sharing between the Indian and the non-Indian. There was a stillness about him that was comforting. His long, slender hands rested easily on his knees, and as I began to speak he nodded, understanding, knowing.*

*I told him about the biography I was trying to write.*

*"The subject of the Indian schools is very complex and requires certain wisdom—perhaps more than you have at the moment," he said kindly. "I went to Holy Rosary here in Pine Ridge, the school your Katharine Drexel founded, but I ran away when I was nine. I was lucky; others had tried but were caught and dragged back."*

*Shyly, I asked if he had called me on this journey.*

*"Sometimes I appear as an eagle."*

*I waited for further explanation, but none was forthcoming. I asked if he thought I should drop the project. After a long pause he said, "Understanding comes in its own time."*

*We talked on for hours, long after the sun had gone down. In the Lakota [Sioux] language there is no word for time. I would learn this and much more in many talks with the man I came to call "Grandfather" over the next four years.*

In days long ago, in the old world, before the time of the white man, this land was known to us as Turtle Island. The grass was waist deep on the prairie where the buffalo grazed. Ferocious animals, bears and wolves that ran in packs, threatened the herd. The bull buffalos would stand at the perimeter as sentinels, ever watchful, guarding the females and young ones.

As the legend goes, the oldest of the bull buffalos was standing there one cold and windy day when he heard a voice crying in the wind. He put his head down close to the earth to try to follow the sound. It was difficult because of the howling of the wind.

"Help me," the voice cried out. "I'm hungry, I'm tired, I'm weak, I'm cold . . ."

The voice sounded pitiful, but the old bull couldn't make out what it was. It kept saying over and over, "I'm hungry, I'm tired, I'm weak, I'm cold." He kept following that sound until he came upon a clot of blood. It was then that a great transformation took place. The

Great Spirit was working there to guide the Lakota people to the future that was to come, because as the legend goes the buffalo adopted this blood clot as his younger brother.

The buffalo told the blood clot, "You say you're hungry and cold and weak and tired. I'll make you my younger brother and you can have all of me. I'll sacrifice my whole being that you may live, that you won't be hungry or cold. You will live and be strong. Look at me. Look at the world. All that you see is food to me. And when the greatest blizzard comes and it is bitter cold, I face the north wind, that's why I have so much fur. I'm never cold. Use my hide to make your tipi and your moccasins and clothing. Use my flesh to eat, survive, and live and to be strong. And up here on the hump there is medicine. Use that to cure your people. My blood is the same as yours. We are blood brothers. You may live on my blood." So from this clot of blood came the Lakota people.

We are brothers with the Buffalo Clan, and it is the Buffalo that the Great Spirit chose to bring the Sacred Pipe to the Indian people.

There's a ranch nearby that raises buffalo. It's where we get our buffalo for the Sun Dance. I had been Sun Dancing for eight years. One year I told them I wanted to go with them when they butcher the buffalo. My son, Peter, was with me. We went in two cars, one a pickup carrying canvases, towels, knives. The group selected a two-year-old bull, and the rancher shot it. We drove up close and started skinning it. But first they bled it. When they got the guts out, I took a cup and filled it with the buffalo's blood. They were all looking at me. I drank all of it. My son asked me for the empty cup, and I handed it to him. He filled it with blood and drank it, too. The others were nearly gagging. One went around the pickup and threw up. And he's a full-blooded Indian! This is what the government has done to us.

It is our custom to use buffalo blood to paint the base of the Sun Dance Tree. This particular time I was asked to paint it. I took a bunch of sage, cut it in half, and dipped it in the pail of blood, using my hands to paint the tree. We want to be so clean; do we detest the blood of an animal that we use in a sacred rite in the Sun Dance? I eat with my hands, I work with them. When I finished I wiped my face with the blood. We went to the ceremony and to the feast afterwards and prepared for the morning ceremony. I was in charge of the tree ceremony. I was the one to fill the pipe. The buffalo's blood is part of my blood.

I never wanted the gift of medicine that the Creator gave to me, but then I had a dream that I knew was a sacred dream:

I was Sun Dancing, and I was crying the whole time, crying without end. . . . I had a pain in the upper part of my leg that was too much, too much. The worst pain I've ever known. The dream was so clear, even to the smallest detail. The songs that were sung, the tree as it stands . . . I look up at it . . . the flag is flying, the offering flag, from it . . . there were five singers. . . . I am pierced. The rawhide thong that pierces the skin over my breast is attached to a rope tied high on the Sun Dance Pole. . . . All day long I struggle to free myself, dancing, one leg all but useless, in step to the drums. The skin stretches and stretches, but it never breaks, never comes free. . . . A storm approaches and the sky grows dark. I raise my pipe to the heavens. The storm parts in two . . . and the sky above the Sun Dance grounds is suddenly blue. . . .

I spent sixteen years trying to get away from that dream. I knew what it was telling me, and I didn't want it. I ran from it. My father and his father and his father before him were all medicine men. They tell me my father was a good medicine man, but that he couldn't live with the knowledge of whether or not someone he had treated was going to live or die.

I was born in 1912, right at the peak of the movement to Christianize the Indian. Catches is a name the government gave us in place of our Indian names. We were originally Hunkpapa from the Sitting Bull band, but my grandfather came to the Oglala tribe to get married, and that's where my branch of the family comes from. One great-grandfather went to Arapaho country and got married there; my other grandfather went to the Cheyenne tribe in Montana, and he got married there. My father was a medicine man until he decided to become a Christian instead. I, on the other hand, was baptized a Christian but turned back to my own religion and eventually became a medicine man.

I moved from place to place—Colorado, Nebraska, Wyoming, finding work on ranches—anything to run from that dream and what it had told me I must do. For two years I was on the tribal council; for five years I served as a catechist in the Catholic church. I even tried to enlist in the service during World War II, but I was rejected because of a scar on my lung that I got from the Spanish flu in 1917. The dream followed me wherever I went.

First I took jobs breaking horses. I was pretty good at it because I have a lot of patience. I knew that whenever you take a horse from his home you'd better watch that animal closely because the first chance he gets he's going to take off for his home ground. But when I brought in a new horse, I'd corral him with the other horses. Of course, the other horses wouldn't like the new one; they'd try to bite him and push him aside. But I talked to the new horse, "You stay around here. This is your home now, and you and I are going to work together. I will teach you something, friend, and you'll be able to use what I teach you in your life. They'll like you for that, so stick around." And then I'd turn him loose. None of my horses ever took off; they stayed right with me.

My father-in-law, whose ranch it was, used to ask me, "How is it that before you came we could never have new horses come to our place without their sneaking away the first chance they had?"

I didn't get paid for training horses, I just had the use of the new horse. I'd talk to him, and I knew he understood me. I'd keep him until I saw that I could trust him, then I'd return him. Such was my life then.

I had a large family, and sometimes we would run out of food. Then I'd have to ride out on horseback to Nebraska to find seasonal work. When I had earned enough money for groceries, I'd come home and break horses again. Sometimes I'd be gone for two or three weeks at a time. Except for the dream that never stopped hounding me, I was content with my life.

In the 1950s, I worked in the Platte Valley in the sugar beet fields. My wife, Amelia, and my oldest daughter, Christine, who was a teenager then, were with me. It was a very large field. There were three families of Mexicans who worked there, too. They worked one side, we worked the other. We were slow, but the Mexicans were fast. We worked there day after day. I got along with those Mexican people. They'd call me over and we'd joke around; we'd share an orange or an apple. Sometimes they'd invite me to their place, but we were so tired after a day's work, we'd just eat and go right to bed.

One day one of the men came over to where we were staying. "I guess this is our last day here," the Mexican said. "Our women folks will stay here. But every year we men work at the sugar factory, and tomorrow it opens. Will you look after our family?" he asked. So from time to time I'd look in on them.

One day I heard screams coming from where they were working. I dropped my hoe and ran to see what was wrong. The women were jumping up and down, pointing to something on the ground. It was a bull snake. He was coiled and ready to strike. I realized he had probably been fast asleep when they accidentally turned him over with their hoe. That snake was mad, really mad. I explained that the farmers keep them around to take care of the bugs and the mice. I picked him up to take him away from the field. I told him not to be frightened, but he was still mad. He wasn't paying attention to me; he was mad at those women. I put him around my neck. He was full grown, a big one. As I walked away, the snake stuck his head around my shoulder and kept glaring at them. He reminded me of an angry child. I took him over to the next field and put him down. Then I talked to the snake. "Don't go back there now until we're finished working." My wife and daughter had stopped their work to watch me.

Quite a coincidence occurred after that. We had moved back to the reservation. I was on a baseball team, and every evening we went to practice. One evening on the way home, I cut across the hills and saw my girls jumping up and down, running toward the house. I knew exactly what it was. I took off down the hill, and sure enough it was a rattlesnake. Amelia was in the house cooking. She came running out. I grabbed the snake and killed it. Amelia got mad. She accused me of showing off for the good-looking Mexican women by playing around with the snake and carrying it off, but "here you just go and kill the snake." "That was different," I explained. Back there they had a purpose, to get rid of bugs and mice, but here where the snake lives, we have our children. If I had taken him away, he

would have come back here, and somebody would get scared or bitten. One has to be in tune with nature.

I took a job at another ranch. The boss, McNurty, would buy wild, half-thoroughbred horses cheap and then hire a cowboy from Gordon, Nebraska, to break them.

One day seventeen wild horses were being unloaded from a huge van, and we all went over and sat on the fence railings to have a look at them. The boss asked me which one I liked best. I stood up on the top railing to watch the horses run in a circle. A dapple gray caught my eye. When the horses came around again, the gray was close to the rail. I jumped on him. He couldn't buck or run because he was crowded. But as soon as he got clear he did start bucking. When he got near enough to the railing, I fell over and hung onto the top railing to get off. They called me crazy. I didn't just tell him which horse I liked, I had to get on him to show him.

But all the time the dream was with me. It was right there beside me no matter what I did or where I went—the dream never left me. Finally, I had to give in to it. I guess I thought if I went through with it and lived out the dream once, I'd be released from it. And maybe I wouldn't have to become a medicine man. Up to then I had never Sun Danced, I had never intended to. But I made the commitment to dance that coming summer.

In the month when the moon rises as the sun is going down, and the chokecherries ripen, preparations for the Sun Dance begin. The lodge is put up, and arbors are built. Then a cottonwood tree is selected and marked with red paint. The medicine man who was conducting the ceremony invited me to go with him and the Sun Dance singers to cut down the tree. It is our custom that no portion of the sacred tree must ever touch the ground, so while it was being chopped down we all stood in line to catch it as it fell. I stood closest to the base of the tree.

It began to fall slowly at first. But then all of a sudden it came crashing down and landed on my leg, at the point of the thigh. "I'm caught!" I hollered, and they came rushing to me. Two or three of them raised the tree while the others freed my leg. The pain was excruciating. I saw sparks in my head, but I managed to limp my way back to camp, sweating all the while from the pain in my badly bruised leg.

We set up the tree and surrounded it with sweetgrass, sage, and bison hair. As a Sun Dancer, I was expected to show bravery, endurance, and integrity, so I continued on despite the pain.

That night I lay in bed unable to sleep. I took aspirin, three, four, five at a time, without relief. I cried and cried. I couldn't help it, the cries just came, all through the night. My bed was soaked with perspiration, and twice during the night I had to get up and change the sheets.

The next morning a young man who'd heard I needed help came and parked his car in front of my door and came to the side of my bed. He asked me how I felt. "I'm in great pain," I said. "But what shall I do? This is the day that came to me in a dream, and it's all happening as I dreamed it. So now I must go through with it." The young man picked me up and carried me like a baby to his car and closed the door.

Up to this point in my life I had never cried. Nothing could bring me to tears. I thought I had done all my crying when I was in Catholic school, when they whipped and punished me. The wrongs that were done in that school hurt me, and the pain remains with me still, but I never cried.

The participants were already gathered in the sweat lodge for the purification ceremony that precedes the Sun Dance. The young man drove around to the back of the lodge and removed his jacket. Again, he lifted me in his arms and carried me to the door of the lodge. Setting his jacket underneath me, he slid me inside.

I had never been in a sweat lodge before, I didn't know what the songs were about, I didn't even know what the medicine man prayed—all I could think of was the terrible pain. And all I could say was, Great Spirit, pity me. "*Tunkashila, onshimalaye.*"

Afterward, the young man came in and slid me out of the door of the lodge. I picked up my pipe, stood, and walked with him, limping, stopping from time to time to rest.

My brother had said, "You're foolish. You're in such pain. Postpone your commitment. Postpone it until next year, why don't you?"

I said, "No. This is exactly how I dreamed it would be. I must go through with it. If this day passes without me doing the thing I'm supposed to do, I'll regret it the rest of my life."

When I arrived at the arbor, the singing had just begun. I went and stood by the tree and said my prayer, "*Tunkashila, onshimalaye.*" Great Spirit, have pity on me. Then I walked around the tree and took my place and began the dance. I got through one round. The next round I was pierced with the rawhide deer thong. It was terrible, but it was exactly as I had dreamed it.

The rawhide thong that pierced the skin over my breast was attached to a rope tied high on the Sun Dance Pole. All day long I struggled to free myself, dancing in step to the drums, stretching the skin, but never able to break it. I danced, one leg all but useless. I had a very difficult time. The skin stretched more and more, and still the pain was not as severe as the pain in my leg.

This was the first Sun Dance ever held out in the country away from Pine Ridge. It was a dry camp; we had to carry our own water. At about three o'clock the sky began to grow dark. Suddenly, bolts of lightning were all around us. People began to get nervous. They knew if it rained hard, they'd never be able to get their cars out from that area to the blacktop road. So they were anxious to get going. As in the dream, I called to someone to bring me my pipe. "*Tunkashila, onshimalaye,*" I prayed. Tears streamed down my face as I held my pipe up toward the heavens and repeated the prayer, "*Tunkashila, onshimalaye.*"

Suddenly the clouds parted. Clearly, visibly. They parted dead center. One side of the storm went south, and the other went north. In both instances the storm did a great deal of damage. The part that went up north along the White River, through Kyle and Rosebud, brought hailstorms so bad they tore roofs off. The part that went to the south did damage, too. Hailstones damaged crops and cornfields. Some areas were flooded.

You see, the sacred pipe is very powerful, especially when you've been given a sacred dream, and when you use that power to interfere with nature it can make the spirits angry. That storm was an expression of nature, and who was I to part that storm? Something good that was coming for this portion of land I divided in two, and they in turn showed destruction. The spirits might have gotten angry enough to turn into a tornado.

In our culture, we look upon the spirits as one of us, one of the Lakota people who have gone before us. When we hear the rumble of thunder, we envision the spirits on horseback, galloping across the distances. When we see the lightning, we know their spears are aimed at something. They respect the pipe, so must we. We must not misuse the power of the pipe. I realized afterward, that when the storm had done its damage, that it was I who had caused it by parting it. And I thought, what if it had developed into something more serious? What if someone had gotten killed?

In the area of the Sun Dance only a few heavy drops fell, and the people settled down. The ceremony was completed in joy, with love in the hearts of everyone present. Even my older brother, who had thought me a fool not to postpone it, was happy. But there was something that no one who was there ever knew: The hurt, the pain that had caused me to cry all day long, all through that ceremony, had disappeared. When the Sun Dance was over, I walked away from the grounds, and I wasn't even limping.

This was the sacred dream, the gift that Tunkashila had given to me. At first I felt that if I lived out the dream as it was given to me, that would be the end of it. I could go back to living my normal life. But that was not to be. Because after that I began to receive visions in which I was given the medicine man's way.

After the Sun Dance, I did my first Pipe Fast, what some people call a vision quest or *hanblecheya*. First, I went into the sweat lodge for a purification ceremony, and then I was taken by my helpers to the place I had chosen. It was on the side of a hill, close to the top. I went to that fasting place with my whole heart in it. Fasting is the separation of the self from all things of the world. We leave our families and our work behind. We do not go there to rest or sleep; we use all our power to make sacrifices so that we may receive a sacred vision.

I stood and faced the four directions, my pipe raised in reverence to the Great Creator. It was just me, the sacred pipe, and the Great Spirit. Evening came, I wanted to sit. Night came, I was tired and wanted to lie down and sleep. I was hungry. But I kept standing. The pipe grew heavier and heavier; my arm got tired, and gradually it began to fall. It took all my strength to raise it up again. But this was my commitment.

The next day the sun was hot. So hot my shoulders and back felt like they were on fire. The skin on my face was burning. I folded my star quilt, our traditional blanket that we wrap ourselves in, into a square the size of a cushion and placed it on my head for a bit of shade.

It was on the third day, when the sun was way up past the noon hour, that it happened. I was standing holding my pipe up level with my eyes, staring beyond it. Suddenly, about twenty yards away, to the left of my pipe, I saw a man walking. I watched as he turned to the right and walked on, appearing on the other side of my pipe. Before him was a huge fire, like a sweat lodge fire. He walked slowly toward it and knelt, his back always to me. Then he carefully moved some sticks aside and reached into the fire with his bare hands. A moment later he removed his hands, and I saw he was holding two handfuls of hot coals. They gleamed red in his hands. The man then turned to the left and circled the fire, and I saw his face. I gasped. The man I was looking at was me. At that moment the figure and the fire dissolved, and I knew I had received a sacred vision.

On the fourth day, when I finished my fast, they came to take me back to the sweat lodge for a pipe ceremony. During the ceremony I told Frank Good Lance, a great medicine man who gave me my teachings, what I had seen. The old man sat silent, thinking for several moments, then he said, "This vision was meant for you alone, and in time you will understand the meaning of it."

I remember the time early in my life as a medicine man—after the Sun Dance and my Pipe Fast—that I was called in to heal an old man. I was in my forties by then. They were smudging the area, purifying it with sage, when I got there; I could see the smoke coming from the doorway. The family told me to come in; they were expecting me. I stepped inside, and the old man's son came forward, holding a chair. He led me to his father's bed, placed the chair beside it, and went to the bureau where the pipe was already filled, waiting for me. He got the pipe and lit it. I accepted it and puffed it. I sat there smoking, my head bowed, thinking and wondering with my closed eyes. I wanted to see God, the Creator, the Great Spirit in my mind's eye. I had something big to do, and I wanted to be worthy and humble to do it.

I felt somebody staring at me. I slowly raised my eyes and saw it was the old man lying there looking at my face. I could read his thoughts. Is this son of a bitch trying to cure me? Does this son of a bitch think he has the power to cure me? I closed my eyes again and kept on smoking. When I was finished I called a young man over.

"When the hot coals are ready, you bring the sage and crumbled sweetgrass and sprinkle them on the hot coals."

The young man cut off a piece of sweetgrass, crumbled it, and got some sage. At that time, every home on the reservation had wood fires; it was how they cooked. And they know boiling water is needed standing on the stove for a ceremony. So the stove was going full blast, and the water was boiling so that we could make the medicine.

I got up and walked slowly, very slowly, as I had in my vision during my Pipe Fast. I opened the firebox, reached in with my hands, and pulled out two handfuls of burning hot coals and walked slowly back to the bed. When I reached the bed, the young man stepped forward and placed the sage and sweetgrass on the hot coals, and I smudged the old man. When I was finished, I walked slowly back to the fire box, the door still open, and I put the coals back. No marks showed on my hands.

It was a terrible responsibility to bring that vision back into this physical world. I am committed to it till the day I die. This is what it is to have the power of a medicine man. I've done that Pipe Fast twice since, and I have one more to do yet before I die. I'm waiting to see when. My name became Petaga Yuha Mani, He Who Walks with Hot Coals in His Hands.

In 1976, when I was in Maui giving a talk at Hawaii University, I went to the beach one day wearing a hat and boots. Since I was the only person on the beach fully clothed, I drew a lot of attention. I noticed some people sitting in a circle staring at me, especially one young man with very bushy, long hair and a full beard. After a while he motioned to me to come over. I obliged. They were passing around this short little stub of a cigarette and sucking away on it. I didn't know anything about marijuana at the time, so I thought, these guys are really poor. They're even poorer than I am, to suck away on a little bitty stub. They even had some sort of a pincher to hold it so their lips didn't touch the paper.

The bushy one asked me where I was from, and I told him I was an Oglala medicine man from the Pine Ridge reservation. He said, "I had a vision. In this vision I've seen God, and he spoke to me and I spoke to him."

That got me mad. After all I've been through, the sacred dreams, the visions, the pipe fasts, and nowhere had I seen God. Here was this half-clad man with half-clad women sitting on either side of him sucking away on a piece of cigarette. I told him, "If you'd really seen God, and he'd spoken to you, you would not be here. You would be walking the highway trying to save souls, preaching his words, and healing the sick." He didn't answer me, and I walked away.

Nicholas Black Elk was my adopted uncle. Frank Good Lance was my teacher. They were both truly humble. One day early in the morning I was standing at my window looking out. There was a car stopped at my brother's place where Good Lance was staying. I saw some people go into the house. After a while they got in the car and drove off. So I knew he was alone. I went to see him. He said to me, "They all went to town; they won't be back for a long time. They left me my noon meal. I'm glad, because I wanted to talk to you." He got up and put on his coat, his hat, took his cane. "Come with me," he said.

He shut the door behind us, and we walked along the trail. We passed my house and went to where my sweat lodge was located. When I saw that's where he was headed, I assumed he was going to ask me to build a fire in preparation for a sweat, but he didn't. Instead he told me to sit down, and he sat facing me. A sweat lodge fireplace is a few feet from the lodge itself. Between the lodge and the fire pit, to the west of the doorway, is a mound of earth where the pipe is rested during the ceremony.

He pointed to the mound of earth and said, "I want you to use your mind to visualize what I'm going to tell you: This continent, this Turtle Island, has some very high peaks, and across the big waters in other lands there are some more huge mountains. But those are nothing. They are just the part of the earth that their height distinguishes as the earth's pinnacles. People who seek glory for themselves, who seek to conquer the laws of this physical world, scale those heights every month of the year. They write about it and talk about it to glorify their egos.

"But this little hill here," he said, pointing to the mound of earth, "This is the highest point in the world. This is our church, our way of salvation, where we will enter one day into the next world. This is the place where many good men and many good women have tried to scale this highest of mountains. They topple and roll down clear to the base. Little brother, use your pipe in a good way. Never do anything wrong. Use it to make the people happy and well. Heal their sicknesses, and when they fall, bring them back to the red road of life that is health and love. And whatever you do, little brother, try to get to the top of this huge mountain. Even if you have to crawl with your elbows until your elbows are raw, you must always keep your hands on that pipe. When you get to the top of this highest of mountains, there you will meet the Great Spirit. This is what I wanted to tell you."

Throughout the years I have remembered those words and have pictured him in my mind sitting there opposite me. Especially during the year 1991 that I just went through, when I was so sick. There was no joy in all of that year. I remembered what he said: Determination, throughout my life in all areas. The little pebbles on that hill are huge boulders which represent the problems of our everyday life.

In 1980, I was in the hospital after a serious operation and required a round-the-clock nurse. The doctors were not certain I would recover. One day the nurse was sitting in a chair next to my bed reading a book. I must have fallen asleep, because when I woke up she was bent over, dozing, the book open on her lap. I thought I heard something on my right. I moved my head to see what it was. There, standing beside my bed, was an old Indian. I could see him plainly. He had war paint on and wore a buckskin vest, a shirt that had no collar, and a string with some kind of ornament around his neck. There was a pouch of Bull Durham tobacco sticking out of his vest pocket, and a sash of some sort was around his waist. His pants were of buckskin.

He was looking down at me, and in Lakota he said, "When I was young I had twelve fingers. I was told I was to give one of those fingers to somebody who needed help. I did. Now I have eleven fingers. I was supposed to give one more to somebody, but I haven't until now. I've brought you that finger so that you can live."

On one hand he had five fingers, on the other he had six. The finger he gave me is unseen, but it's there.

[Pete holds up his right hand and spreads his fingers. The space between the fourth and fifth finger is wide, as though a finger were missing.]

From that moment on I recuperated quickly.

Last year, I was invited to Russia to lead a tree-planting ceremony with the children of Moscow. The day was cold and windy. I filled my pipe. The tree was already set up, but the hole hadn't been filled yet. There was a large crowd of people, children and adults. I had an interpreter, but of course he didn't know Lakota. I did the ceremony in my own language, then in English I told the interpreter, "These little children standing here, I want them to go first, to get a handful of dirt and throw it around the tree." He translated what I said to the children and they all moved forward. "You children gathered here, and Russia itself, will grow to see peace, and to learn to love one another. This tree is young; like you children, it will grow as you children grow."

I love this life, with all of its misery, with all of its pain. I lie in bed in my trailer house, suffering, unable to sleep at night. At first light showing in the east, I lie listening to the coyotes howling and the owls in the canyon hooting, and I do nothing but listen. Pretty soon, on the eaves of my house, little birds begin to sing their morning song, the waking song. And in my pain I see all of that in my mind. I see them half looking at me, thankful that I have arrived at another day. Tears stream down my face, and I sing a sacred song. My voice is weak and racked with pain and suffering, but I join in the glory of the coming day. Because I am a part of them, and it seems to me that they know.

# Arvol Looking Horse: tomorrow's elder

*Seventeen miles north of Eagle Butte, South Dakota, is the million-acre reservation of Green Grass, the place where the Sacred Pipe of the Lakota Sioux nation is kept hidden. Arvol Looking Horse is the Keeper of the Pipe, which has been in his family for nineteen generations.*

*The pipe was brought to the Sioux by the sacred White Buffalo Calf Woman. Its stem is made from a buffalo calf's lower leg bone, and eagle feathers and bird skins are tied to it. The pipe is kept wrapped in buffalo hair and red trade cloth; it is so brittle with age that it can no longer be smoked. The* chanupa *is the most sacred object of the Sioux. Its red stone is said to be their flesh and blood, their heart. Its bowl contains the whole universe.*

*Green Grass, population less than one hundred, stretches from Swiftbird to Cherry Creek. It is a peaceful, timeless place where horses roam free over verdant, rolling hills, which stay green throughout the year. The Moreau River flows through the reservation from the sacred Black Hills, creating underground springs and streams.*

*Carole Anne and Arvol live in a large, modern trailer with Carole Anne's nine-year-old daughter, Cante. Carole Anne and Arvol both travel extensively. Arvol has led prayer services at the United Nations and lectures at Harvard, Dartmouth, and Berkeley. During the Middle East crisis Arvol traveled to Baghdad to hold prayer ceremonies.*

*Carole Anne is a partner in an organization in Bismarck, North Dakota, the North Central Indian Technical Assistance Center II, which serves a seven-state area. She conducts workshops on education and parenting skills, and travels around the country for speaking engagements that seek to promote better understanding of the Lakota culture.*

*Together they strike a perfect balance. Arvol represents the ancient tradition; Carole Anne, the contemporary American Indian.*

I am the Keeper of the Sacred Pipe for the Lakota, Dakota, Nakota [Sioux] nation. We, the *ikce wicasa* ["common people"], have a way of life. Ever since I was young, I saw the healing strength of prayer. It pulled me through hard times. To survive on the reservation you have to learn how to cope in different ways, to learn the balance. Four is a sacred number for us. We were supposed to live the four stages of life. We learned to be humble and pray to *Wakan Tanka*.

When I was young, a black widow spider bit me. The venom started spreading and eating away at my skin. I remember my grandmother praying that I would live, and it was the prayer that pulled me through. But it left a bad scar on my face, which made me very shy

when I was growing up. I stayed away from people because I was ashamed of the scar. I rode my horse and spent time sitting on the hill in Green Grass, looking at the beauty of the land and thinking about how it must have been a long time ago. I'd feel secure and at peace. I'd find my center.

Another time, after my brother died, I decided I wanted to do something to honor him because he was so good in everything he did. At that time, I was just the opposite; I had no confidence. The day he was being buried, I thought about how he was so natural with horses and that he would have been the best rodeo rider. So I made a commitment to ride rodeo for him, in saddle bronco riding, which he loved.

The first time I put on spurs and got into the chute, I was so scared that I could hear my spurs rattling. I kept thinking how my brother always told me to be brave, so I tried to set my goals like he would have done. I started in small rodeos and eventually got into bigger and better ones. By 1980, I was into pro rodeo—until I got hurt in 1983.

The night before, I had ridden at Pine Ridge Rodeo, and I had drawn a good horse. The next day I went to the rodeo in Deadwood, but my body didn't feel quite up to it. I got ready anyway because there were a lot of friends from the reservation who had come to see me. I saddled my horse and was feeling good. I looked up at the grandstand. I got on the horse—he bucked and went straight up in the air. Then he spun around and fell backwards—right on top of me. I heard a crack in my backbone. When the horse stood up, I was just lying there, shaking. I couldn't feel my body. The ambulance came, and then I was lying there in the hospital. The doctor was telling me that I'd never walk again, that I was paralyzed from the neck down. I had broken three vertebrae, cracked one, and had a concussion.

I remembered my grandmother once saying to me that when a person is getting ready to go into the spirit world, their relatives come to them. At different times I would open my eyes and see them standing there.

Then the phone rang, and a voice—a spirit voice—said, "I'm your grandmother, and the people need you." This grandmother chewed me out about the rodeo and said I had done this to myself. I felt my mother and father entering the room, but I kept my eyes closed because I didn't know whether they were real or not. My dad started talking to me about the Sun Dance they were having. In my mind I kept thinking about my grandmother saying that it didn't matter how many people prayed for you, if you didn't pray for yourself, the prayers wouldn't be effective. So I was trying to relax my mind. I kept picturing the Sun Dance with all the people circling around the Tree of Life in the center. I prayed so much, humbly, from my heart.

When the Sun Dance was over, my bones healed back together. The doctors couldn't believe it. A week later I walked out of the hospital. I knew deep down in my heart that my prayers had been answered.

My grandmother used to tell me when you walk this balance of life you must pray for direction, because if it is not part of your life you will get hurt. In the mid-eighties we had a walk and a run to Pipestone, Minnesota, where the red stone for our Sacred Pipe comes from. From the blood of our ancestors, the elders say.

We have a prophecy called "Mending the Sacred Hoop." From the time of the Wounded Knee massacre, in 1890, to its centennial commemoration in 1990, it was like a concentration camp on the reservations. We could not practice our way of life until the Freedom of Religion Act of 1978. Today, we have a high rate of alcoholism on the reservations and a lot of suicides because of the lack of self-esteem and the lack of identity. But we set a goal for the year 2000 to be alcohol-free, and a lot of the people are working to get themselves back to our culture. So the prophecy is coming true, the sacred hoop of the nation is mending.

There was a time in my life I felt so low, I started drinking for about two weeks straight. I was alone, I didn't want to talk to anyone. I remember one night I was so drunk I took off and didn't remember anything. Next thing I knew I was lying inside a car, the car I had just wrecked. I felt my body packed in the car, so squashed I was barely able to breathe. I squeezed my way through a little opening and got out. I remembered I was mad, thinking I wasn't ready to die. The next day there were cuts, and I was squeezing glass from my skin. I went into the sweat lodge and prayed. I decided then I'd be a stronger person. That was in 1988. Since then I stopped drinking.

In January 1991, right before the Gulf War, we made a journey to Baghdad with a group of Lakota elders to pray for world peace. Only our prayers got us there and back safely. We were there in Baghdad the first week of December 1990, when the bombings started, and I thought my life was in danger. But I thought it was better to die for the people than to die in a car wreck. We went because of a dream an elder had about black smoke in the air where the sun rises. We were supposed to go to this place and offer the pipe of peace and pray. Our people say that we are the caretakers of Mother Earth. They say that when you make a spiritual journey the spirits will meet you halfway.

We have a simple way of life, but some of the things we have to go through to fulfill our commitment to the Great Spirit are difficult. The commitment is between you and *Tunkashila*, the Great Spirit. You have to humble yourself and say your own prayers from your heart. *Tunkashila* will hear your prayers because he made everything upon Mother Earth.

Traditionally, we are given a baby name when we are young, and we must earn our Lakota name when we get older. We use our Lakota name in ceremonies and in meetings. We say our Lakota name first.

The highest honor a person can receive is an eagle feather because it represents knowledge. A long time ago, when people went to the spirit world, they were put up on scaffolds to keep that knowledge high, because everything in life works in cycles. That's one reason why we don't let babies lie on the floor. The mother carries them on her back, or puts them in a place that's at eye level because that's where the knowledge is. In our way of life, a child is born sacred.

Our ceremonies reflect the four stages of that sacred life—from the time you're born through to the time you're a grandparent. We learn how to pray for health and happiness with the Pipe. When you pray for something, you must always give thanks for all good things. We also learn how to take care of ourselves by learning from the animals—even the prairie dogs. We can tell how high the snowbanks will be that winter by how high they build their homes. We also believe that how much you put into something is how much you will receive in return. So it's a really good life when you look at it that way. We learn from the animal nation.

My grandfather believed in both ways, Christian and Indian. He said, "It doesn't matter how you pray, there's only one Creator." Out of respect for our grandfather, we continued to go to church until an Indian preacher called our prayers with the Pipe "devil worship." My dad got up and left in protest and took half the congregation with him.

When I was young we were told not to talk about the Pipe. That was before the Freedom of Religion Act was passed. I have enough respect for other churches that I never put them down. I know whatever you believe will work for you.

I learned a lot from my grandfather. I slept at my grandparents' house when I was young, and as soon as the sun went down he'd start the *iktomi* [trickster] stories. He helped me understand about people. After my grandparents died I went to live with my parents, and that was quite a culture shock. But people still came at night to sing and dance and tell stories. I was so filled with happiness, I thought that this was the way it would be all the time.

My parents only knew Lakota. When I was growing up I used to think my life would only be from Green Grass to town. I never thought I would travel and talk about world peace. Sometimes I wish my grandparents were still here. In our language there is no word for good-bye. When you see someone off you say, *toksa,* meaning "We'll see you."

When I look at the land I feel secure and at peace. *Ma Lakota,* I am Lakota. The elders taught me to set my goals and to go for it. It's a lesson for everyone who had to learn from their mistakes. Even though we grew up with a lot of different ways that hurt us. I grew up living on the reservation, but I feel that I have accomplished a lot of things for myself, and I always try to be a better person. Today, I encourage the younger kids that they can do anything they put their minds to. I did it, and I know they can, too. The sacred hoop of the nation has no beginning and no end.

# CAROLE ANNE HEART LOOKING HORSE: TOMORROW'S ELDER

My name is Carole Anne Heart Looking Horse. I am a Rosebud/Yankton Sioux from South Dakota. My Indian name is *Waste Wayankapi Win*, or They See Good, which literally means that people see something good in me.

My dad, Narcise Francis Heart, was a Yankton Sioux and my mother is a full-blooded Rosebud Sioux. The Rosebud Sioux are "Sicangu," which means "Burnt Thighs." The name traces back to the Indian wars when the people would burn the prairies for protection. Some people were burned when the fires backed up, so they called them the "Burnt Thighs." My great-great-grandfather was Horn Chips, who was one of the Rosebud Lakota spiritual advisers to Crazy Horse. My great-grandmother's name was Stands Alone by Him. My grandmother on my father's side was Aberdeen Zephir Heart.

I grew up on both the Rosebud and Yankton reservations and was a straight-A student both at St. Francis High School and at Marty, so I skipped the fifth grade and upon

graduation went straight to the University of South Dakota. At that time there were only seven Indian people attending the college; among us was Tom Shortbull, who eventually became a state senator. When one of the Indian students murdered the town jeweler, the entire town became afraid of us. People in the stores treated me as though I were the guilty one. I learned then that racism and bigotry come in many forms. After college I went to law school at the University of South Dakota and worked in Washington, D.C., in the office of Trust Responsibilities, the legal arm of the BIA [Bureau of Indian Affairs]. I also worked for Legal Services in Mission and handled everything from landlord-tenant problems to DWIs, and even a murder case.

I thank my grandmothers for my strong sense of self-esteem and cultural identity. They taught me that everything happens to you for a reason and that you must always look for the lesson in whatever occurs. Looking back, I realize that these outstanding women were the ones responsible for giving me the strength to be who I am. Not only were they extremely generous, but they knew how to honor people in simple ways, thereby empowering one to realize their potential.

It took me at least four years to agree to marry my husband, Arvol Looking Horse, even though he wanted me to marry him a month after he met me. I was more reserved because I knew who he was and I wasn't sure if I wanted to choose that kind of life. When I finally agreed, we had a traditional wedding in Green Grass on October fourth. We picked that date because four is a sacred number.

Eagles came to our wedding, which was just amazing. They appeared just as the ceremony began. Richard Charging Eagle, who is a Lakota speaker and pastor at the Green Grass church, and Harry Charger, an elder and a supporter of the Pipe, conducted the ceremony. Richard told us that the eagles had come to remind us that they mate for life, and that our union would also be for life. I listened to these words and took them into my heart.

During the ceremony, we formed a big circle with our relatives and friends at the Sun Dance grounds. This is different from a non-Indian wedding because usually people stand behind you and can't even see your face. We both held an eagle feather between us, and I read something special about how marriage represents the coming together of two people and how important it is to also maintain individual identities within the relationship. Afterward, Richard and Harry asked our relatives to form a smaller circle inside the larger one in order to symbolize the joining together of the families. His family then became my family and my family became his, all joined together as one family.

The four seasons also visited our wedding. It snowed and rained and then the sun came out. When the ceremony was finally over, and everyone was hugging and congratulating us, someone noticed a horse standing alone on top of the hill looking down at us. Someone said, "Hey, it's a *Looking Horse!*"

As the wife of the Keeper of the Sacred Pipe, I have many responsibilities. Sometimes it's hard because of the expectations people have of me. I try to do the things that positively promote our culture. When Arvol and I are asked to speak, we have to ask ourselves, Is this going to benefit the Indian people? Is this going to educate the dominant society about who we are? I think it's really critical to do that. It's equally critical to work with our own people in order to assist them to reconnect and reinforce our own cultural values. I'm not talking about living in a tipi and wearing buckskins; it has more to do with the values of generosity and respect that we as Native people have.

If I were to summarize what Arvol's and my responsibilities are, it would include the preservation and reinforcement of our culture, our spirituality, and the language and ways of the Lakota, Dakota, and Nakota people. What is most difficult about our roles is that people tend to expect us to be better than everyone else. This is especially true for Arvol as Keeper.

There is also the expectation that his life should be a role model for others, that the Keeper and his family should be a model family. I think a lot of people are surprised to learn that we're human beings, too. We're just regular people, and others shouldn't attribute characteristics to us that they don't have themselves. Take drinking, for example; we've been affected by alcoholism, just like every other Indian family. It's affected everybody. I don't think any Indian person can say that they have escaped it in the past generations, because it's been with us for such a long time. So the expectation that people have of Arvol is very high, and sometimes it's hard to live up to as a normal human being.

The role of Indian women has been changing. It's been hard to maintain the same roles that existed in the 1700s and 1800s because the times have changed economically; contact created different roles for all of us. Many Indian women now find themselves head of the household, even though traditionally the woman owned everything, including the house. If a woman kicked the man out, he would have to go live with relatives. What's changed is that men no longer have to hunt to provide food. Now they have to work to pay the rent and put food on the table. That has changed our society, and changed our relationships to one another.

I've learned that marriage, in order to work, has to be mutually supportive. In the old days, it was the man who used to bring home the buffalo, and the woman would honor him by waiting on him. Nowadays, it's often the woman who not only "brings home the buffalo," she cooks it, too. This has created a certain amount of conflict among men of traditional families and more modern women.

I've belonged to the White Buffalo Calf Woman Society on the Rosebud Reservation since 1974. A friend and I wrote the proposal that got the first Domestic Violence Shelter in Indian country funded. As a group we decided to tackle the issue of family violence directly, because it was never a part of our culture. We observed Indian men abusing Indian women and decided we should try to bring it to the surface so people could start dealing with it. We found that much of the abuse was caused by the man not having a job, forcing the woman onto welfare, which was a switching of the roles within the culture. And the frustration and tension that kind of situation created precipitated power and control issues.

Traditionally, our society was matriarchal and was based on mutually dependent relationships. Decisions were never made without consulting the woman. Men had to consult with their wives before any important decisions were made. All the men consulted with their wives—not just Mr. Crazy Horse and Mr. Red Cloud—because it affected the entire family.

People coming from another culture sometimes don't understand. Non-Indian writers write from their own cultural perspective and propagate misconceptions, which is why we've been misperceived throughout history. This is changing now because our own writers are now offering a true perspective, and so are other people who really care about who we are and that our story be told accurately.

Even *Life* magazine misrepresented our language in the April 1993 story about the White Buffalo Maiden. They described our sacred Spirit Woman as a "squaw." I just about fell over. *Life* magazine is a publication of international reputation with the capability to educate its readership about Native people, and more specifically about the Lakota Sioux's prime spiritual leader. In the article, they called our Spirit Woman who brought the Pipe to the Sioux a "squaw," a word that has a real negative connotation to Indian people. What's so ironic about this is that that same week an article came out in the *Lakota Times* with articles about what "squaw" really means. In one Native language, it means vagina. And in whatever Native language that came from, which they think was the Naragansen, it was a derogatory term. They also called the white men who were with Indian women "squaw men," which is negative. The *Life* writers were not thinking when they decided to choose this word. It's like calling the blessed Virgin Mary a slut.

It's critical that we acknowledge this language barrier and work to make a positive change for the Indian people, who were denied access to their own culture. We were punished for speaking our languages, which led to the belief that our culture was inferior to the dominant culture. We learned we were savages with no religion. Now there's a major push to return to our spiritual way of life, so we can regain what has been lost for so long.

In the schools that are Indian controlled, we can help our students feel proud of their ancestry and help them to understand their history as an oppressed people in this country. Once they realize this they can begin to understand why they feel what is now termed "historical grief," and healing can begin. People can now understand why their parents weren't loving to them. Our mothers and fathers didn't know how to be parents because as children they were taken away and put in boarding schools. The cycle couldn't be completed because their own parenting was interrupted.

We have begun a spiritual journey. People want to go back to find that missing link, that hole in their being. They want to fill it with all the possibilities of what we can be. The passage of the American Indian Religious Freedom Act in 1978 was a beginning for us.

If the United States had the same philosophy as Native people, we wouldn't have many of the problems we presently have. The lack of respect—not only for other people, but for the environment and the animals—is amazing to us. I always stress how important it is to speak to our youth about these things. In our work we try to accommodate all requests from the youth because I think it's important for the youth to know who Arvol is and how important he is to us as a people, and to reconnect them to the culture from whence they come.

I believe that the American Indian Movement was a good and positive force in Indian country because they brought pride back to our people. They brought back the old ways that people thought had been forgotten. I like the fact that they felt the power to make a positive change and did what they felt was necessary to create changes in the Indian community. They're still going strong, but the reason people don't hear about them so much now is because they've developed more peaceful tactics.

What I would like to see for the future—ten, twenty years from now—is a community that honors our children. In order to create positive changes within our communities, we have to begin with the children, because they are the foundation.

In keeping with the idea of beginning with the children to mend the sacred hoop, for the past two years we have submitted a proposal to build a school on the Green Grass Reservation.

This summer we plan to reunite our families and give everybody an Indian name who doesn't already have one. We are going to put up the family tree and complete it, and ask each matriarchal member of the family to continue to keep it up, so that we know what our sacred relationship is to one another and reaffirm our ties. We will bring back the ceremonies, live our culture, and honor our elders. In doing so, we will strengthen and mend the sacred hoop within our own family, and thereby start mending the world.

# HOPI

## MARTIN GASHWESEOMA: THE PROPHECY

*The Hopi are descended from the Anasazi cliff dwellers who lived in Chaco Canyon, New Mexico, and Mesa Verde, Colorado, for at least 10,000 years. They built extraordinary multistory apartment villages, some of which still stand. During a drought the Anasazis moved south and west to form the twenty or so pueblo villages in what is now New Mexico and Arizona. The group that became the Hopi built a village, Old Oraibi, in central Arizona in A.D. 1100. It is believed to be the oldest continuously inhabited settlement in North America. Other Hopi villages sit atop three mesas in the surrounding fifty-mile radius.*

*In 1906, the traditionals, led by Yukima, were driven out of Old Oraibi by the white-influenced progressives. Yukima's band, carrying only what they could hold on their backs, moved to the sand country four miles west, to what is now called Hotevilla.*

*Yukima's nephew, Martin Gashweseoma, became the keeper of the sacred stone tablets containing the Hopi prophecy.*

*There is a gentleness about Martin Gashweseoma, an inherent kindness that seems to quiet one's troubled spirit. His gaze does not pierce; it rests peacefully on the listener even when he speaks of dire prophecies. For he lives only in the present moment, one that has no beginning and no end.*

*Martin has difficulty speaking English, so his son-in-law, Emery Holmes, a medicine man, sits beside him. From time to time they discuss some point in Hopi before Martin feels comfortable answering my questions. Emery is married to Martin's daughter, Mildred, and it is in her roomy kitchen where we sit. Mildred serves* piki, *a deliciously crisp and flaky, blue corn bread baked the old way, on a stone. The children watch TV in the living room. There is a riddle in so many Indian homes: no indoor plumbing, but always a TV.*

*At bedtime, I climb a ladder to the sleeping loft. As I drift into a peaceful, dreamy sleep, I think, there is magic somewhere. There is this place of pink sands and canyon walls carved by wind spirits, where the four sacred mountains keep the harmony of the breath and spirit of land and life.*

*It is said the Hopi are the guardians who hold together the balance of the whole world with their prayer and ceremony. I can't speak for the whole world, but for tonight, this day, I feel in perfect balance.*

It's been a long, long time since our prophecies have been handed down. In the late 1920s, my Uncle Yukiuma, who was what they call a "Hostile" or Hopi traditional, would come to our house and tell us about what would happen in the future. At that time I didn't notice anything unusual, and I thought he might be joking. But I listened to my uncle and always went out to greet the sunrise to pray, and then down to the spring to bathe with cold

water. That way you can have a big heart, so if something bad happens to you, you don't have to be afraid of anyone.

I think something was pushing me toward this traditional system. My uncle was teaching me the right things. Even if he had to keep some of them secret. I knew some things, and I prayed for this secret knowledge. So I kept going month after month, thinking I was doing something wrong because I didn't understand. I just kept continuing with my life, until one year I had no dreams. Then, one night, some kind of dream spirit came to me. It was like a dream, but it wasn't. A spirit woke me up and took me to the kiva, a subterranean chamber for sacred ceremonies and meetings for men. When I was inside the kiva, this spirit gave me something to hold so that the people inside would not see us.

When I went inside the kiva I listened to the conversations and learned the teachings that were passed down through certain societies. When I asked my uncle if these things were true, he asked me how I knew about them, and I told him I had been there. He told me, "You have good ears. You have good eyes. Because you know, everything is true." This is how I learned about their prayer feathers, their shrines, and other important things. But they could not see me.

Now I live my life according to the ways my uncle taught. I can see that the prophecies he talked about are happening, just like he said. This is my purpose, to continue living by the Creator's teachings. My brothers are on the wrong side of the road. They have chosen the white man's path, the materialistic way of life.

In recent times, everything in our Hopi life has become corrupted. Our elders told us that when the plants blossom in the middle of winter, we would need to go to Santa Fe to warn everyone of suffering and destruction to come unless they changed their ways. Last year, in the middle of winter, the plants began to blossom. We had a meeting with the elders and wrote letters to Santa Fe telling them that we wanted to come.

Many aspects of our life here are now subject to the federal government. If we lose our tradition, we will be sorry. The increasing earthquakes foretold in Hopi Prophecy have already started, as well as the beginning of worldwide martial law. We knew the earthquakes would start in California. I have told visitors from there that they should move out this way, toward Flagstaff or Sedona to be safe. Even the sickness and starvation, the AIDS and homelessness, are all part of the prophecies handed down.

The very reason this village was formed was to respect the Creator's laws and ways and to live off the land. No one was supposed to bring in electricity, water, or sewage systems, because all of that makes our land become the government's property. The government has already come in and taken up land along the edge of our property in order to install such things.

Our elders taught us that people would come to this continent in search of the Creator. Just as the Bible was written to tell the true story of world-shaking events of the past, I have asked the public to write down my statements so that, when the purification is over, it can be published afterward. In our prophecies there are two brothers, a dark-skinned younger brother and a light-skinned elder, whom we call the "White Brother." Together they will decide how the purification will be accomplished.

Life has become out of balance. When people are so out of balance, someone will hear our voice and our White Brother will answer the call and clean away the evil ones. According to the Prophecy, when the purification is over, only a handful of people will survive in every nation overseas. Then they will come to this continent, which we call heaven. This is where the Creator first lived and that's what he called it. The Kingdom of Heaven. He sent his own son from Oraibi, a village in Hopi, to Bethlehem in order to be born there. The Hopi already knew that the morning star would rise one day and someone special would be born.

The two brothers were with us when we first came to this continent. When their father passed away, the elder brother went out in the direction of the sunrise and the younger brother stayed here. They had agreed the elder brother would go, but he would not stay away too long. He would return when people would travel on a road built in the air. At that time we would know that the earth had been corrupted to the point that it must be purified.

We've come to that point now. Everything has been corrupted. Because we're out of balance, we don't obey the laws. Like right now in California, in spite of our warning, bad things are happening. It's too late now for gradual voluntary corrections. People say that they'll worry about it next year, but next year might be too late. So that's why we warned the people, "Wake up right now! Do something for yourself." So that they might stop all the wrongdoing and get balanced.

As Hopi, we don't own the land; we're just the caretakers. We use it, but not with electricity and coal mines. We're calling for the purification because it is our obligation. We're ready; we want it to happen. We know we can't get people to change, but we're near the time. Very near. We pray to the Creator and tell him it's not what we want, but we feel there's no choice. We've already gone over the time limit that was given to us in the Prophecy. Even the leaders of our village have put it off because they don't want to see it happen in their lifetimes.

A lot of people are looking to the Hopi right now for answers. Those who are ready will survive, but they will be tested. Last year we met with the people in Santa Clara Pueblo and kept a fire going all day and all night. They are Indian, but they have lost their language. When I saw them I wondered if they were really Indians. So many tribes have lost their

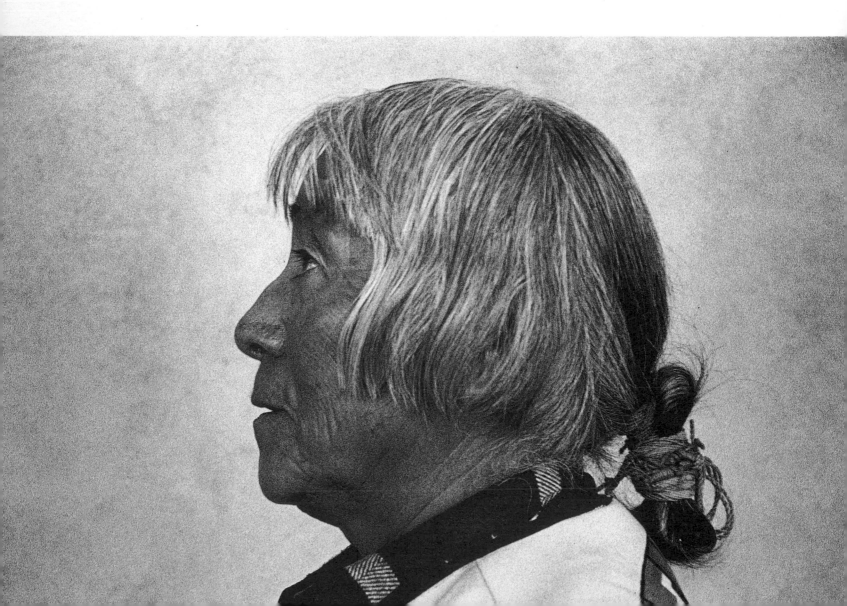

language, and that's how the culture has been corrupted. Nowadays they have computers to hook up everyone; this was also talked about in the Prophecy. It was said that we Hopi were going to become lazy and that when we would go to visit a friend or relative we wouldn't walk, we'd float around without ever touching the ground. They were talking about cars. They also talked about a highway in the sky, which are the planes. And that we would look into a window to find out what was going on—the same as television.

One of the first things our elders taught us was that when the time of purification comes a big mirror will be brought in. We will be judged in front of the mirror, and it will reveal your judgment. Now I would say that it may be like a computer. They will ask you a question and check your answer against the years of information that are stored in it.

The Hopi were also the first ones to travel to the moon. They traveled in a gourd. Long ago they were great magicians. They knew what the moon looked like long before the white man ever went to the moon. When the white man brought back pictures, they were the way the Hopi described them a long time ago. They were very powerful people, but nobody wants to heed their warning.

I'm sorry to have to tell you this, but it's true. Those are our teachings, so I have to tell you so you'll know about it when the time comes. It will depend on what you have in your mind at that moment. If we are on the path and have a pure body, maybe we'll be safe. If you don't have a big heart, you might get frightened and have a heart attack. You can conquer fear with prayer and by building up your body by bathing with cold water. This will help make your physical and spiritual body strong.

## Thomas Banyacya: the house of mica

*Thomas Banyacya is the translator and interpreter for spiritual and traditional leaders of the Hopi Independent Nation.*

*On December 10, 1992, the worst storm of the 350-year history of New York City hit at the very moment Thomas Banyacya was fulfilling his thirty-three-year attempt to reach the world's government leaders in the United Nations. As he delivered his Hopi message of peace, the storm began to rage. Ninety-five-mile-an-hour winds shook the towers of the United Nations and subways flooded, paralyzing traffic in New York. Huge waves from the Atlantic roared inland, washing away part of the freeway along the coast. Over half a million people in New York City were without electricity.*

*One third of the United Nations' employees were dismissed because of the blackout. The next day, the few who came back to work asked Banyacya if the storm could be stopped. "Yes," he said. "It can be stopped." He asked them to form a circle and pray, to ask forgiveness for all the wrongs the people had inflicted on the earth and to promise to uphold the laws of the Creator in the future. They did, and almost immediately the storm stopped. People in Hopi were not surprised when they heard of the occurrence. The name* Banyacya *means water.*

I was born around the first part of June, 1909. My mother had another baby boy about the time I had just started walking. Both my mother and the baby passed away that day. My father had a little grocery store with his brothers, the first village store in Moenkopi, which is near Tuba City, about thirty, forty miles west of here, close to Grand Canyon.

I had my own name, Banyacya, when I was born. It came from my father's clan, the clan of the rain clouds, water, springs, oceans, anything water and corn.

We are all Hopi in this village. My mother belonged to Wolf, Fox, and Coyote clans, and you are a member of the clan your mother belongs to. The main one in village ceremonies is the Coyote Clan. I belong to that. Our mission as the Coyote Clan is to watch all other leaders to see if they hold onto their laws, rules, regulations, and spiritual instructions,

to keep this land alive and in balance. When I was initiated into the society, the elders told me that I had the same mission that the coyote has here. The coyote yells out sometimes during the evening and gives you a message. They can welcome you or they can give you a warning. That is part of our mission. That's why they selected me as one of the interpreters or messengers for the elders and religious leaders who met in 1948 in Shongopovi Village in Second Mesa.

The old people were eighty, ninety, a hundred years old. They had a four-day meeting. They said that we have lived a balanced life, a good life, and so nature acted in a way that wasn't destructive. But now we have entered a most critical moment because somebody made this gourd full of ashes and threw it on Hiroshima and Nagasaki and burned everything; thousands of people died in a few seconds.

This land belongs to the Great Spirit, Maasau. This land is our Mother, everything came from her body. Animals, birds, trees, grass, everything that came from this Mother Earth is a powerful living being, just like human beings.

Being the first people here, the Hopi know how to take care of this land. We learned many songs, ceremony, activities or rituals, and every month we perform them so that this land and life will be in natural order. So that gentle rain will come, no flooding, no destruction of crops, no strong winds, just gentle winds that will bring a cloud, and it will rain and drizzle day and night for three or four days with no run-off, no flooding. That's the life that was here. There is a lot of grass here, knee high, a lot of beautiful flowers of all kinds, and all kinds of butterflies and birds. We were placed here by the Great Spirit. We were led here because this is the spiritual center, this Four Corners area, surrounded by high mountains in the four directions. When our ancestors first came, they put shrines in them. So this is like a sacred chamber.

It's from here, according to the Hopi, that Native people moved off into all four directions. Many of our grandfathers went up to Alaska to the edge of the land and planted shrines there. And they left a baby boy and baby girl there. People went south, through jungles, animals—"wildlife," they say, but we always say natural life, not wildlife, because it is the natural life of living things. Then they got down to the tip of South America, Argentina, where they placed shrines and left a baby boy and baby girl. Some of our clan people went west from here and covered the land up and down and built shrines. And those who went east did the same things at the edge of the land. So now there are shrines in four directions.

When our white brothers made this gourd full of ashes and threw it on Hiroshima and Nagasaki, our elders felt that they needed to have this message spread out. To warn all people, because we are all one people; first world, second world, third world, we speak one language. But now we are in the fourth world, the last world, the last life that we will have.

We believe the Great Spirit lined up all the human groups and asked each leader to come and pick up the ear of corn they wanted for food in this world. The first one picked up the longest ear of corn, until the last was a very small ear of corn. The Hopi brothers waited until last and picked that one up, the smallest one. Then the Great Spirit came and told them, "I'm glad you picked up that last ear of corn. I see you have patience, you have wisdom, and you have picked up the real corn; all the rest are imitations." So the first corn, they said, maybe it contains wheat, the white brothers using the wheat mostly. The others might be rice; maybe that's the Asian group and others. But the Hopi got the real corn. And so they told us never to let go of planting this corn. Because when we pray, fast, and meditate for this corn to grow, we make all vegetation, the grass, everything to grow, too.

We were trained in our societies to pray for plant life, animals, birds, all of the foods that we receive from Mother Earth, and always with a prayer we accept those things. When we go to the field when our plants are coming up, they are just like babies, so we go and sing to them. Sometimes in this valley you can hear them early in the mornings; you can hear them singing out there. They go to the field and talk to their plants as if they were human beings and encourage them. That's how they take care of this life out here.

After that 1948 meeting I went around in the four directions. I went east first to the Six Nations and the Grand Council of the Iroquois Confederacy. We went to all of the pueblos and villages and talked about these things. We formed a caravan of five or six cars full of food and money and traveled to Ohio, Iowa, Wyoming, Washington, down to San Francisco, Los Angeles, and back to here. We went to New Mexico, Oklahoma, and on into the eastern part, and then we went back up to the Six Nations. And we went over to Lake Ontario in Canada. By the end of six years, we had been to all the four directions.

The last meeting was in Canada. I didn't make it up there, but they said over two thousand families from all over gathered there for a whole week. They camped out, just like a new community. The old people cried when they saw that. This is how it was in the early days. We used to meet here and there; we were just one family spread out. So we didn't ask, what tribe do you belong to. We knew that we were all one people at one time, only now our languages are different. In some places, their words are still very similar to the Hopi, but some of the meanings have changed. The clan system that we have here is the same clan system that they have in the Six Nations.

Some said that this country is always throwing its power around. They threw it at Korea, Vietnam, and at Japan, Hawaii, and other places. Originally, they threw it at the people in New Mexico. Now they throw their power at foreign countries like Iraq. Are we going to live in peace, justice, and happiness by doing that kind of thing around the world? Get to the senators and congressmen. Get your leaders and organizations together and see if you can stop these things. Because if we don't, we are going to be faced with the most terrible thing in the future.

The reason that the elders selected me in 1948 was because I had a little education and I speak English a little. In 1921, they sent a bunch of us to a government school east of Riverside, California. I spent six years there before I was allowed to come home. It was like a military school. We didn't understand why we were there. I found out later that the United States government tried to destroy the Native people. They were trying to wipe out the Lakota people. But they couldn't defeat them, so they decided to destroy all their food, the buffalos. And they forced them into starvation. Then they still wanted to get rid of other Native people. So they decided to form what they call reservations. But somehow the Native people survived, and there were a lot of children coming up. That's when the government came up with the idea that maybe they should send them off to a foreign school and brainwash them so they would no longer have any interest in their cultures, religions, or languages. That was why they set up these government schools, to wipe out our cultures, religions, and ceremonies.

In 1930, I graduated from high school. Somebody gave me a two-year scholarship to Bacone College, an all-Indian college near Muskogee, Oklahoma. I spent two years there studying comparative religions. I found writings very similar to what the old people teach us out here, how to live and respect each other.

When I came back, I met with many elders and finally they talked to me and opened up. Before, some young people who were rebellious like me would say, "Oh, that's old stuff, we don't need that. We don't listen to old people." But I know now that they know so much. So I spent days and nights in the Hopi villages of Hotevilla, Oraibi, Shungopovi, Mishongnovi, Walpi. I went to all different pueblos and sat down with the old people.

Each village has different versions of what happened in the first world [the first phase of human existence]. It was destroyed by nature, everybody knew that, and only a handful of people came out and went from the first world into the second world. Later, they didn't correct themselves or their leaders, and they misused the power that they developed and started going against nature. The word *koyaanisqatsi* means to completely turn away from the law of the Great Spirit, the law of nature. Now, in this fourth world, it is the last world; there is no other place where the people live like this. This world is supposed to last forever, and it's up to the people living today, all around the world, to make sure it does.

We are one people, but we have different languages now, different colors, like flowers, and we are all to take care of this land and this life together for the Great Spirit. But it seems like people want to grab everything for themselves; they don't care, they just destroy. There

will be terrible things that are going to happen. These are things that the Hopi have always known, and they were concerned that we must bring this knowledge to the world.

In 1972, four of us went to Stockholm and spent five days in Belgium. From there, I traveled to Switzerland, Austria, Germany, Moscow, Yugoslavia, France, Rome, Puerto Rico, El Salvador, Hawaii, and Japan, and up north to the Yukon, close to Alaska. I met many Native people all over. I carried out my commitment to my elders. In 1948 they told me, "It's going to be hard. Some religions are going to call you crazy or a liar."

We have high spiritual leaders in this country that have never been listened to, never been given a chance to speak. I think that it's time to do that. I'm just an interpreter, a messenger, and I carry this message wherever I can. I delivered my last message to the United Nations in December of 1992. I fulfilled that commitment.

We are the living people of this land, just like the trees and the animals. People from South America, Brazil, Argentina, Peru, Guatemala, those people are praying through ceremony to keep this land alive. They lead a simple life, and they are now speaking out for what is happening. Big foreign people down there, big corporations are taking everything away for money and power. And they are destroying everything. Trees can't speak, rocks can't speak, rivers, springs, animals, and birds can't speak, so those living people finally have to speak out.

That's why, after knocking on the United Nations' door since 1949, the United Nations finally decided to open it to Western Hemisphere representatives. On December 10, 1992, they had twenty speakers, and they declared 1993 as the Year of Indigenous People. I was the last one to speak. I had a speech written, but I had to deliver from the heart. Because it's the spirit within you that has to speak to the spirit of another person.

The United Nations people talk about human rights, equality, justice, and religious freedom, but they have never helped the Native people. They have just about destroyed every culture, religion, and language of Native people. So it's time that you help with your laws and regulations. If the United Nations doesn't do it, then nature is going to be acting. That's why this great wind came and shook them up with a big snow storm, tidal waves, flooding, and blackouts.

We need to clean up the mess that we created. If we don't, Mother Earth is going to shake us real hard. We are all breathing this air, which is a part of nature; every living thing on this earth has to breathe in this air. We are all a part of it. We have no business destroying any other life. Right now we have terrible earthquakes, terrible wind, tornadoes, volcanic eruptions, and now this flooding in Mississippi. And other things are going to happen soon. From now on, things are going to happen fast. This is why the Hopi are so concerned. It's time to stop and look and weigh what we're doing.

We have to look at each other as one people; we have to work together and help each other to restore a balanced life on this earth for ourselves and the next generation and the generations coming. This is my hope, and I want to thank you and others and every nation, every individual who has helped me since 1948 with writings, with statements, with money, whatever. I want to thank them for helping me fulfill my part.

# DINEH

## Roberta Blackgoat: Declaration of Independence

*The Navajo, a nomadic people, are descended from the Dineh Indians of Northern Canada. In about A.D. 1400, they moved southward to a range east of the Hopi villages, where they co-existed reasonably peacefully, trading and even intermarrying.*

*When first the Spanish, and then the white settlers, invaded their territory, the Navajo, unlike the Hopi who resisted passively, made repeated attacks on the invaders. In 1863, General Kit Carson led his huge cavalry against the Navajo, driving them into a canyon where they were trapped and thousands starved to death. Survivors were forced to walk across New Mexico to an internment camp at Fort Sumner; those who managed to escape fled west toward Hopi country.*

*The Hopi were less concerned with the encroaching Navajo than they were with the white settlers. Their status as a sovereign nation had been guaranteed by the Treaty of Guadalupe Hidalgo of 1854, and they argued for the eviction of the whites. The government responded by reducing Hopi land by 60 percent. Even worse, a portion of the land declared Hopi reservation by the United States was land that the Navajo were already living on. This is the area that is currently in dispute.*

*Under a new law, ten thousand Navajo and Hopi are to be relocated, moved from land on which many generations of ancestors have lived and been buried.*

*The traditionals say that the United States and their BIA puppet tribal councils (traditionals have never had anything remotely resembling tribal councils) want to get people off the land to make way for coal strip-mining and uranium exploration.*

*The Navajo are a matrilineal society. Among traditional families women control the herds of sheep as well as the households. It is not surprising then, that whenever violent confrontations between U.S. agents attempting to enforce relocation occurred, women over sixty years of age carrying rifles were invariably in the forefront.*

*On October 28, 1979, a declaration of independence was signed by sixty-four elders of the Independent Dineh (Navajo) Nation at Big Mountain, with Roberta Blackgoat as chairperson. It is excerpted here:*

> *The United States government and the Navajo Tribal Council have violated the sacred laws of the Dineh nation . . . [dividing] the indigenous people by boundaries of politics, Euro-American education, modernization, and Christianity. . . . Our sacred shrines have been destroyed. Our Mother Earth is raped by the exploitation of coal, uranium, oil, natural gas and helium. . . . We speak for the winged beings, the four-legged beings, and those who have gone before us and the coming generation. We seek no changes in our livelihood because this natural life is our only known survival and it's our sacred law.*
>
> Signed by ROBERTA BLACKGOAT,
> Chairperson, and sixty-four of the Council of Elders.

Everything is changing. There is no rain, and only the wind is coming by and sending messages of how it is out here. All the suffering going on in this country with the tornadoes, floods, and earthquakes is carried on the breath of Mother Earth because she is in pain. Even the animals are talking now, and we can see some of them disappearing from the earth.

I was born here in 1917 and know this area very well. I know all of the trees; each one has a name. All my relatives are buried here, including my great-great-grandmothers who escaped the Long Walk to Fort Sumner. They are buried on Dzil Assad, or Big Mountain in English. There's still a lot of medicine up there that my ancestors used for healing. These are my roots. Our original name is Dineh, not Navajo, so I call myself Dineh.

Our troubles over the boundary dispute started in 1977 when the U.S. government put the Hopi Partitioned Land [HPL] fence around us, which was the worst thing possible. We pulled out the fence that came through here. Just cut it up. And we've been fighting ever since. This is not the Hopi Reservation; this is the Dineh/Navajo Reservation.

The dispute is really between the U.S. Government and the Hopi and Navajo traditionalists, who are fighting to keep their land free. We want to have a healing for Mother Earth because the more coal and uranium mines they put in here, the greater the suffering of

our Mother Earth. I've been saying this all along; this is my fight, too. Many people around the world have heard me talk and understand what I mean when I say this area is sacred. My grandfather told me that the Four Corners is our Holy Land, which includes Arizona, Utah, Colorado, New Mexico, and parts of Texas. This whole area contains Mother Earth's guts.

What I mean is that—just like us—there are a lot of things that happen inside of Mother Earth. The white man wants part of her insides, which will eventually kill our Mother. Right now the Peabody Coal Mine is causing a pitiful pain to our Mother Earth. My grandfather told me that coal is like the liver, and uranium is both the heart and lungs of Mother Earth. She's been living on these minerals underneath the surface of our land.

You know how it is when you have a pain—if you get a little cut, it hurts. That's the way the earth is now. And we need to heal her in some way. If the government understood us, they would leave her alone and allow her to heal, but they never say anything. All they do is push the dust and ashes back in there. They don't put in anything to replace what's been taken, like they do with human surgery. They're not patching up anything for our Mother Earth, and she's not healing; she's just getting worse with the pain. They are trying to take her precious guts out for money. People are told they can dig here and get rich. But we are even making the air sick with all these smokestacks, and the spills are flushing into our spring water.

The BIA [Bureau of Indian Affairs] keeps asking us to move and to reduce our animals. We even have to have a permit for cutting the timber out here for our firewood. Now they are coming to us and saying we have to pay for our grazing area and for our house, that we have to pay tax.

I told them, "I'm not going to pay any tax. I'm not allowed to. This is our land and this is where we've been set. We're not allowed to pay tax. That's what I was told long before you were born." I said, "You were not even in diapers when our spiritual law was made for the Indians. The Indians were the first ones to live on this land."

It's mighty hard to follow the white man's laws, especially for people who don't speak English. Because those people don't know what it means; they don't know what's going on. This makes me so sad. I was with some people who didn't speak any English when the BIA man came and gave them a paper to sign for the relocation. I just sat there and didn't say a word. They didn't understand him, but he gave the paper to each one of them to sign. One put a thumbprint on it, and the other one signed the paper without knowing what they were signing.

Then I mentioned it to the BIA man, saying, "Why do you have to do that? These people know nothing about these papers. It's not the way they have been raised. They have been using this land all their life, and you shouldn't be warning them. They might sign it even if it meant they were to go to jail."

We argued, and he said he was going to send all the leaders over here to see me. I told him, "Go ahead and send them right now. I really want to talk with them, too. This is serious—this is not your business, and it's not your law. You are just hungry for money and that's all. They are trying to kill the Mother Earth by putting the Peabody Coal Mine in here. After you move all those Indians, you are going to have a lot of money in your pocket. And you're just going crazy over it. You are destroying yourself over it."

I know where I belong. There's nowhere else I can go. The BIA used to come and say, "Do you want to see the new land where your people are moving?" I would say, "No way, I'm not going anywhere; I'm staying here. No matter what happens to me, I'm going to stay here. All my ancestors are buried here, and I'd rather be with them."

Senator Barry Goldwater came here once to talk to us, and he said, "We'll let people live out here. You are not going to move; you just stay and live here." This is what he said. But about two or three months later, I heard that he had ordered all the Navajo off their land. This is why I went to Shiprock, Santa Fe, and Albuquerque. I carried a sign saying, "Relocate Goldwater to Europe." I got a funny letter from Germany saying, "We don't want Goldwater."

I'm going to a meeting in Florida to speak about our forced relocation. They told me that I may have to be there for about two weeks or so. But I told them, "I can't stay two weeks. My animals would be hauled away. I would rather they be hauled away with me."

The BIA told me that if I didn't do anything with my sheep or horses, they could be taken away five days later. So I said, "Okay, you just let me know and I'll call my lawyers, who will stand by me and witness this illegal action." When they asked me who my lawyers were, I said, "I'll never tell you names, but there's one in New York, Minnesota, Florida, Washington, San Francisco, and Germany." These are the places I go and talk to people.

That happened after I was arrested and went to jail, which was really kind of embarrassing. They came around one day and said they were going to redo that old dam and make it deeper. I told them, "No, you can't do it today, tomorrow, or the next day, because we just had an offering for our Mother Earth yesterday. So, we have to respect her for four nights and four days. Then we can talk about it, and then whatever comes up, you can do what you wish to do. But not now, *please* understand me." I kept chasing them away until they sent out policemen to surround us.

When the policemen and policewomen came I was sitting right in front of the blade of the bulldozer. Someone started the motor and the blade was going up and down in back of me. I got up and walked over to the policemen and said, "Please understand me, we had an offering for our Mother Earth yesterday and nothing can be done to her, not even cutting down any trees or anything that's on the ground. We can't do it. We have to respect this and keep it that way for four days and four nights. Please, please understand me."

I said it three times standing there. Then the policeman said, "If you don't leave, we are going to arrest you." He said it right in the middle of what I was saying. I was still pleading when they started grabbing people. I told the others to just follow them and to not fight back. But the first person they grabbed started to use his fists and threw himself on the ground. They grabbed his hair and dragged him away.

I was so mad at that moment I turned around and saw a survey stick and threw it. I told the policeman, "You are breaking the law, too. My law is very sacred to me." They started dragging me away. They were so rough. I told them, "Don't try to make me walk; I'm not a baby." I just kept on talking. They pushed me into the paddy wagon and I said, "Oh boy, I'm going to have free beans." I was so hungry and starving.

I spent about seven and a half hours in the jail, in a cold room. That's where I got sick the next day and almost became blind from an infection.

The main traditional people on both sides really don't want to lose their land because it's where we have been planted, just like plants in the soil. Wanting us to move is like trying to pay us off for our prayers and our song. That's the way we feel.

The four sacred mountains—Sisnaajinni [Mount Blanca], Tsoodzil [Mount Taylor], Dook'oosliid [San Francisco Peak], and Dibe'Nitsaa [Mount Hesperus]—are all part of the room inside our hogan. It is more important to say that this is like our church; the Creator set these mountains down for our hogan posts. These mountains are sitting with prayers and songs that we call the "Home Song." It's been voiced by the Holy People to have this be part of the room in the hogan for the Dineh people.

We put corn pollen and corn meal on the east side by the doorway. On the south side is Mount Taylor, and on the west side is San Francisco Peak. On the north side is Mount Hesperus, where we sprinkle some corn grain and pray with it. This is how the room inside the hogan is kept.

It's mighty hard to break somebody's life. To tell them to leave their homeland. I imagine that it's like a broken rainbow. The four sacred mountains are home to Dineh people, made for us by the Creator. The dirt is the rainbow surrounding us. Now oil has been drilled up in Four Corners. Peabody Coal Mine is drilling here. Uranium is being mined in Mount Taylor, and another coal mine is happening between Window Rock and Gallup. So it's going on right inside of our hogans. This is how it is, they don't respect our home, the home womb. That's why I call the miners "mice." I say, "The mice are going into our hogan, digging here and there and making homes." I'm saying that you're killing your Mother Earth, that's what you people are doing. It's so painful.

The BIA has created a dispute between us and the Hopi. That's the reason they are saying this land belongs to the Hopi. But the Hopi are not going to use it. The government is going to set up mines, and nobody is going to live out here. The Hopi aren't going to move out here. They know they cannot live out in this big open sight. They have their traditional way of not pushing and spreading out. They are not allowed to. But the government is doing it for what they know is underneath the land. And that's why I say they are trying to kill the Mother Earth.

This is my sweet home. I had a rug that said Home Sweet Home. That's the way it is, this whole area is a sweet place. No matter how hard it is without green grass or water nearby, it's still a good place for me. I can't go anywhere. That's what I've been telling them. "If you are trying to transplant me to an unknown place, do you think I'll grow? It may be a week later, but I'll die. Like the way some plants do when you transplant them, especially an old bush or an old tree; it won't grow."

People are talking about how we have to do something because a lot of things are going to happen. But it's the government needing money, money, money. It's mighty hard to have other people, other nations, understand what we are telling them.

I wanted to use my life for my nation. To fight against whatever is wrong. I want to stand up for my people. I pray for all the people of different colors, the people who live in the water and in the wild, the flies, and the four-leggeds. All these people have the same struggle we are having here. Harassment is everywhere, and that's why we pray for all people. If you can stand strong and do the things to make yourself a better life, maybe your people, your families, will be proud of you. This is what I teach. My message is a hard one to take to other nations, but this is my purpose.

## JANET MCCLOUD: THE ELDERS' CIRCLE

*Janet McCloud's large, rambling house is on ten acres in Yelm, Washington, adjacent to the Nisqually Indian Reservation and about an hour's drive from Seattle. She and her husband, Don, were able to buy the house thirty years ago with only a three-hundred-dollar down payment. For the past several years, Janet has used the house and its grounds, named the Sapa Dawn Center, for ceremonies and conferences.*

*In August 1992, I was invited to attend the Seventeenth Annual Elders and Youth Circle. I arrived a day early; tents and tipis were already set up. Elders were put up in bungalows next to the house. By the following day, three hundred people, young and old, had arrived. Janet's daughters took charge of the cook house, which was equipped with two refrigerators and a restaurant-size stove. Under a large arbor were rows of picnic tables, and beyond, a huge thriving vegetable garden. Down a hillock were the prayer grounds and two sweat lodges.*

*Chiefs Oren Lyons and Leon Shenandoah had just returned from the 1992 Earth Summit in Rio, and they spoke discouragingly about prospects for change. Other elders stood in turn to speak of matters concerning their tribes and to offer prayers.*

*On the fourth day of the circle, an Indian law student brought to the attention of those gathered that there was documentation from the Catholic Church that overturned previously held notions concerning the "humanness" of the indigenous people. The Papal Bull of 1537 clearly stated that even though Indians were not Christians they were humans and therefore had rights to property, and they were not to be enslaved. According to this documentation, "Notwithstanding*

*whatever may have been or may be said to the contrary, the said Indian and all other people who may later be discovered by Christians, are by no means to be deprived of their liberty or the possessions of their property, even though they be outside the faith of Jesus Christ . . . nor should they be in any way enslaved . . .*

*The Papal Bull of 1537 was ratified and verified by all the secular powers of Europe. This declaration of human rights was also verified almost word for word in the first important Indian law of the United States, the Northwest Ordinance of 1787, adopted two years before the federal constitution, a constitution in which the guiding principles were parallel to the Northwest Ordinance and the 1537 Papal Bull.*

*At the gathering, it was further stated that, "Not only has the United States never upheld even one of the 372 treaties it has made with the Indian, it continues to repudiate the constitution of the United States by refusing to recognize the legal and just property and political rights of the Indians who are in their own homeland." This documentation, the elders explained, opens up new questions over the sovereignty issues that all the tribes are facing, and it will have an impact on further Supreme Court rulings.*

*Although Janet can be an imposing and at times intimidating spokesperson, when she stood to speak of the Indian youth who are committing suicide and dying of alcoholism, drugs, and AIDS, tears streamed down her face. "I'm weary and heartsick of burying the children," she said.*

I was born on the Tulalip Indian reservation on March 30, 1934, during one of the biggest storms to ever hit the Northwest. My mother wanted to name me Stormy, or Gale, but she owed sixteen dollars to my Aunt Jane, and Jane insisted that I be named after her. That's how I got the name Janet. I have always had a stormy personality, so the name Janet doesn't tell you much about me.

My Indian name is Yetsiblu Talaquab, which means a "Mother to All and One Who Speaks Her Mind." It was given to me by my Aunt Marge, because she was raised by her grandmother and she was the last member of my family to speak the language. I am descended from the Chief Seattle family.

You have to go through a ceremony to get a name, and you must also get a clearing of that name. You have to pick a sponsor to help you with the give-away ceremony, and it must be declared in a longhouse that this person is now taking this name. If anybody has any objections, they have to state them. If anybody wants to challenge you and take the name themselves, they must hold a give-away and feast twice as large as yours just to bring it to the floor so that the elders can decide whether that person has a case. If they decide in favor of that person, then that person has to hold another give-away and feast twice as big as yours once again. This can get to be quite expensive.

At that time I was still pretty materialistic. I told my sponsor, "I'm just a poor Indian. How many blankets and stuff do I have to give away?"

My sponsor laughed and said, "It doesn't matter how little money you have, you still have to have a big give-away."

And so I just kind of thought, Well, yuk, I want to get, not give. I finally decided that I would go ahead and do it, and that it would be held around the time that my daughter got married.

My daughter Julie married a Mohawk man. So we had both the leader from our longhouse and the chief from his longhouse do the ceremony. I decided to hold my naming ceremony afterwards. I went to my tribe up in Tulalip to ask if the elders could be brought here to do the naming, and they agreed. Now we had to have two give-aways, because at an Indian wedding the families of the couple have to throw a give-away. But it's not the couple who get gifts; they only get advice.

It's the mothers who take the wedding vows. During the wedding ceremony, I was asked, "How do you like this young man that your daughter has picked? Are you going to accept him in your heart as a son? Are you going to help them through the rough times?" And they ask the man's mother the same questions. The reason we take the vows is because it's not just the couple who is joining, the families are joining too.

After the wedding I had my naming. I had been coached what to do and when to do it, but I was still tongue-tied during the ceremony. After that I loved give-aways; I started having them all the time. I still have them and it's great.

The original Yetsiblu was Chief Seattle's sister. Schewabe and Skolitsza were the patriarchal and matriarchal heads of the big longhouse there. I am related to them through my great-great-uncle and my great-great-grandmother, who are buried right next to them. It will be three generations after I die before someone can take the name Yetsiblu Talaquab again.

Some people say that taking the name of someone three generations past is you coming back here to take back your own name. That it's like a hat that you wear. You never let it touch the ground, you never let it get dirty. You want to live a clean life, because whoever gets the name after you will have to take the good with the bad of it. Since I have taken my name, I haven't really had a lot of bad, so I think whoever had it before me must have lived in a good way.

My tribe, Tulalip, in the Northwest, comes from fishing people. All of our legends are linked to the salmon. Salmon was like corn to the Iroquois, or the buffalo to the Sioux. We had ceremonies that were outlawed for over a hundred years in Washington state. Our potlatches, give-aways, were considered a threat to the economy of the U.S. Our reservation was one of the first to revive the salmon ceremony. We had a song for every different species of salmon, as welcoming ceremonies. When the salmon were coming upriver to spawn, you weren't allowed to make loud noises, because it was like a nursery.

We have a legend about the time when there was no sun. The Changer went to steal the sun in the spirit world, and he brought it back in a box. He told the people, "You can't get too close to this. You're going to have to learn to deal with this light. So just wait now and let me explain things to you."

But the people pushed him and pushed him, and they cried, "Let us see! We want to see!" They shoved him so hard the box lid flew open and the sun came popping out—everybody got scared. Some jumped in the waters, and they became the salmon and the seals and whales. Others ran into the forest, and they became the deer and the antelope and all the animals there. But the others, the pushiest, stayed and became white from the sun. Others remained in the background; they stayed black. And that's how we got our different colors.

I lived both in cities and on reservations as a child. We'd go back to Tulalip or to Quinault, then back to Seattle. I have some happy memories. I remember experiencing the beauty in nature. Oh, it was so awesome. I would go off by myself into the woods and stay all day with the big trees and the animals and birds. I lived in an imaginary world there. I loved it. I felt something there that would always draw me. When we lived on the coast, I would go to the ocean and walk the beaches all day, or if we would be on the reservation, near the mountains, I would be on the mountains all the time. But I would always be alone, just taking in that beauty. I remember a spring that was so pure and clean—and I would drink out of it.

The springs would tell me stories about the Little People, the Sasquaches, and the beautiful wildflowers. So it wasn't all negative; there was a lot of beauty in my childhood. There was a balance there. I found healing in nature. A lot of times I would go out and cry, and it would be as though somebody was soothing me, and I would feel better. Even now if I feel bad, I'll go out among the trees and sit and watch the sunrise or sunset and drink in the beauty until everything is peaceful within me again. I am empowered again.

I believe that all these problems that we Indians face go back several generations. For me, when I was seven, I distinctly felt that there was something wrong with our lives. I don't know why, but I started going to churches. I was looking for something. Of course, they would all try to indoctrinate me, and I would listen very intently and ask questions, but if they couldn't answer my questions, I wouldn't stay. One thing I couldn't understand is why they all believed in Jesus Christ, and yet they would tell me not to go to another church because that church is bad and only theirs was good. To me that was very argumentative, and at that time in my life I was very tired of anything argumentative. I was looking for some truth even at my early age.

After a while I found the Christian Science Church. I really wanted to believe what they taught, that if you have faith you can move mountains. And that there is no pain; it's all in your head. You only think you hurt, but there really is no such thing as pain. And so I took this into my personal experience. One day my stepdad was going to Seattle to find work. We had a Model A car, and he had to crank start it. That day it wouldn't start. I got out in front of the car with him and looked at him seriously and told him, "You know Punk,"—that was his nickname—"if you had faith in God, that car would start. You have to have faith."

He didn't make fun of me. He just laughed a little and said, "Well listen, you'll have to have faith for me. You pray, and I'll try and start the car."

Well, I got down on my knees and prayed. When it still wouldn't start, I thought, "There must be something wrong with me. I must not have enough faith."

I kept going back to that church. Then one day I did something really wrong, and my mother gave me a spanking. I cried for all I was worth. My mother said, "Why are you crying? There is no pain; it doesn't hurt. It's all in your head." My bottom was stinging. I looked at her and thought, "Well, my butt sure hurts."

That was the end of Christian Science for me; as far as I was concerned, two strikes and they're out. I gave up going to churches for a while until I was a little older.

I went down to stay with my grandma, who went to a Pentecostal church that believed in one God, but my girlfriend went to a Pentecostal church that believed in the Trinity. My grandmother would get mad at me because I would keep switching every other week to keep my girlfriend happy. My girlfriend used to talk in tongues, and try as I may, I couldn't talk in tongues. All night long I would read the Bible and pray and pray. And I would try and talk in tongues. I thought the fault was in me that I couldn't make it as a Christian. I assumed that everybody else in the world was saved, and I was unsavable.

When the fishing rights struggle started I remember thinking, "Boy, when the Christian people hear how badly they are treating Indians, they are going to rise up and take these Game Department men and throw them all in jail!" I had some rude awakenings when I realized that Christians weren't saved either, that it was just another mind trip.

When I went to Los Angeles for one of the first meetings on our fishing rights struggle, I met all the traditional people for the first time. It was the first time I met hippies, too, and that was a real culture shock. They were all smoking dope on the Los Angeles freeway, going seventy miles per hour, and the guy at the wheel was going to sleep. Boy, was I scared. We finally arrived at the house where we were supposed to eat, and they were passing this pipe around. I didn't know what to do with it. Thomas Banyacya was sitting next to me. He said, "Just put it to your lips and don't smoke it." Then it came time to eat. The hippies jumped up and grabbed all the food, and there was nothing left for us. By the time we got up, there was only cheese and olives and stuff we had never eaten before. It was getting late, and we were hungry.

Finally, they took us to some house in Pasadena. It was a Hopi house. The Shoshone and Ute people got out their drum and began to sing. They told us to get up and dance. Well, I had never danced to anything except bebop-type music. So I watched this Yakima Indian woman dance, then I got up and followed her movements and danced just like I had been dancing all my life. All of the sudden all of my tiredness left, and I got on this high. I thought what a marvelous thing this dancing is. I felt so good, such a wonderful sense of well-being. It was almost like the glow you get when you first start drinking. But with drinking, from that point on it's all downhill.

The next day we went to the forum that had been arranged for us. Everyone was traditional and very spiritual. At that time I was just a political activist and I was thinking, "What am I doing here with these people? I am sick to death of the hellfire and brimstone of Christianity, what am I doing here?" But when the Hopis sang their Creation Song something stirred right inside my solar plexus. It was as though something opened up within me. I sensed there was something that these people had and that maybe it was the very thing that I had been searching for. So I went home thinking about that.

Later I was invited to Oklahoma to a spiritual unity conference. The things that I experienced through the ceremonies and talks gave me a good sense of the natural love that everybody had for each other. I got on such a spiritual high that I swear I didn't need an airplane to get back home. From that point on, I knew that this is what I had been looking for. And I made sure at that time to keep in contact. I still spent time as a political activist, but if there were gatherings of elders, I would do anything I could to get to them. That became my school. I also sought out the elders in my own area and listened and learned from them. When I found our traditions, my mother said to me, "I'm glad you finally found what you were looking for, Janet, because all your life you were searching for something."

In my radical days, during the fishing rights struggle, when I was put in jail, I was called a militant and communist. I even had people call me an intellectual once, and I said, "What!" That's a new one, I only had a formal eighth-grade education.

In 1960, I was named spokesperson for the Nisqually Tribal Chairperson by Mildred Ikebe, an elder and one of my closest friends. My first overseas trip was in 1973 when Wounded Knee II was still going on. It was front-page news over there, but here there was a blackout. In the early sixties, when we first started out, my objective was fighting for the health and educational benefits that we were supposed to have as Indians. We had no health care at that time.

Indians were in a terrible, terrible state. I was just getting into studying about treaties when the McCoy case came down from the Washington State Supreme Court in December of 1963. It was a real racist decision that gave the state the power to regulate Indian fishing. According to this decision, we didn't have any fishing rights; the only fishing rights that we had were like a bear's to go get a fish, or a deer to get a drink of water. We had been trying to get the BIA to support us, but later we found out that the BIA had secretly sided with the State. So when the McCoy decision went against us, we decided we had better do something to nip this in the bud right away. At that time, Governor Rosellini had plans to make Washington State the "winter wonderland for sportsman's fishing," and number one on the agenda was getting rid of the Indians. Get them off the rivers. He used all of his police power to terrorize us and to frighten us. The police harassed us, confiscated our gear. People came down and started shooting at us, ruining our boats and canoes, slashing our tires. That's when I first began to organize a resistance in defense.

On October 13, 1965, during the first big fish-in, I was arrested. The objective of a lot of the fish-ins was to bring some attention to the problem, and if a celebrity was there we got more coverage. Marlon Brando and Jane Fonda came to support us. Dick Gregory was a master at getting the best coverage. I think that he was the one that sacrificed the most because he actually went to jail. He didn't do the six months the judge sentenced him to, though. He went on a fast of distilled water. I think he spent forty-five days in jail, all told, without eating. The reason he got such a stiff sentence was because of the prosecutor's hatred of us. He said that the eleventh commandment in the state of Washington is "Thou shalt not fish with Indians."

At the same time that Dick Gregory got six months in jail, right down the hall a woman was on trial for murdering her baby and stuffing it in a garbage can, and she only got six months suspended sentence. So fishing with the Indians was a crime worse than infanticide. When we would go to the store in Yelm to buy groceries, white people would say to us, "You know you had our moral support and sympathy until you had that goddamn nigger out there fishing with you." I would get mad and ask them, "Will your moral support and sympathy buy us a basket of groceries?" And they would say, "Well, no." Then I told them, "What good is your moral support and sympathy then, when we're drowning. We're drowning, and this man comes and offers his hand to help. And we're supposed to say, oh no, it's a black hand; I'd rather drown than have a black hand help me." We faced a lot of that. Dick Gregory could have avoided the jail sentence—he had the money to avoid it—but he chose to go to jail to bring more attention to our cause.

We get a lot of people who want to help, but some are really exploiting the Native people. One time Thomas Banyacya was at my home, and this woman comes in talking about flying saucers. Here she was, telling this Hopi elder all these crazy stories. Thomas was hard of hearing, and he didn't have a hearing aid, so he was going "a-huh, a-huh." And she was saying, "So you agree that I should be the Hopi representative in the Northwest?" And he said "a-huh." I said, "Thomas! Wake up! Do you hear what this woman is saying?" He said, "What?" So I told him. And he said, "Oh, no, no, no, I'm not telling you that you represent the Hopi and all that." So that's what happens to the elders.

A lot of times what happens is similar to Brooke Medicine Eagle and what she has been doing. She went among the Cheyenne. There was an elder Cheyenne woman there who was really deserted by her kids, who all moved out to the city. She moved in with her and began to help her gather wood, doing all these things that her children and her grandchildren should have been doing. And the elder became so filled with gratitude that she adopted her and began to tell her all these things. Then Medicine Eagle talked and told everybody that she was a medicine woman.

The Cheyenne were really upset about this. But I can understand how this can happen because our people neglect their elders. I see them even do it here; they don't support their elders. They never worry if they have wood, water, groceries. Then when somebody else comes along and helps them out, our elders get so filled with gratitude that they do talk to them and they do tell them things and sometimes even adopt them.

Everything is a dichotomy in this country. That's why I stick with the elders. They are not like these people who preach one thing and practice another, who have laws for common people but not for the elite. People argue about who we are as indigenous peoples of the Western hemisphere. We come from many different nations and tribes. When I go to Europe to speak, I see that they're still fighting and hating one another. The Germans hate the French and the French hate the Germans; the English hate the French and the Germans and the Irish, and it just goes on. And then they have the gall to tell me, "You Indians could really do something if you all got together."

We had no place to practice freedom of religion. No place where we could build a fireplace and sweat lodges and worship the Creator in the way that we felt we needed to connect with Him. We need that connectedness to feel like living again. To stop feeling suicidal, wanting to kill ourselves with alcohol and drugs. We had to find our connection again, and we found it in our ancient ceremonies, which are still as valid today as they were way back then. People say you can't go back in the past and live in a tipi, but the living laws that we were taught are still with us today.

When I travel to Europe to speak, I look out into the audiences and I see all different colors, with all different views, and I think of the Creator. He could make us all the same color, with the same kind of hair, same size, and all looking alike. Wouldn't you just hate to see yourself going down the road every day, to look and there you are? Isn't it beautiful having diversity and differences?

But so many forms of discrimination, racism, and exploitation are practiced today. In Santa Fe, I saw Indians' jewelry and artwork for sale. I'm glad they don't charge you to look, because I couldn't have paid the price to. I have seen this before with our artists in the Northwest who carve. Indian art isn't worth anything when the Indian owns the artwork. But when it changes hands to the white dealers, all of the sudden it has about a one-million-percent markup.

We Native people have had a shattered past. Now, today, we are trying to pick up all the pieces and put them back together so that our future will not be so fragmented. We want to transform our future. And I, as a grandmother, want to see these young people grow. I want to see them healthy with clean air and clean, pure water to drink. I want to see them become a grandparent like me one day and sit watching their grandchildren talking and singing, knowing who they are, and being proud of who they are. That's what I live for.

The great beautiful thing I learned from the Lakota people is *mitakuye oyasin:* all my relations. When they say that, the way it was explained to me, it's so beautiful. It's so immense because it includes everyone who was ever born, or even unborn, in the universe, all the two-legged, the four-legged, birds, animals, rocks, and everyone who's here today. The trees, plants, mountains, sun, moon, stars, and everyone who ever *will* be born! How immense can a statement be? All my relations. I marvel at the beauty of that word, it's so powerful.

We are ruining the earth with technology; we are polluting the waters and the air. Only 1 percent of all the water on this earth is drinking water; now they say at least one half of that is polluted. You just can't keep moving to a pretty place and then start polluting it by continuing to want the same type of things. Like the way people are leaving California. "Well, we've polluted California because of our lifestyle. It's time to go somewhere else." Then they move someplace else, and they want the same comforts and the same technology that they had in California. You can't be in balance and harmony with nature anymore because all of nature is upset by man's misuse of the natural world.

The cornucopia is almost empty here in America. You know, most people who came from Europe came for riches and land. Although they say that they came for religious freedom. I mean, what kind of freedom? Look at the history of what they did to our people under the guise of religious freedom. It was terrible. The Catholic pope put out the word that we weren't animals but we weren't really human beings either, so our rights didn't have to be respected. We had no right to own the land because we weren't Christians, we weren't saved. The Lutherans said the same thing, and we had no rights that needed to be respected in their laws. We are still fighting those battles.

The salmon are disappearing because of the pollution and dams, just like the buffalo, the passenger pigeon, and many other species that have disappeared. But the most endangered species in the world today, let me tell you, is us. We are the endangered species.

Young white kids come to me, New Age kids, and oh god, I love them, but sometimes they are a handful. They come to me and say, "Oh, Janet, please, please, you got to help me. I've got to get back to nature." I say, "Do you need a laxative, or what?" That's crazy, how can you get back to nature? We *are* nature! We are a part of nature, we are part of this earth, we are a part of everything that lives. We are a part of you and me and this air that connects us all together. There is no esoteric chant or mantra or anything that's going to give these New Agers instant spiritualization. "Give me a pill, give me a chant, I need to be spiritual, right now!" I say you have to learn to be a human being first. If you don't know how to be a human being, you'll never be spiritual.

What we do have to learn is to respect ourselves. So many people don't like themselves. They are always trying to change themselves into something else that they see on television. Slim and trim—everyone is dieting. In Somalia they're starving, but here in America people spend millions on diets when they could just shut their mouths.

And we need to heal our own families. As Native people we know that. We still have alcoholism, AIDS, and drugs, batterings, violence, corrupt leadership—and bingo. I hate bingo! We have all this to contend with, and it creates dysfunctional families. I say, yes, we have that. But you know, since I heard about dysfunctional families, I've been trying to find a functional one. I've looked all over for one. I'm beginning to think that this whole country is dysfunctional. It suffers from schizophrenia. On the one hand you teach a child, "Thou shalt not kill," and then when they're eighteen, you put a gun in their hand and say, "Go for it. Go kill those SOBs because they don't believe in our sacred principles of 'Thou shalt not kill.'" What kind of dichotomy do we put on our kids? What messages do we give them? And what are we feeding them on television?

Children learn by imitating. When I was a child growing up with alcoholic parents, I played grown-up by filling empty beer bottles with water and drinking them. And I'd find a cigarette butt and stick it in my mouth and stagger around, pretending to be drunk. They were the role models that I had.

So if we want a better future for our children, no matter who we are, we have to remember that we are their first teachers. If we want a good world, a good earth, free from racism and hatred and violence, we have to look in our own hearts.

One legend that I like is the one about the bear and the eagle and how they became the leaders. They say that at one time in our distant past, our ancestors were killing animals just for the pleasure of killing. Not for food or survival, but just for fun. They were threatening whole species with extinction, so Creator gave every living thing the power to react against injustices. He also gave them a way to connect with Creator if the injustices were so over-whelming that their own power couldn't handle it. He gave them the way to do this in their original instructions.

So the animal people put all of their power together and formed a circle to petition the Creator to give them relief against the false leaders with lies, like the fox and the coyote—the tricksters. These animals would trick the others, then gobble them up and eat them. So after a while Bear said, "I'll be the guardian. I'll pick the site for the circle and protect everyone against anyone creating any type of disturbance. So all paths leading to the site would be protected by the bears." And Eagle said, "I'll watch from afar and warn you bears of anyone creating a disturbance."

So finally, all of the animals and the bird people were able to come together. They put their minds together as one and prayed to the Creator for relief from the human beings. The Creator had pity on them and helped them. And that's where all the sicknesses come from that the human beings have. As a result, the numbers of the human beings began to drop by the millions in this land. The plant world got alarmed, and they thought, If the two-legged all die, it will create a vacuum that will suck all of life down with them. And so they decided to provide an antidote for every sickness the animals would give. Today, those human beings who pray, meditate, fast, and are at peace with nature can go out and a plant will manifest itself and say, Take me, I'm the one you need. That's how our people learned of all the medicines in the days long ago, and it still works today.

# ONONDAGA

*Nedrow, New York, five miles south of Syracuse, is the home of the Onondaga nation. It is a village of winding, hilly lanes lined with tall, stately elm trees. The name Onondaga means, "Place of the Elm Trees," a place, according to the prophecy of the Law Giver, to which the people will flee for sanctuary during "the last days."*

*On the late-April day when I arrived, an internal crisis was troubling the village. Cars and trucks were parked along the road, blocking the entrances to stores and businesses. The Onondaga nation had ordered them closed for non-payment of taxes. The owners of the businesses were refusing to pay, demanding better accountability of how their tax money is spent. The controversy was over whether Indian-owned businesses should be required to pay taxes to the Onondaga nation. The Onondaga clan mothers would make the final decision.*

*I spent the day talking with Chief Leon Shenandoah, Clan Mother Audrey Shenandoah, and (Dewasenta) Alice Papineau, who took me to the longhouse dining room for dinner.*

*Alice, a tiny woman, speaks with the eagerness of a young woman, in a voice soft and whispery. Over dinner we talked about Indians we knew in common, those from the many reservations I had visited, which, it turned out, she had visited as well.*

*A young man sitting near us was listening, smiling. "Women are all the same everywhere," he said, shaking his head. "Don't matter what color you are, you all gossip."*

*Alice drew herself up. "We are not gossiping. We are exchanging information."*

*He stood up, gathering his dishes. "I always wondered how that moccasin telegraph worked."*

# Leon Shenandoah: head chief

I am the *Tatodaho,* Head Chief, of the Onondaga nation. I was chosen in 1969, but even before that I conducted the ceremonies in the longhouse using the wording of the Peacemaker.

The Creator sent down the Peacemaker to set up our way of life and our Confederacy. In order for people to get along, the Creator tells us that we must talk softly to one another and use a good mind. To use wording that makes the harmony of living with one another because it makes a good relationship.

There are eagle feathers in my bonnet because the eagle is the leader of all birds. Here in the northern part of the country, the maple tree is the leader of all trees, and the red whip, or medicine whip, is the leader of all medicines. There are some other medicines that are leaders of the ground, including the deer, which is the leader of the four-legged animals in the Northeast.

I am originally of the Eel Clan, but because of my status, it is as though I am of no clan. It's made out that way so that then I cannot favor any particular clan, or even my own mother—if she's wrong, she's wrong. There are fourteen principal Onondaga chiefs and twelve sub-chiefs, twenty-six of us in all. The chiefs are elected by the clan mothers. But I was originally elected by the chiefs, so the clan mothers had nothing to do with it.

My mother was a Faith-Keeper. Faith-Keepers are mostly women. They help out as a group and announce the time for ceremony. Their duty is to uphold our way of life. My mother used to tell me, "You're not going to school today, you're going to ceremony," which is not like it is now. That's why I learned a lot.

When I was three or four years old, I had a bad accident that almost took my life. I was creeping around the stove, and one of the women working there accidentally spilled boiling water all over my back. My mother took me to a lot of ceremonies and used medicine, trying to keep me alive. They thought they were going to lose me, so she went to Seneca, which is about two hours away. She had to ride all night in an old Model T, which only went about fifteen miles an hour.

They had a ceremony there, and an old man stood up and said, "When this boy grows up, he's going to have a high position that has to do with a lot of people." So my life was laid out already. My mother wasn't sure if I was going to live or not, but he was saying that I wasn't going to go; I was going to live, and when I was selected as head chief, she told me what the old man had said.

It's pretty hard to be a leader, though; there's lots of pressure. If anybody has trouble, you have to go and help them iron it out. I conduct the weddings, and the other chiefs take care of the funerals. Once someone asked if we have any ministers, and I said, "Yes, we have twenty-six of them," because we're all preachers. We're working for the Creator, who set down that all leaders must have the peace and welfare of the people in mind. That's what a chief's got to carry. You can always define a good mind for yourself if someone is considerate, talks softly, and is truthful. That's a good mind.

It's hard for a chief to carry on in a bad way because it will come back to him. For instance, he cannot say to someone, "Look, you're not supposed to be running around with this woman, because you're married," if he's doing the same thing. In our way there's only one marriage. We have no such thing as divorce. Sometimes people leave their marriage and stay with someone else, but it's not good for them. The Council won't give them permission to do that. It's already made out that you live forever with your spouse, and the only thing that will separate you is death. If people need help, or have problems with the family, I try to go out and correct them. It's not easy because there aren't many people who would like to meddle in other people's problems. I really don't like it, but I have to go when they ask, so I do the best I can.

When someone wants a Six Nation meeting, I call all my chiefs together. We'll all sit down and agree on whether we need to have a meeting. When that's decided, we send a runner out to each nation. We still do it the old way, by sending a runner out to deliver a message, except now he goes in a car. Sometimes we use a phone, but we really don't like to.

When the runner goes out, each nation sends back a piece of wood with beads made of clam shell and a message in Onondaga. This tells us how many clan mothers are in their meeting and how many will come, so we'll be prepared to provide housing for them.

In our greetings (we have greetings instead of prayers), we thank everything on Mother Earth that was put here by the Creator. I never pray for money because the Creator didn't make that. When he came into this world, he made the earth and planted the human beings. He planted all kinds of grass, weeds, and all kinds of medicine to help human beings survive. He also gave duties to the water coming from underground, and to the rain and the thunder, to wash the Mother Earth and water all the things that were planted. So all the greetings tell us what the Creator was doing and why we give thanks.

For instance, the moon controls the cycles of women and also brings human beings into this world. She also controls the water, so when you're saying your greetings, you're also referring to all of the works that the moon and the sun do. That's how you get to know what these gifts are for. It's our duty to thank everything. That's why I sometimes say that our work is about being the guardians of the country. We're only here visiting, and we don't know when we're going to leave. Only the Creator knows that.

We don't call him God. I don't know what God means. The Creator tells us that we were made from Mother Earth and we will go back to Mother Earth. But the spirit goes back to the Creator. That's why we have instructions. If some don't follow the instructions and do bad things, they won't return to the Creator. That's why we leaders have to keep preaching about what is good and what is bad. Because that's what breaks down the community. They call it a "changing of the mind." Drinking will make you do things that you wouldn't do in your right mind. It "changes your mind."

You can talk to the young people who are drinking, but you can't make them quit. They have to quit themselves. In this world, it's true that a lot of them drink, but they won't quit until they're ready to do it themselves. They lose their pride, break up with their women, and try to forget it, but they're just hurting themselves. Sometimes either their peers or the grown-ups tell them, "You're not any good," and they believe it. But these peers and grown-ups never tell them to be themselves, or that they're as good as the next person.

I was young when I started with ceremony. Education didn't interfere then because ceremony was much more important. I only learned a little bit in school, because at that time it wasn't necessary to go to high school or college. Now you have to go at least through high school, but it's important in this world not to forget your ways. Education's fine, but don't forget your language.

This is a difficult balance. When I was five years old, my mother talked Indian to me all the time. My father also taught me a lot because he could speak English and his own language. Nowadays, some of the young ones don't even know their own language. And if you don't know the language, you miss some of the messages that the Creator left. Even though I learned when I was young, there's no end to the learning, because the Creator left us all these messages about what's going to be.

We have four seasonal ceremonies, in the spring, summer, fall, and midwinter. The midwinter ceremony goes for fourteen days continuously. Once a year we have our ancestors' ceremony, usually in March before the plants begin to grow, because you can't mix death with life.

There's a monument to Chief Handsome Lake near where I was brought up. Handsome Lake was a Seneca back in the 1700s. It was a time when they used to go hunting before the lake froze. They'd go and get meat for the winter and trade fur at the trading post. When the spring came, they'd send back a runner to the shore to see if the ice was gone so they could go to the trading post to trade their fur. The first thing the trader would do is give them some rum and get them drunk so he could help himself to whatever they had.

Since the trader got them drunk, they didn't care about the cost much and may have given some of the meat away. When they returned to the village the people could hear them

singing because they were drunk. Handsome Lake kept getting sick from the drinks, and it made him think about who made all the trees, the sky, the moon, and the sun. He kept thinking about this until finally he got pretty sick and died.

When they were having a wake for him, his half-brother, Corn Planter, touched his body, and it felt a little warm. He felt his heart and said, "It's warm yet." So everyone waited until even that spot was cold, but they didn't notice Handsome Lake's spirit getting up and going outside the door. When Handsome Lake went outside, he met the Four Protectors, sent down by the Creator. They told him that he had to get rid of something before they could take him with them. Handsome Lake thought they meant his singing, and they said no. He tried three or four other things, and they said no to each of them. Finally he said, "Maybe I drink too much." And they said, "Yes, that's what it is."

Then they made him some kind of medicine out of berry root and made a potion to make him quit drinking. They left and came back the following day, and he was cured. When they thought he was ready, they took him to the Creator and told him all the things that were coming in the future. He looked down and saw the earth and saw a highway from one ocean to the other. They also knew there was going to be a buggy running without anything pulling it, and that things invented from then on would take a lot of lives. They also told him that there would be a time when a sickness would eat the inside of you. Now they call it cancer.

The last thing they said would happen is that all those born would return back to the Creator right away. That they would just come to live on the earth a little while, but they wouldn't reach manhood or womanhood.

I measure the length of time of each of these events by all the things we were told. When I see each one happen, I know that pretty soon time is running out. But our prophecy doesn't say that there's going to be a next world. That's just something I see. The chiefs are always talking about the Creator's messages in order to keep us going in a good way. There must be peace among us, that's first. Then, the leaders that are put up are supposed to be caring for the people. That means that you're not working for yourself, to make a better living or more money; you're working to help other people.

I was at the Earth Summit Conference in Rio in 1992, and it was overpowered by the leaders that were against the environment. When President Bush arrived, there were about two thousand people from all over the world at this one hotel. He had them cleared out so he could bring his own people in. Even though he talked outside for ten minutes, nobody clapped when he got through. It was not a good welcome, like a cold shoulder; he didn't make a big impression. There were three of us speaking there, including myself, Vince Johnson, and Oren Lyons. They kept us pretty busy.

I didn't think too much of the Summit itself. Some groups were concerned about the environment, and others were more interested in progress. If people aren't careful, the environment's going to take over. The water will not be drinkable, the air won't be breathable, and the land will be so polluted nothing will grow. You know it's going to happen, but you don't know how soon. We could lessen this if people cut out all the things that are polluting the air, land, and water. But the way I see it, we're near the point of no return. Everybody seems to want to make money and have a nice car. That's the thought, so how are you going to win? Nobody wants to start walking, but they're doing a lot of running for exercise.

We still carry on our old ways. We are governed by the clan mothers' chiefs, and that's what makes us strong. We are different from the European people because we don't ask for help from the outside. That's what gives us power, because we're not dependent on other governments. Even though they want to give us education, we have our own teachers in the school here teaching the Indian language and history.

When the Hopi came here, they were pretty amazed that we could still carry on our ceremony even though we live so close to the city. It's true we're losing our language, but everybody all over is. We're having some problems right now between the businesses and the governing body here. In the beginning, the businesses had to come to the Council, and we had an agreement that each one would pay a twenty-five-cent tax for each carton of cigarettes sold. For a while they paid, but suddenly they stopped. The Council, not the chiefs, pressed for the money, and then they blockaded the entrances to the businesses not cooperating. They still refuse to pay because they want an accounting of where the money's going. They've got their own excuses, but you can't tell the state government that you're not going to pay because you don't know what it's being used for.

It's the same with bingo. Two summers ago, some outsiders were pushing to put in a big bingo house. We had a lot of problems with that idea, so we stopped it, because it ends up that they're the ones making the money, not the Indians. The ones running the businesses only have money on their minds; they don't know their own way. Money isn't everything. They lose respect for the Mother Earth.

Only Onondaga can build or buy land here. That's why we have to keep track of everyone, but we're not interested in how many there are. The U.S. brought their census in because they would like to tax us, but we chased them out. We have an agreement that if they want to teach us their way, then they pay for everything through the treaty. If they use part of the road through here, then they have to maintain it. Now they have to ask permission to come in when they need to work—even the telephone company does, if they want to fix the lines. That goes for the police, too. We don't ask the state troopers to come in; we only work with the sheriff's office.

I have learned that there is no force in spirituality. That's what we follow in our way of life, or "religion." This is how we conduct ourselves with the earth and everything on it. We don't do it for business or for money. It's an altogether different way of living and doing things than in the United States. We don't tax people's land or their homes. They're free. And when they're visiting, they can make themselves at home.

It's said that we're all visitors. That none of us stays here forever. The time is set, but nobody but the Creator knows when we're all going to go. So that's our whole outlook—we're just visiting and trying to make the best of it.

## Audrey Shenandoah: clan mother

I am an Eagle Clan Mother of the Onondaga nation. In my nation, that position is chosen by the clan people. It used to be that the eldest female in any given clan was entitled to that position, but over time we have been robbed of many of the people who would have been eligible as clan mother. Those who have turned to Christianity, or to the American form of government, cannot be involved as a clan mother. She must be someone who is able to perpetuate and teach the ways of our Longhouse. She must stay within our own governmental structure, and take a position on the different issues as they come up. So today, it's not always the eldest female, but the eldest *eligible* person who is chosen. This is a lifetime position.

People choose a clan mother by watching how she has lived her life and cared for her family. She has to be someone who has a family and knows the responsibilities of being a mother, because that's evidence that she will take care of all the people as if they were her children. Those are the qualifications. The duties of a clan mother are many, beginning with being a counselor. She has to be there for people in times of family crisis, or for their own personal problems. She must be someone who is able to give advice on how to handle difficult situations. This goes back to someone who has followed the Longhouse way, because that's where we get our teachings.

One couple who got married last year came to me on a regular basis for about a year. We'd talk about raising a family and caring for each other and taking on the added responsibility of looking after everyone around you. When you become an adult and take on the responsibilities of marriage, you also have the responsibility of looking after everybody within your space, especially the elders.

Clan mothers also have the duty of selecting a candidate for leadership chief in the clan. To select a chief, first we bring that person to our clan members. If they accept him, then we move on to the rest of the people in our house. If he passes their inspection, we take him to the opposite house, which has the right to question him and discuss any objections.

If the candidate is rejected at any point along the way, then we must start over and find another one. But if both houses of our nation have accepted him, then we present him to the other nations, and they, in turn, have the right to question and reject him. So it's a long process. The candidate must be accepted by a lot of people along the way before he is finally installed in a position.

The installation ceremony is done by our opposite house, which means within our *Hodenausaunee* [People of the Longhouse], which are the elder and the younger brothers. The elder being the Mohawk, the Onondaga, and the Seneca, and the younger brothers being the Cayuga and the Oneida, who sit on opposite sides of the longhouse. The Onondaga sit in the middle, at the head of the Council Fire, which is what I'm referring to when I say the opposite house.

So the Oneida and the Cayuga would be the ones to install Mohawk, Onondaga, and Seneca. If the Cayuga or the Oneida needed someone, then it would be done by the Mohawk, the Seneca, and the Onondaga.

There are also two sides in everyone's respective longhouse. Certain clans sit on one side of the fire, with the other clans on the opposite side. There is always a balance. The same goes for the distribution of duties; there are always two people—one from each side of the house—to carry out whatever needs to be done, such as whenever an ambassador, or runner, is sent out on a mission.

If a chief has to be replaced for behavior that is unbecoming to his position, it's our responsibility to find someone to take that place. If we see him going on in a way that is not acceptable, we must approach him and remind him of his responsibilities. In our language, it's called "bringing him back to his feet." This does not happen often, but it has happened a couple of times during my lifetime.

It's a very difficult thing to deal with. The clan mother must approach him to talk and then seats him back in his place. If he continues to do wrong, then she takes a Faith-Keeper to speak to him. And together the two of them try to "bring him back to his feet." The third time, she takes one of the young men from the clan to speak to him.

Molesting a woman is considered completely unacceptable behavior for a clan chief. That calls for him to be immediately dehorned [to remove his hat of office], which he does himself in silence. There are no words when that occurs; he is immediately cut off. This demonstrates the respectful place that the women have within our society.

The same applies to someone with blood on his hands from killing another person. But there are other reasons as well, such as a person who is not trustworthy, who "speaks with a forked tongue" as they say in English. Or, someone who just doesn't come to the Council and doesn't attend to his duties and ceremonies.

There has got to be someone to attend to the ceremonies and keep his responsibilities as a leader. It is also necessary that that person speak his own language. My brother-in-law Leon Shenandoah will be very difficult to replace as a clan chief when that time comes, and that is on all of our minds. But we do not actually make preparations for that ahead of time.

I was born a member of the Onondaga nation on May 5, 1926, near where the longhouse is now. My parents were both Onondaga. My grandparents on my mother's side were Onondaga. My grandfather on my dad's side was Mohawk, and my grandmother was Onondaga. There has always been a lot of travel between our nations, so it is not unusual for our people to intermarry with other nations. My mother wasn't a clan mother, but my grandmother on my father's side was a Faith-Keeper when she was young. My mother and my mother's family were all Christian.

My grandmother went to Hampton Institute in Virginia and then on to a seminary. When she married my father's father, she became a Christian. But I remember as a little girl that she was always consulted about longhouse ceremonies. She remained informed, although she didn't go to the longhouse herself and continued to go to the Christian church.

My uncles and my father went to the longhouse, and some went to both. When I was a little girl, I went to church, sometimes three times a day with my grandmother, but I also went to the longhouse with my uncles and my father and my next-door neighbors, and my mother never objected. She never had anything bad to say about the longhouse, never denounced it in any way. So then I began to go to the longhouse more often.

When I was ten years old, I joined the Girl Scouts. Because we were an Indian Girl Scout troop, we were asked to go to a lot of events in central New York. They always asked questions about our people, because we were different. I felt a curiosity to learn more about my people. There wasn't really anyone in our group who could answer the questions that the other Girl Scouts were asking completely enough, so I began going to the longhouse more and more.

I was very young when I began attending longhouse meetings, discussions, and ceremonies. Since I was raised by my grandmother, who was over sixty when I came to her as a nine-month-old infant, we spoke only the Indian language in our house. She was an elder, and all of the people that came to visit were also elderly and only spoke the Indian language, so there was a lot of discussion on the things that went on among our people.

My father's relatives spoke Mohawk, and my grandmother's father spoke Seneca, and if you really listen, both languages have a lot of similarities. So I heard the Indian language a lot while I was home. Learning the Longhouse way was easy for me because I knew the

ONONDAGA

75

language. A lot of people my age were born of parents who had been through that boarding school era and had come back not knowing their language, so they couldn't pass the culture on.

My mother didn't know the language. She was a Christian and totally inclined toward the dominant culture. That didn't cause too much of a conflict for me because I didn't live with her. I only visited her during the holidays. My parents weren't together when I was born, but I had such a full life with my grandmother that I didn't suffer the difficulty of a broken home. When I look back I must have been pretty spiritual because of the things that I would hear in the longhouse. Chief Irving Powless, who passed away a few years ago, used to be amazed about all the things that I knew. He would say, "How do you know that? You're not that old." But I would remember all the people coming over to my grandmother's house and talking. We lived right near the longhouse, so when there was something going on which involved all the Six Nations people, there were always people staying over from different places in our house.

I don't think I was spiritually gifted as a child, but I was exposed more than other people my own age. When I was only fifteen, I was asked to take notes at a Six Nations meeting because the person who normally took notes was unable to come. I had been seen there enough that they knew I understood the language and what was going on. I remember being so nervous, but I was also impressed and elated that I was being asked to sit among all these great chiefs and take notes. That was a very high point in my life.

It was a long time before I finally cut off all ties with the church. After I was married I just stopped going and went to the longhouse instead. But my little children were going to both the church and the longhouse. One Easter, I finally told my aunt that my kids weren't going to go to church with her anymore. She cried as if I had died, probably more than if I had died. A couple of days later she came to my house with the minister to pray and talk with me. My mother had passed away, but my grandmother had not told me anything about why you should or shouldn't go to church; she just said to go wherever you were happy. So even though she was a Christian, it didn't bother her if we went to the longhouse. But it made me very angry that my aunt brought the minister over. We had a bad time right up until she passed away five years ago. Every time we met at birthdays or whatever, she always managed to get in some digs about the heathens and pagans.

Now I teach language and culture at our school. I have been working here since 1972, but I was an aide until 1978, when I finally got a provisional certificate to become a teacher. I was asked to take the job by the Council of Chiefs while we were doing some community investigating into the school system.

That investigation was initiated by some high school seniors who were willing to give up their graduation and senior year to bring changes about for the kids who were following

them. At that time, nothing was being taught about our people, maybe a single paragraph in a whole textbook. So we threw a lot of books out. State monies allocated to the education of Native Americans in New York were all put into a general fund. We formed a committee to look into what funds were being given to the other schools and found, by comparison, we had nothing.

Later that year, we had a very formidable group investigating different areas of the whole educational system. That was when the Council asked me to come in and teach language. It was a difficult personal decision for me. Our culture has always been against formal education because of what it has done to our people. So I had to deal with my own personal inner convictions and those of the longhouse community.

One of my deepest concerns right now is about our youth. We live so close to the city—we are one of the nearest of all our nations of people to a big city—which makes it hard for the teens to keep in mind the importance of being who they are. These are the years they usually get into trouble, and it's especially hard because they have this other culture coming at them from all directions. They have a hard time being different. Some can manage, the ones who have parents who are strong. But with television, radio, magazines, and the papers, it's hard. After they reach the age of, say, nineteen or so they usually can see the value of their own culture.

In kindergarten until about the sixth grade, they soak up just about everything that you can give them. They're really excited about their language and culture. But by the time they're in junior high, other things become important to them. They're not home all the time anymore; they're out in society. If they can just make it through those years remembering our laws and our ceremonies, then they will make the right decisions. I keep pointing out that, in what we call the "Great Law," we have all of the rules and guidelines for living.

I tell them, if you find yourself in a position where you have to make a major decision, think about the things that are taught in the longhouse, and ask yourself, "Is this going to bring harm to myself, or to any other living thing?" Basically, that's what we call respect—respect for yourself, respect for people around you, and respect for the earth.

As women, we have a very special privilege and responsibility here on this earth, to bring forth life and to nurture it in its very beginnings. We should respect ourselves for that. It's a very, very high position, and it's sad that a lot of women don't feel that and carry that self-esteem. We don't have to go beyond our means to be equal to men, which is how we differ from so many feminist organizations.

A fallacy has been perpetuated from back in the old days about women doing all of the hard work. It's true women cultivated the land and did the planting, but that was because of the special relationship for growing things that our culture felt women had. Women all over the world do the planting anyway, and always have. When the children came of age, around nine or ten, they knew everything they needed to know about survival. They knew how to plant, how to harvest. They knew how to gather food and how to preserve it. And they knew how to take care of themselves and one another. All under the nurturing and protection of the women of the village.

By the time boys and girls were old enough to go out into mixed society, their talents were usually visible. Some were going to be singers, some speakers, some dancers. So all the stories about the little boy going out with his arrow and bringing home a deer were not true, because they were only taught about the bow and the arrow and the spear when they had the physical ability. The saying, "Don't send a boy out to do a man's job," came from our people. As times changed, there weren't any restrictions on a woman's physical activity. Whatever she was physically able to do, she would do. Except for sports that overdevelop the muscles and organs in a young woman's body that she needs to carry and deliver a baby. A lot of colleges began having girls' lacrosse teams a few years back. But our way does not allow us to let our girls play lacrosse; it says so right in our ceremony that this game is given to our men and the boys.

We are a very tight community because we still utilize our clan system, and that keeps everyone aware that we are all family. People still know who their family is beyond their third or fourth cousin, but it's getting more like the white society now—not as close. In our culture, your aunts are your mothers. Your mother's brothers are also your fathers, and everybody is your grandmother. All elders are our relatives.

# ALICE PAPINEAU: SECRET MEDICINE SOCIETIES

My name is Alice Papineau; my spiritual name is Dewasenta. I am an Onondaga clan mother of the Eel Clan, and I have lived at Onondaga all of my life. I was born right here on August 1, 1912. My mother had six of us, and she never had a doctor or a nurse. In those days everybody used midwives. It was the way of life here.

We still have our own health laws for pregnancy, what to do and what not to do, and how to take care afterward. At birth, there was a cleansing that a woman had to do, since she hasn't had a period for nine months. She would drink about three or four gallons of these herbs. It was made from the bark of a wild cherry tree; it would cleanse the woman and make milk. That's the way that I was born. When you drink this, you don't drink coffee, tea, or water; you just take the medicine.

We didn't have big families. Six children was considered a huge family. We usually only had four in a family, because of this purification medicine we took. It wasn't made to keep

the population down; it was a health law. And now that they have discouraged women from taking this medication, we have larger families. It was in a way a natural birth control, but we didn't take it for that reason. The cleansing is what gave them the safe menstrual periods. So now we have people with nine kids.

The habit of being in bed during childbirth and after you have a baby is something brought over from the royal families in England. The queens thought lying down during birth was a luxury, but really it's an unnatural position. The natural position is to either stand up or squat. So immediately after the woman bore the child, the midwife would have her stand up straight and drink a bowl of this medicine. All of us children were birthed like that, and mothers all nursed their babies for about three to three-and-a-half years.

We never drank cow's milk, and we didn't put our babies on cow's milk either, because it doesn't agree with us. We don't have the enzymes to digest that milk. When the U.S. State Health Center came out here, they would try to brainwash us. They told us our breast milk was no good, "Don't nurse your baby with breast milk because you have blue milk." I don't know what made them think that. Everybody here had bad milk according to the government. So mothers put their babies on formula.

I remember this because I had my first child when I was twenty-five years old, and they were discouraging breast-feeding then. I would put the baby on formula, but cow's milk didn't agree with us—it had a lot of mucus, and it also gave our babies earaches. That was something brought in by the Europeans; it was not our way for nourishment.

I am glad today many of the young mothers are going back to having their babies at home. The hospitals did away with our purification after the birth. Of course, you can't do that in a hospital because they have you lying down in bed for ten days. Eventually, they found out that this was bad, too, so now we have been liberated, and mothers can nurse their babies again. As far as the purification tea, they don't do that anymore because it was discouraged so much. It came to the point that if a midwife delivered a baby, she would be arrested. We were always told that our natural way of doing things was bad according to New York State law.

My mother wasn't a clan mother; she was a Faith-Keeper. She lived to be eighty-six years old, and my father lived to be seventy-three. The Faith-Keeper works to keep the faith. It's like an auxiliary organization, like the firemen's auxiliary. Her duty is to work and cook at ceremonies, while being the timekeeper, too. We don't follow the calendar; we go by the moon and the seasons. We just had our Planting Seed Dance Ceremony. My mother used to always say that the time that you can actually start planting your corn— "Gehet" is the Indian name for the tree that you see on our hillside—is when the tree has the white blossoms. We have our ceremonies during the growing moon, not on the receding moon.

My grandmother was Onondaga Deer Clan. During the wars, when they were burning the villages, she and her family went up north to run away from all the trouble.

They don't have a Deer Clan among the Mohawk. My grandfather went up there to compete with the Mohawks in a lacrosse game, that's where he met my grandmother and brought her back here. She proved that she was Onondaga Deer Clan, so she was given the role here. She passed away here, but was actually born in the Mohawk country. That's the way it is, we have so many Onondagas up there because their great-grandparents moved up there when we had trouble. They always knew who they were and where they were from because of their clan.

My grandmother only had two sons and a daughter. My mother's mother was born here and was Onondaga and lived here all her life. She was also Eel Clan, whatever clan your mother is, that's what you are.

I was mentioning the ancestor ceremonies. Early in the spring, when the trees are still asleep, before they bud and come back to life, that's when we have our ceremony to our ancestors. The women—the Faith-Keepers and the clan mothers—gather information as to when the ceremony will be. Then, two weeks before, they go to every home here and ask for food or money to be used at this ceremony. And everybody that enters into the longhouse always says, "Oh, is it that time again?" And they gather whatever they can. It's something that is accepted here. Even the people that don't go to the longhouse have grown up with that custom and willingly give.

We used to have a lot of corn soup for this gathering. We start at about nine in the evening. For every song the men singers sing—they sing about eighty altogether—the women sing the same song after them. They are our ancestor songs. It takes till about midnight for all the songs to be sung.

Then we have a give-away. We give all new things to the people who worked, who cooked. Everybody gets something, like a towel, socks, shirts, all bought for the give-away. It's about 1:30 when the food is given out, and that usually takes about an hour and a half. Everybody brings their own basket with dishes, and we give them food in their dishes. We don't sit at a table—there is no table there at all—you just sit down and eat on your lap. Traditional food and modern food are both served. The traditional foods we use are corn soup, squash, different kinds of pumpkin, boiled corn bread, and all kinds of beans. Then, after everybody eats and all the food has been passed out, we have pies and cakes. Like I said, ancient food and modern food.

When everything is cleared away and put back into the kitchen, we have social dancing until dawn. When it first starts to get light we have another ceremony and singing, then everybody goes home. People come from all over, from Cattaraugaus, Allegheny, Tuscarora, Niagara Falls—the whole confederacy is there to visit. And we support one another. Different nations all have this ceremony to the ancestors—*Okawa* we call it. They might have a different way of saying it, but it's the same songs. The Seneca song is the same as the Onondaga song that we sing. Different tempo, but same words. Some wear traditional clothing, some don't.

We have four major ceremonies during a year for the four seasons. During the winter is the equinox, which used to be in December, but now we have it in January because of Christmas. So many of our people have intermarried with Christians, we moved it to January because Christmas time is a busy time for the Christians, and it's pretty hard on our youth not to celebrate Christmas. It depends on the family, how strong they are. With all the lights and the glitter, radio and television advertisements everywhere, it's hard on our children. Some give presents, and some may drag a tree home, but it has no meaning of Christmas. It's just an exciting time of the year. But it can be a great burden, too.

Our winter solstice ceremony takes three weeks. We don't follow the calendars, so the date that it could fall on could be anytime—the beginning of January, the middle, or toward the end—it depends on the moon. In the spring is the Planting Dance, and that takes six days. The next one would be the Green Corn Dance, which also lasts six days.

And then, besides the four seasonal ceremonies between the equinox and the planting dances, we have the Running of the Sap Ceremony. It starts in February. At the end of that, you make maple syrup candy, which is hardened in pans and made into squares. In June, for the first fruit of the year, we have the Strawberry Ceremony, which only runs one day. And then in June or July, we have the Bean Dance, for the corn, beans, and squash. We don't use the yellow corn that has been crossbred since the Europeans came over.

We also have many medicine ceremonies in between. We are known to have secret medicine societies. Only those who have been inflicted with a particular sickness or disease are allowed to go to the respective healing ceremony. I belong to four medicine societies. They are held in homes. The medicine people are very strong here, but you would never know it. And we would never, never get invited if we didn't belong to that particular society. We have many in the wintertime, especially.

I belong to one society that holds ceremony only at night. I belong to another, the Bear Society, that holds ceremony in the late afternoon. I also belong to the Fish Ceremony and the Grandfather's Ceremony. The Grandfathers are healers. They are the ones that wear the medicine masks, the false face, which is very strong here. That's a medicine ceremony that takes place during the winter solstice. The reason why the winter solstice ceremony takes three weeks is because we have many medicine ceremonies in the morning, but not too many at night.

We have singers and drummers in our medicine ceremonies. Nobody would ever know it because we don't allow non-Native people at all, because right away they go and write about it. And as I said, only people who have been afflicted by the sickness are invited to a ceremony. There's much cooking—every society uses a particular kind of food. We have one big ceremony to the Grandfathers, the Thunder Beings, to the Wind Spirit.

I had a healing when I was about nine years old. A woman who was one of the greatest medicine women at the time cured me. Her name was Electa Thomas. Most of our medicine people have been women. They have knowledge of different herbs. I believe in the medicines. I probably would have been a cripple if I hadn't been healed by them.

Something was festering on my arm. I have a scar now, but then it looked like a boil. My mother called a white, state Indian doctor. He came out from South Onondaga in an old Model T Ford. He lanced it, but then it moved further up my arm. He didn't lance the second one because he didn't know what it was. He told my mother, "It isn't a boil. It isn't a carbuncle." He said, "Use your Indian medicine." That's before they started taking your blood to the hospital to be tested. He was just a country doctor. So then it pussed up and went to my leg. I was laid up for a while with that. I had to keep my foot up on a chair.

My mother finally took me to see Dr. Electa Thomas. She took care of me. I had to have three ceremonies. I drank about two gallons of the herb tea she made. It cleared up and it never returned after I had those ceremonies. There are different kinds of medicine that you take with each ceremony.

I grew up across from the longhouse. People are familiar with the term "longhouse." When you go into a state hospital they ask you what your denomination is, for your last rites, I guess. So if you say "Longhouse," they accept that. Everybody born under the Iroquois Confederacy is Longhouse, or *Hodenausaunee.* Even the Christians are *Hodnausaunee,* even if they later turned to Christianity. They are still People of the Longhouse.

I used to deliver a quart of milk to Electa every day because my father owned a couple of milking cows. I thought she was about the messiest housekeeper I had ever seen in my life. But she was a busy woman, she gathered her own medicines, and she had bottles and jars of herbs all over her house. People used to come to her in horse and buggy; she had quite a reputation. She even doctored non-Indians from the city, and she would help them. Finally, she bought a house in the city in Syracuse, and she had an office there where non-Indians would go. She spoke both English and her own language well.

She made a lot of money from the people in the city. With the Native people, she exchanged gifts and things. She finally died, but she was my favorite woman. I always keep a picture of her. I would like to give a copy to the school—they keep all those pictures in the hallway. If you go to the historical society in Syracuse, you'll find her life story there. She had no children, so she never trained anybody.

We never train anybody unless they are interested. That's one thing you cannot force on a person. They either take a liking to it and they are readily interested or they don't care. That's what happens with our young—they don't have these values that the older people had. Anyway, roots and herbs are not my talent. I have trouble identifying plants where other people can identify any kind of plant immediately. I had trouble remembering the names of the herbs.

I don't ordinarily tell these things. Some people think that only the western Indians have any knowledge of medicines because we are so secretive about it. There were two men that I know of that capitalized on their healing. They had an office, too, where the non-Indians came. Of course, they had a lot of money. We really don't care for people like that, who go around and make money on healing. We do give for healing, but it's usually a blanket or some other gift, not with money. That's how we pay, not with money. Even if we went to an office, we would probably give a blanket, just like the western Native people do.

We have our own sacred tobacco that we use. Not just any tobacco, we use it from a particular seed. We are the only ones that have that seed. The only reason I am telling you this is because we do have our own kind of medicine. Everybody thinks that you have to be a Sioux or a Crow to be traditional. There are so many that have accepted Christianity. Even Leonard Crow Dog did a ceremony out here at our longhouse, and he had a suitcase with his paraphernalia in there, and he had a cross.

You will never see a cross in our homes. Because we have our own messiah. The stone, that rock, that came way out from Ontario, at the head of Lake Ontario. It's where our Peacemaker was born. Last year I went on a Peace Tour, to the places that our Peacemaker had traveled. The Peacemaker was Huron by birth. But the Hurons didn't accept his vision; it wasn't accepted by his own people. So he went east by foot until he came to the Mohawk valley. The Mohawks accepted him and believed him. This was two thousand years ago, but the legend still goes on. Nobody can set the date. His name is not permissible to say because we don't want to make it common. The reason that we are not allowed to make it common is because they will take the name and use it in vain, and swear, say it when they are angry. So we all say Peacemaker. Maybe it is all right to tell people who don't understand the name. But the only time we use his name is during a ceremony. It's nice to keep it sacred.

On the tour, for nine days they took us through the Mohawk valley. And then we saw where the Peacemaker and Hiawatha met. We had meetings in different places. In Troy, the

ONONDAGA

church invited us and had a dinner for us. The man who led the tour was Jake Thomas, who is from Six Nations up in Canada. He is Cayuga and one of the most knowledgeable men of this generation. He lectures on the *Hodenausaunee*. He would tell about the Peacemaker briefly, explain who he was. I'm sure he had a divine mind to be able to establish a confederacy. We didn't have just Native people on the tour; we had other people who were interested, who knew the history of the Peacemaker. So to me that is a very sacred story. We saw the place where he was born, then we saw the place where he grew up, and the place where he was last seen with his canoe going east on his mission of peace. All the way up past O'Hara Creek, where he and Hiawatha met. Before we confederated, that's the trail that we took, his path.

For me it was a very sacred tour. It was like the people going to Jerusalem, on a pilgrimage.

# SIX NATIONS

## Sara Smith: Under the Tree of Peace

*In October 1992 I flew to Buffalo, New York, and rented a car. First I visited some of the reservations in upstate New York, then my plan was to drive across the border to the Six Nations reserve (as they are called in Canada) in Ontario, where I had an appointment to meet Sara Dale Smith. The day was overcast when I arrived in Buffalo; by five o'clock the sky had grown dark with angry clouds that had swirled in from the west. Within an hour rain and sleet were pounding my windshield, all but obliterating my vision. I had told Sara to expect me before dark, so I pushed on, straining to find the Peace Bridge, the signs seeming to disappear at every turn. Rush hour traffic bore down on me, horns blaring, refusing to let me change lanes; monster trucks sped by me hurling more water onto my windshield—and all the while I was thinking, Indians were driven onto reservations to make way for this?*

*By the time I crossed the border into Canada it was night, and I had perhaps another hour and a half to go before I was supposed to exit. Then, carefully following Sara's directions, I found myself on long stretches of unmarked, unlit country roads, and it was getting on toward nine. I drove on, wondering if I had missed a turn, until to my enormous relief I saw the lights of a small store ahead. I called Sara and was given new directions similar to the "right-at-the-tree, left-at-the-rock" ones earlier, except that it was night, the distance great, with no one to stop and ask.*

*She described her house, which she assured me was only ten miles from where I was, and promised to leave a light on. It was eleven by the time I found it. Sara opened the door and*

*without a word hugged me. She had herbal tea and biscuits ready, the bed in the guest room was turned down, and I nearly wept.*

*It was clear that if I was going to be doing this time travel, back and forth into Indian country, cursing modern highways, I'd better improve my navigational skills.*

*In the morning, after breakfast, we went into a sun-washed living room that looked out onto a sloping yard and a giant shade tree and began our interview.*

*Sara is a young elder, soft-spoken and gentle, who possesses the wisdom of all the elders who have gone before her. From the time she was quite young, her spiritual quest has been the focus of her life. Her teachers, she explains, came into her life when she called them to her.*

My given name is Sara Smith. I was born on the Six Nations of the Grand River Reservation in Ontario, Canada. I am of the Mohawk Tribe, Turtle Clan of the Iroquois Confederacy. My ancestors had been actively involved in the movement and affairs of the nation territory and community before and after the migration from Mohawk valley in New York State. Several of my great-Dodahs [teachers, not always biological grandparents] were interpreters and spokesmen for the Confederacy because they spoke several of the Iroquoian dialects, as well as English and French. My grandparents understood the language but never spoke it, and my parents did not understand or speak the language at all.

Then our generation came along, so far removed from the traditional language. But there were other ways of instilling in us who we were and why. So it was up to us to begin that search for our roots.

The Iroquois were people of the Great League of Peace, and I have honored, loved, and respected that, feeling that it was a blessing coming into this incarnation. I believe that we are reincarnated individuals, that we have had many lives. And that today we are a sum total of all those past lives. It is my understanding that we enter into this Earth Walk because we have made mistakes in the past, and we come back to work toward perfection. We work toward perfection so that we can attain the ultimate goal of becoming Spirit People again. I recognize and embrace that we are given many options and choices along that pathway.

We were instructed to search our roots, and in so doing we would find the peace and protection under the Great Tree, which is our symbol of the Iroquois Confederacy, the original five nations who chose to govern their people by peace. What I feel is so important today is that we work toward getting back onto the Pathway of Peace again.

My Dodah used to say to me, "How far back do you want to go?" And many people ask me today, "Why would you want to go back?" I feel that it's not so much going back as it is coming full circle, and going on again. We have been off our Pathway of Peace for a long,

long time. We, as so-called "Red People," have got to admit that we have been off our path. Otherwise we wouldn't be under the strife that so many of our settlements are in today. So much chaos, confusion, and internal strife. But if we were living according to the Law that the Great Mystery, the Life-Giver, Creator, God—the One of Many Names—gifted us with, we wouldn't be in the turmoil we are in today. I don't think that there is a family today that isn't hurting and in need of healing.

It has all been prophesied by our people that the time would come that we would be in this state. That we would be wandering around in darkness, even though the sun is out. And that the heads of the chiefs and the leaders would be rolling like tumbleweeds in a desert storm.

There is much to these prophecies. In our settlements there is a great deal of controversy over who is the rightful one to carry the title, who is the one to make the decisions to govern the people. But before, when we were walking on that Pathway of Peace, there was no dispute; everyone knew and embraced that way of life without question. The prophecies talk about the Sacred Council Fire that burned so brightly here on Turtle Island once, because the people had made the decision that they would govern by peace and not by power. There is a big difference between a government built on power and one that embraces peaceful co-existence of all life.

Understanding the duality of life is important, whether it be winter or summer, hot or cold, left or right, day or night. The balance of day and night is critical. We have gotten out of balance with the daytime and the nighttime. It has become "seemingly" necessary to work sixteen to eighteen hours a day, and rest for five at the most. We allow the children of today to go off to school by themselves to a teacher who is not a family member, for six to eight hours a day. They have to get up early in the morning to sit on a bus for an hour, and when they return at night they watch television until suppertime, then more TV, and then to bed. We no longer spend that quality time with them, so there is no longer any interaction between the old and the young.

Children need the balance only their parents and the old people can give them. There was a time when the evening was story time for both, when they could share the day's message. The children are also our teachers; we have forgotten to honor that, too.

In the times of the Good Life there were twelve hours for work and play and twelve hours for rest and healing. Nighttime is a precious time for rest and healing. Today, we find ourselves with so much "dis-ease," and we wonder why.

One of the most precious things that occurs during the night is the dream time, when there is a personal connection to the upper, spiritual realms. Today, we operate too much on the physical plane. We are too materialistic and physical-minded, and there again we are out of balance. We need to put ourselves back in proper perspective. It is important for the little ones now to understand their dreams and to work with them.

I consider it a blessing that I entered into this Earth Walk as a dreamer. My earliest and strongest recollections of my childhood are my dreams; they have always guided me. Dreams have limitless potential. Part of the teaching of our forefathers was about the dream-world. They never, ever sat on a council and raised their arms to vote on something instantaneously. The wise decisions they had to make, to provide for their people for seven generations to come, took time. Divine guidance came to them through their dreams and visions.

Some of the dreams I had as a child were seemingly negative, what one might call nightmares, but I would like to encourage people to share my understanding that there are no such things as bad dreams. It's only when we allow ourselves to be led into thinking that there is a negative force that it becomes just that. Inside every dream, which is so uniquely ours and so personal, is something pure that comes from Spirit. Teachings may come repeatedly to us to impact on our minds, to tell us that we need to do something about the dream. If we don't react, then we allow the dream to go to sleep. We have to learn to see the beauty of the teachings in our dreams, and let them become our guides. It's like us walking on this pathway. We know goodness is there, but we do not always know how to find it. It's when we begin to examine and turn things around to see the many facets both in life and in dreams that we can appreciate the beauty that is within. And that same beauty is within every individual as well. One complements the other. When children have these so-called bad dreams, it is because they need to begin their own personal search.

We have got to come to the understanding that if we allow fear to crowd our physical life, then we are shutting down the natural forces that are in our being. Because fear and jealousy are two of the greatest destructive weapons that there are. The Creator, the Great Mystery, has given us many natural ways to reverse those "negative forces." The wind can sweep them away, water will cleanse and purify, and we have medicine plants, if we honor our traditional ways.

We are given choices. Which ones are we going to make? Where do we see our lives taking us? And what about the little ones and the ones still to come? I think it is time to begin the deepest search within ourselves for the coming generations. Being a granny, I would like to leave them with a legacy that will put them back onto this Pathway of Peace. I have confidence. The children today themselves realize that. They are coming into new understanding with their new thoughts and many of them are coming with a good, clean mind. We must listen to what the children are saying.

There is a legend about why the rabbit has such huge ears. It's because he has been made to listen. So we have got to become like our brother, the rabbit, and develop the spiritual ears to not only hear what is being said but hear even that which is not being verbalized. We no longer hear the wind, we no longer hear the language of the stones, the colors, any of the forces of nature; we don't tune in to them anymore because we have long closed our ears and allowed them to go to sleep. It's time to wake our own ears up and listen. Every other living thing has maintained and is carrying out their duties and responsibilities; it is we humans who have forgotten to do that. We have taken things for granted. We have used and abused all of the sacred gifts that were put here for our use so that we could learn from them. The elements are our greatest teachers, the wind, the four-leggeds. Each comes to us with its unique teachings. All birds are messengers; they teach us to rise above the situation, to be free and rise above. Right from the tiniest winged ones to the eagle, their message is the same, to rise above situations and be free.

As a child I was influenced by the talk of my parents and the elders. They would talk about the *Hodenausaunee,* or the Original People, and I would always feel a sadness in my heart, and at the same time I would feel pride. Being born with lighter skin, brown hair, and light eyes, many would ask, Where did you get this child? I looked different and that made me do a lot of going within. Later on, I used to think, People don't understand or know what is going on inside of me. It doesn't matter what's on the outside, it's what's on the inside that counts. Even today, as I manage a gift shop and speak about traditional ways, many will ask, What part of the states did you come from?

I was fortunate in growing up on the reservation. My father was my schoolteacher. He was very much a nature lover, and he instilled that love within each one of his students. He graduated from a Normal School, which certifies one to teach. I would have to say my father was anything but normal, even in his teaching methods. He taught by experiential learning. It was nothing for him on any given day to say, "Pack up your books and go get your coats and boots." And off we would go into the woods. We learned so much. They were our science, health, and history lessons—everything all combined into one. He taught many lessons using legends, pictographs, and poetry of our own Indian poetess, Pauline Johnson. And in history, he always included the Native perspective versus non-Native concepts.

My natural instinct after high school was to become involved politically and try and contribute whatever I could, so I served a term as an elected council representative. I found that the answers for me did not lie within that system. It taught me to go out and do a lot of searching and a lot of questioning of the traditional people of the Confederacy. That is where I found my Dodah, or my grandfather, the one who contributed so much to my learning. He was able to give me direct and specific answers to my questions. I spent a lot of time learning from him, and his teachings will live on. He was my inspiration and mentor. Even though he has entered into another dimension of Life, he speaks louder and clearer today. The Original Way is in my heart now, and I am willing to share whatever little I do know whenever I am asked. What I have learned is to revere life, to be at peace with myself, and whenever possible to help others. If we can help one person, our mission is fulfilled. I think of myself as only an echo, to pass on the gift that has been given to me to whoever wishes to hear it.

We do not force our point of view upon anyone, that is not the way of our people. When I was seeking these traditional teachings, Dodah would say to me, "You have to learn to think four times greater than what you are hearing because I can only tell it to you in English, the common language that we know today. You have to learn to think four times greater." Then when I got to be a teenager, and was like all other teenagers who think they know all there is to know, he said, "Now you have to learn to think ten times greater than what it is that you are hearing." And I know now that I still have to learn to think even greater than that; many, many times greater than that. And so the search continues.

It's a joyful search, and there are many teachers out there. We have to learn to listen to many of them in order to come to our own decisions. I am grateful for so many from different nations. I was always encouraged by my grandfather to go out and hear as many people as I possibly could. My husband gave me the freedom to travel, sometimes not even knowing where I was going. I would go and listen to these people, and always I would learn from their kernels of truth or words of wisdom.

I have gone through some pretty traumatic challenges, which I couldn't have come through without the strength and support of these people who assisted the building of my foundation. Twenty years ago we had a fire; we lost our home and all of our material possessions that we had accumulated over the years. We basically had to start over. That was a great teacher for me. But the greatest challenge I had was when I had to face the possibility of losing a child, not once, but twice. Then it was always that inner voice that spoke to me and told me that these children are not your children, they are a gift to you to be cherished for only so long. Be grateful for the time you've had with them, to care and to comfort and carry them in your heart forever. These experiences made me become stronger in my beliefs.

We have four children, and they have brought us another four, and now we have ten grandchildren. Of course, they didn't always walk the path that we would choose them to be on all of the time. Now I see that in allowing them freedom to go out and experience whatever life holds for them is where our only responsibility lies. We have to be understanding enough to allow them to do that, because we never know what experience they need in order to perfect themselves.

We may have to go through this walk many times. These children chose us to be their parents. We all enter this Earth Walk knowing our connection, who and where we will learn all the lessons we need. We make that covenant before we ever enter into this Earth Walk.

It's what our soul needs, not what our physical self wants. If we can teach that to our children, then that's all we can do. We can't force them to walk the pathway that we would have them walk. But always, always give them your love.

Whenever we are gathered together, even if there are only two, and we are speaking with an open heart and a good mind in order to create an understanding, we sit in a circle. Because there are always the Unseen that have gathered there with us. Once you get up from this circle, you will never be the same individual that you were when you sat down. We have sat and shared the vibrations and the energy that have traveled the circle in us and through us. Our hearts and minds have been opened, that's the law that our people knew and practiced. That was their way of teaching.

Sometimes when it's not possible to sit in a circle, and we are seated in rows, we can quietly envision being in a circle. What we can do with the mind, collectively, even in a small way, is create change. Our thoughts are energy, they go out and manifest. Everything occurs on a spiritual plane first, before it manifests on a physical plane, and it has to have a physical vehicle in order to do that.

Humankind has stopped carrying out its duties and responsibilities as that physical vehicle because of its desire to control all of life. I think one of the reasons why governments of every nation are failing is because there are so many people wanting control. Until we learn to live in coexistence with all of life, not forsaking even the tiniest part of this total creation, we will not be able to stop the devastating effects that lie ahead. All of this is in our prophecies. It talks about the hole in our Lodging—long before it became known as the ozone layer. We referred to it as the Web of Life. The prophecy said that the time would come when there would be a hole that would appear to be irreparable. I know from our teachings that the time will come that we will be moving into a change. They always said to pay attention to the cycles and circles of life. We are now ten years into the new age and approaching the year 2000, which is a total new cycle, a new beginning. We have come full circle in this time.

They said there would come a time when blood would be on our Grandmother, the moon, and the eagle, our Guardian Bird, would warn us of approaching danger. When the astronauts landed on the moon, the first thing they said was, "The eagle has landed." The eagle is also the symbol of the United States, and it has been warning the people of approaching danger for a long, long time. Iroquois people witnessed this experience as a dual fulfillment of their oral prophecies.

Our way of teaching is through nature. For instance, the Tree of Peace that was mentioned earlier is the white pine with four roots extended to the four corners of the earth to embrace all people. It has the guardian bird—the eagle—perched on the top to warn the people. The eternal central sun, the source of all life, is beyond that tree.

Colors are another energy form, another healing dimension. The Native people know and understand the gift of colors. Even those people who do not see, feel colors.

I would like to see a returning to the Original Way, when we walked the Pathway of Peace. It would be wonderful to see all living in harmony and unity, with love and respect for one another. To embrace each other with pureness, dignity, and peace in our hearts. We have a choice and it's up to every individual to exercise that choice, and there is no greater crucial time than now. We have to let go of all of the things that we have held onto for so long. That's not to say that some of them don't have their purpose, but we have to put them in a new perspective.

When our council fire burned bright, and the Peace Confederacy was in operation, we lived according to that way of life. It was known that the time would come when the council fire would almost be distinguished. They tell us that runners were sent to take the embers of that original council fire into every nation when this time came. The runners were to tell the people that these were the embers of the original council fire, and that they would have to tend them until the time came to bring them back and rekindle them. Then the fire would burn in its original form again.

According to the prophecies, the Three Big Sisters, North, South, and Central America, are coming together to pool resources and to gain strength from one another. We are coming together to find the thread of truth intertwined in each so that we can rekindle the Sacred Fire and weave the Tapestry of Life again. The art of weaving is inherent in our people, that and the knowledge within certain tribes of how to build a fire. I believe we can do this again with all the help and concern that people have today.

We are moving into a new cycle of lunar and solar timing where man's time is going to be obsolete. Everything within the last hundred years has speeded up to such a degree—with the radio, jets, television, telephones, and the computer—that it has been impacting our minds. In prophecies it is said that the time would come when there would be a fork in the road; many would stay on the path of speeded time and only a few would move into the new cycle. The prophecies say that the two paths would seem identical, like two pointing fingers of one's hands, yet totally different.

There is always hope, and we have to maintain hope for the children. As I said, my children were once my teachers, now my grandchildren are. One night not long ago, there was a particularly bright light in the sky, and I was captivated by it. I asked my husband, "What is that? Is it a star or a light of a plane?"

My husband looked and said, "Oh, that's a plane."

My five-year-old grandson, who was also watching, said, "Granny, it's a star."

I was mesmerized by it because normally you don't see a bright star that early in the evening. It wasn't quite dusk yet, and we had not yet seen the sunset. Finally, my grandson said to me, "Granny, are we winning or are we losing?"

I looked at him, surprised, wondering where this was coming from. I thought deeply about what he had just asked, wanting to be truthful but to put it into perspective. I finally said to him, "Roggie, I think we are losing."

And he said, "No, Granny. We are winning."

Roggie's statement confirmed that we have to maintain hope for the children. We have to keep striving that we will come out a stronger people—and winners in the game of life to save humanity from the destruction told in the prophecies.

We can do it with pure hearts, trust, and forgiveness. Children know this so well, but then we clog their good minds right from birth. Then, when they're twenty-one, we say, Well, you're old enough to know your own mind now. We forget all of the things we have done in between to clog their minds. So we have got to allow them to find their own expression within themselves. And to learn that where all of the answers lie is within.

We practiced this once; it was our teaching and Way of Life, but gradually we forgot or strayed away from it. No one took it away from us. No one stole it or borrowed it. We allowed this to happen. We have learned the lesson; now let's become strong enough to admit it and make amends. It can be done in the simplest way, to begin to honor life and to know our connectedness to all living things in the total Universe.

This summer I was privileged to go into the Yukon territory in Alaska. And standing there on the highway, looking down into the valley of the Rockies, where one can see for miles and miles, I was deeply aware of how small we as humankind are. Then I turned and faced the other way, looked up, and fully realized that we are no bigger than grains of sand. Yet everyone is so unique and so different that there are no two alike. Each little grain of sand holds its own vibration. That is a beautiful part of walking on this pathway—nature is always speaking to us, always reconfirming, telling us to pay attention, we are here for you. Couple nature's gifts with meditation and the vibrations can change to constructive energy.

Meditation is much a part of my being. Through an inspirational happening, the lesson of meditating made an impact on my life. At the age of seven or eight, I saw one of my Dodahs in meditation. I will never forget seeing him sitting on a log in his "Indian" regalia, puffing on his medicine pipe that he always carried with him. I watched him for a long time. I knew that something was happening. I felt it in my whole being. It gave me such inner peace just watching him.

All of the sudden he turned—he knew that I had been watching him—and he invited me to come sit with him. He said I could take a puff of his pipe. "Don't breathe it in," he said, "just puff it and let the smoke return to our Creator. It's a prayer." Something transpired there that I could never, ever erase from my mind. I can still see that picture so vividly. Was I dreaming or did this actually happen? I pinched myself, and yes, it was a reality.

Later on I asked another grandfather about the experience, and he said if it was a dream it didn't matter, but if I believed and acknowledged it and wanted it to be a part of me, then I was to burn tobacco. I still did not understand, or maybe I wasn't yet willing to make that commitment.

Years later I began to ask many grandfathers and grandmothers about praying with tobacco and was told burning tobacco was sacred and one has to learn to honor and respect it. Needless to say, I did a lot of soul searching. I had four significant dreams that related the same message over and over. When I went back to see Dodah to tell him, we talked about prayer, meditation, dreams, and daydreams. He said prayer is whatever pure feelings you put in your heart, that's all that's needed to burn tobacco. Burning tobacco is a direct communication to the Great Mystery, and your voice and name is heard.

That led me to the meditative state, which, I now understand, is allowing what is so to pour forth from within one's self. It's not from you, but for you. The more I can sit and still myself, to allow the answers to come from within rather than from me dictating what I want and what I need, the more I come to understand my Dodahs.

If I was faltering in health, no matter how critical it might be, I would hope my family would give thanks, just give thanks. We have much to learn about gratitude. I've seen miracles happen when we are willing to accept whatever is intended to be. Who knows if our mission is to go into the other dimension of life? I believe that our Dodahs work from that other dimension. We always speak about the coming generation; we work for seven generations. My understanding is that we work not just for the coming seventh generation, but we must also work in that other dimension of life. We are not going to be here to see our sixth generation, or maybe our fifth. Few are. I do know that I will not be separated from my great-grandchildren, just as my father, for example, is not separated from our grandchildren. He walks with us. I look at my grandchildren and think how my father so loved children, and I think, Oh, it's sad because he is not here to see these little ones, how proud he would be. Then I have to smile and say, "Daddy, I know you are here now. You're here and you're seeing these children. It's just me and my short eyesight."

Our grandchildren carry a part of their great-grandparents. And I'm sure it's going to be the same when we move into that other dimension of life. I'd like to have my little input into their lives and maintain a contact with them if that's what they desire. After all, one of our missions in this Earth Walk is to provide for the coming faces.

# MOHAWK

CRAIG CARPENTER: A TRADITIONAL MESSENGER

*After my first few trips West, living in New York City had lost its appeal. I took a summer job teaching creative writing at Washington College in Chestertown, Maryland. At the end of that summer I took to the road again, this time to the Southwest to meet the Pueblo Indians. Deciding the east was no place to write about Indians, I rented a small adobe in Santa Fe and went back to collect my things.*

*I had read about Craig Carpenter, a Mohawk, in Peter Matthiesson's fine book* Indian Country, *and had met friends of his in Santa Fe, who told me I ought to contact him. I was given a phone number in northern California where I could leave a message for Craig, but I was told that since he lived several miles from a phone it might take weeks before I'd hear from him. I called, my message prepared, but to my astonishment it was Craig who answered. We talked at some length, and an exchange of letters followed. He said he'd be glad to see me if I'd like to visit his camp.*

*I flew to San Francisco and drove up the coast to Eureka, where I spent the night. In his letter, Craig had given me directions, which I followed carefully: From Willow Creek follow signs to Hoopa—go one mile on the winding mountain road high above the river, at which point it will drop down into a valley. Go another mile and start looking for a pasture on the right with two cows!*

*I passed many pastures, some with four cows, some with six, but none with two. Finally, I went to the library where Craig's friend worked and asked if she might give me more explicit*

directions. *She drew a map of where the pasture with two cows would be found. I headed back,*
*map in hand, doubting. But mysteriously, they were there, right in the middle of a pasture I had*
*driven by three or four times. My next instructions were to climb the wire fence, cross the pasture,*
*and call his name.*

*Craig appeared, tall and fine-boned, in a hooded sweatshirt and blue windband, and he*
*led me to his camp.*

*His three handsome, courteous sons were visiting for the summer, John, Danny, and Mike,*
*ranging in age from seven to twelve. I was surprised to learn that this camp, consisting of two*
*tents, bordered by wild plum trees and an abandoned apple orchard, was Craig's year-round*
*home. He explained that his quarter-acre garden of corn, squash, carrots, beans, giant turnips,*
*rutabagas, potatoes, onions, garlic, and a variety of fruits provided him with all his needs.*

*"It has to," Craig said. "I've lived on under six hundred dollars a year since 1952 so as not to*
*pay taxes that contribute to the war machine."*

*I had told him in letters and in our one telephone conversation that I was recording conversations with traditional elders throughout North America. Now I asked if he would be willing to help. He sat silently for a time, then looked at me. "When do we start?"*

Both sides of my family were Indian, but until I was about thirty-two, we never knew what kind of Indian—because on my dad's side, four generations back, four little boys were farmed out to be raised in non-Indian families to try to acculturate us. That was probably in the Canadaigua area, south of Rochester, New York. One of those four boys, at the age of thirteen, was earning a dollar a day to help dig the Erie Canal. They knew nothing of their Indian background. Down through the generations they moved west into southern Michigan. At thirty-two I met Bear Clan chief Alex Gray, who recognized me as a Mohawk and talked to me for four days and nights.

My mother's family came from Ohio before the Civil War and settled in Temperance, Michigan, a few miles north of Toledo, Ohio. That branch of the family was involved in the underground railroad, helping escaped slaves find freedom in Canada.

We are four generations of teetotalers, strictly against liquor, a curse that's killed more Indians than all the white man's diseases and all the white man's bullets combined.

I am assuming that my father was Seneca, but he might have been from Mohawks who moved west. My mother's side was descended from a Mohawk lady who was probably one of the strongest advocates of Handsome Lake's religious rebirth movement. She'd moved west to Sandusky, Ohio. And I think we're a branch of her family that eventually moved up into the heart of the Great Lakes.

From the time I was a little kid, I was always going back to the Indian ways, even though both sides of my family had been acculturated. We lived on the west shore of Lake St. Clair during my school years. There was virgin timber stretching for miles, starting just one block south of us, where there were giant elms four feet in diameter. I would go off into the woods alone at every opportunity. My grandad was very upset when he saw me going back to Indian ways because he wanted his grandchildren to be lawyers and doctors. Some of them made it. My parents' generation were schoolteachers. My dad was a junior high school principal, my mother was a high school teacher, and my aunt was a schoolteacher in Massachusetts. Grandpa wanted me to be a lawyer, but I didn't make it. I dropped out of college at age sixteen.

I didn't like school. In my third year of high school, I took nine classes so I could get through school in three years. I had mastered more subjects, had more credits, than any other student before me. I went to college on a scholastic scholarship, but I didn't fit in at all. I spent most of my time in the library reading the books that interested me instead of studying. I finally realized that I wasn't going to fit in either in the academic or in the commercial world. So I went into farming. I worked day and night and ended up with the largest corn acreage in our area of southern Michigan, two hundred acres of corn. As I was working that tractor hour after hour, inspirations would come to me.

I had heard about Hopis as a kid from my dad. Later, in college, I saw a little item in the newspaper about Hopis going to prison as conscientious objectors, standing up so strong for the Hopi peaceful way of life that they were willing to go to prison rather than go to war. I felt an overwhelming need to go talk with these people. So in 1947 I started west for Hopi. I had no money in my pocket, no food, no blanket, not even an extra coat. I was determined not to beg for food, or work for food, or borrow money for food, and certainly not to steal food. I just started walking.

By the time I got out of the valley where the St. Joseph River flows through, west of Jonesville, Michigan, somebody picked me up. I refused to ask for rides; if somebody wanted to pick me up, they would. And if I didn't receive food, I was willing to die and say to hell with this world; it's so full of corruption anyway. One time in Nebraska, I remember having a strong impulse to walk over and pick up a brown paper sack that was on top of a bank beside the road.

I said, "If I go picking up every brown sack that I find along the road, I'll never get to Hopi."

"Well," my thoughts said, "If you don't, you might be sorry."

So I crawled up that embankment, picked up that sack, and found a half loaf of fresh bread inside. Another time, as I was walking along, I found a cock pheasant that had just been killed by a car. It was still warm. So that was a good meal for the day. On other occasions food would bounce down right in front of me, so I assumed that it had dropped from the sky. Sometimes people voluntarily gave me food, so every day I had one meal, as the Spirits promised.

As I started across the Great Salt Lake Desert, I thought, "How in the world can I get across that, with no food, no water, no nothing." I was really scared. I kneeled down by the side of the road there and prayed about whether to go on or to stop. I was assured that since I had come that far and had been provided for, the angels would continue to provide for me. So that gave me the faith to go on. I had only walked about three steps when I saw a stick of Adams Clove Gum lying at my feet. I picked that up and figured, well, that will get me across, and it did. Almost immediately somebody picked me up. All I had to do was face the challenge and see if I was faithful enough to go ahead.

I reached Mount Shasta. There was no trail up the western side, but I got to the top. I had heard reports of a magic people in Shasta who had apparently rejected civilization, and I wanted to talk with them. But there weren't any people living there, no magic people on Mount Shasta.

From Shasta I continued on to Hopi, but on the road I spent four years learning psychic research, and then four more years training with the spiritual leaders of the Dineh [Navajo]. At that time, they had the highest infant mortality rate in the nation. As a farmer I thought I might have some ideas that might help with their nutrition problems. My little experimental subsistence gardens were a sort of demonstration.

During the four years I was with them, I worked with the medicine people. They saw that I was leading a moral, righteous life, circumspect and spiritually clean, so they asked me to do things for them, like gather wood for the healing ceremonies, which were four nights of songs that invoked the unseen guardians to come and help the patient. They had to have a spiritually clean person to gather that ceremonial firewood. And it had to be an adult, because one had to climb up those juniper trees and break off dead branches and bring them back in four big bundles on your back—enough to last for four days. They also asked me to spin some of my homegrown cotton yarn, which was used in their ceremonies.

And I would drive the elders around to meetings and ceremonies. By that time I had a 1927 Dodge that could handle those backcountry roads where modern cars could not. Sometimes I would take the people down to Hopi to get doctored by the medicine men there, and I witnessed many miraculous healings.

So I spent four years among the Navajo learning about *chindi* [evil spirits] and "witches" and how to deal with black magic. And how to stand firm and faithful for the first law of this land, which is peace and justice.

Then one morning, a spirit came to me in my garden and told me to stop what I was doing, go and clean myself up, take a bath in the Paria river, and go to the Hopi village of Shungopovi. I was to tell the leader of the Bluebird Clan that "Spring is here," then ask him his troubles and offer my assistance. As a boy I had given myself the name Robin Walking and Looking for Something, so I guess that's why the spirit person, whom I could not see but whose presence I could feel and hear, sent me to the Bluebird Clan. Back in my homeland, those two birds work together to bring the message, "Spring is here."

I arrived in the village of Shungopovi just as the sun was rising—exactly as the spirit told me I would—and rested against a house that turned out to belong to the Bluebird leader. But the people in the village seemed to be afraid of me; I was given the cold shoulder. So after a couple of days I went back to the Navajo. I was pretty disappointed. Very discouraged.

Two years later, I was driving some Navajo to Window Rock, and they wanted to stop at Hopi to see the Snake Dance. So I did, and as a result I met two more leaders, Thomas Banyacya and David Monongye. This time I was accepted. They taught me the basic fundamentals, and within a year I began my duties as a messenger. That was in 1955, and I have been a messenger ever since.

According to the Hopi prophetic instructions, if a gourd full of ashes was ever invented, and if the people became so corrupted that they dropped the gourd full of ashes from the roadway in the sky, and if it hit the earth, it would boil the water and burn the land and leave ashes over a wide area where nothing will grow for many years. If that ever happened—and it did on August 6, 1945, at Hiroshima—then it would be the duty of the Hopi, who were peaceful and righteous, to stand up and declare their message of peace to the world, warning us and teaching us how to correct ourselves and our leaders while we still had time.

I am supposed to uphold the Indian message to try to promote their teachings. I consult with their elders, and if necessary, go off and communicate with the spirits of the ancestors in the area to try and find out what the original language was, where the original homeland territory was, and how they conducted their religion. Because ceremonies are involved with everything Indians do—from gathering food to waking up and taking a bath—there's always a song or a prayer that goes along with it. I encourage people to consider Thomas Banyacya's four words: "Stop, consider, change, and correct." Stop what you are doing. Consider the effects of what you are doing. Is it upholding life on this land? Or is it destructive to the life on this land? If it is destructive, then change your value system and your actions. We are not supposed to be subduing the earth, treading it underfoot, vanquishing the earth and all its life. We are supposed to be taking care of this land and the life upon it. So it's up to you to consider which side you are going to be on.

Eventually, in 1973, I was sent clear around the world, and I found Indians everywhere. They didn't all have brown skin; they weren't all what they call "red men." But they had their sacred original instructions, and they were diligently trying to follow them.

Then we were told by our leaders to take the Hopi message of peace to the four specific groups of the leaders of the world peoples, who would be meeting together in a great house with transparent walls, which would be built on the eastern edge of this great island by that time. To Zrupiki, which means house of mica. The Hopi didn't have glass at that early time, but they did have mica. So they figured that meant the United Nations.

We were also told to use four methods of communicating: The first was face-to-face. The second was by means of a magic cobweb. You hold a little instrument in your hand and talk into it. The person on the other end of that cobweb had a little instrument in his hand, and he could hear you. We would talk back and forth over these cobwebs, which would criss-cross the land. The third method was to use marks on cornhusk, because at some future date these inventive people would come up with a system of sending thoughts back and forth with marks on cornhusks. And the last, the fourth method, was to sit in a little room with no window and talk, and your voice would be heard clear to the other side of the mountains.

The first time the Hopis talked on radio was on the first call-in radio show in history, the Night Owl on KFI in Los Angeles in the early 1960s. The Hopi's message of peace went all the way to the other side of the Sierra Nevada to Bishop, California, and even to central Nevada.

I was one of the early messengers; there were three before me, among them a man named George Yamada, who had been a conscientious objector during World War II and had been in prison with Thomas Banyacya. There were only a few hundred of us conscientious objectors in the whole United States in the early 1950s. I had to face that land of clanging doors, too.

Banyacya was our main communications man at Hopi. We had to get the Hopi message out to those four groups of people by using those four methods of communication.

The prophecy, as shown on the ideogram on Prophecy Rock, depicts Massau at the beginning of the life plan as we humans come up from the underworld. Massau, a Hopi name for the greatest spirit person who walks the surface of this earth, is holding onto that straight and narrow path. The major events in this era are shown, including three world wars. We hope the third one doesn't occur, because if it does it will probably destroy all life on earth. And if that happens, we will have failed in our purpose here, and we'll have to forfeit our right to live upon this earth as human beings.

Massau also appears at the very end of the ideogram. That's the day of purification. Massau said, "I am the first, I am the last. I am the eternal." The message of peace tells where we human beings came from, from the world that was destroyed by the great floods because of the corruption of our ancestors. Why we came here, and what happened to us afterward. It also tells how we met the Massau and what is happening to us now, and what will happen to us if we do not correct ourselves and our leaders while we still have time.

So when Bigfoot started manifesting to the modern world in October of 1958, we were very happy. That was the first public indication that he was returning as promised. By 1992, he was putting handprints on the earth again, on petroglyphs in many widely scattered areas.

Jomo Kenyatta, in his book *Facing Mount Kenya*, traces Bigfoot's ancestors as originally coming from North America. First they went south, then they went across the ocean to Africa. Then this giant man covered with black hair traveled east across Africa, planting people as he went. Finally, he came to Mount Kenya, and he said, "This is where your nation is going to live, and this is what your language is going to be, these are your foods, and this is how you are going to make your fields—long rectangles, and this is how you are going to make your houses—round houses, this is how you are going to have your religious ceremonies, this is how you're going to conduct your family life, your village life," and so forth. He taught the people he planted everything.

And once they had learned it, he said, "Now I'm going to hide myself from you to see if you can follow these instructions no matter what happens to you. Once in a while I might manifest again in a physical form and leave footprints in your gardens to let you know that you are still being watched and therefore are still obligated to uphold these original instructions. But if you add to or subtract from these original instructions, you may be making a mistake. You may be sorry, you may suffer, and you may even die at the end."

This is the same thing that the Hopi were taught, in an entirely different language, halfway around the world, different color of skin, but the same thing.

Bigfoot was here first. Then we human beings were planted here. Not only Indian nations have these teachings; I talked to some of the mountain people from Vietnam, and they call him the same thing, which is Lei, which refers to the monkey-man. Only he isn't a monkey, and he isn't a man. He is a god. The most powerful human-type manifestation on the surface of the earth. They also call him the Monkey God in India, the Father.

In 1992, he started talking to people in Europe and America in intelligible words. Ordinarily, he communicates by thoughts, or with visions, dreams, or in body language, sometimes called Indian sign-language.

Bigfoot is the super god of earth. There might be greater gods with more power, more intelligence, more compassion in outer space. But as far as we are aware, he is the most powerful deity on the surface of the earth.

He is now coming down from the high mountains and appearing in broad daylight at the edges of villages. He is appearing to white people, and because they weren't observant enough to see him, he took the branch of a tree and waved it like a flag to get their attention. So he's really giving us every opportunity to bear witness to the fact that he's here, and from the Indian viewpoint it's the beginning of the fulfillment of his prophecies that he would come back to re-establish justice on this land.

# PIT RIVER

# WILLARD RHOADES: A STORYTELLER

*Craig Carpenter and Sharon Laurence, his wife of two months, picked me up at the airport in Redding, California. Our first stop would be the Rhoades', only five miles west of Cottonwood. I relaxed in the back as they argued about which road to take, content to let someone else get lost.*

*A "For Sale" sign marked the turn-off onto a mile-long dirt road that led to the Rhoades' trailer. Willard was lying underneath one of the half dozen cars parked on the side of the driveway. Indian lawn ornaments, as Craig and I had come to call them. Mildred stood at the door and called to her husband to "come out from under that thing"; they had visitors.*

*We went inside and sat in the living room overlooking the Sacramento Valley. Willard, Craig explained, is the spiritual leader of the eleven independent bands of the Pit River nation. Mildred works at the Rancheria, a center for drug and alcohol abuse, which doubles as a receiving house for unwanted Indian children. She also heads the program that brings food to the elderly who are confined at home. She is a Wintu, of the Shasta Mountain people, and speaks knowledgeably about both tribes.*

*The Rhoadeses immediately asked Craig for information about the activities of traditionalists in other tribes, and in particular, the Hopi. The Hopi is regarded as the least corrupted nation, a stronghold of the old way. Craig, true to his duties as a traditional messenger, told of the battle the Hopi at Hotevilla were waging against the encroachment of the modern world.*

*Then Willard sat in what was clearly his favorite chair and began to tell us his coyote stories. "Old Coyote now, he was a smart fellow, smarter than his own good. . . ."*

I'm from Goose Valley, here in northern California, that's where I was born and raised. I'm from an Achomawi band of the Pit River tribe. My dad came from Missouri; he came over when he was just a little baby. My mother was born and raised in Goose Valley. My grandfather was from Patrick, California, and my grandmother was from Pit River. My mother's grandfather was the chief of the Goose Valley people. He gave his authority to my grandfather after he married my grandmother, and my grandfather gave it to me.

As a boy, I used to go visit the old people; I liked to hear what they had to say. I guess that's where I got my education. They would tell me stories about the beginning of time, the beginning of this world and the destruction of the other world. And they'd talk about how people had been replanted on this planet, how many of them, and about each of the times that they were replanted.

This world has been rebuilt twice already, and it's going for its last go-around now. The time is getting short, according to the prophecies.

In the beginning there was another world that we lived on. I know that because it's where my people came from. They lived through the great freeze, the flood, and they will also live through the fire that's coming. The people who remember their instructions will be taken out of here during the time of destruction and brought back after it is rebuilt. Not just the people who remember but those who believe.

In the other world, we had everything that you can imagine, even more than you have today. You didn't even have to go to work in the other world. You could just sit around in your house if you wanted to, and things would be brought, not by people but by some type of automation. Robots or something. I guess there were airplanes because they flew around in the air. And there were cars because they rode around in box-type things on the ground. There were refrigerators, iceboxes, televisions, radios, everything that anyone would want. Except that they forgot the Old Man. They said, We don't need him anymore, look what we got.

Well, the Old Man got mad. "I fixed another world," he told his helper, Quan, the silver-gray fox. And he told Quan to gather up all the people who remembered him and still followed his way. "Build a web with a pouch in it like the little spiders do, and put the people in it. The web will take you to the other world."

But Coyote—who we call Jamo, the helper of the Devil, or Weblah—begged to come. "I know what you are going to do," he said. "You are going to destroy this world, and I don't want to die."

The other ones said, "We can't take you because of the things that you have done. You have caused the people to do bad things and to forget the teachings of the Old Man."

"I won't do it anymore," he said. "I won't teach them bad things anymore if you'll take me."

But still they said no.

His final argument was, "Your Father said that you can't kill your own brother. If you leave me here, then you will be killing me."

And so they brought him. But on the way over they told him, "If you do wrong, if you do the same things that you did before, we're going to have to destroy this people again."

And that is what happened. First, the Old Man froze them. Then, he rebuilt the world, fixed it all over again. But after a time they went on to do the same bad things all over again.

"Well," the Old Man said, "we're going to have to destroy this people again. They are forgetting. They're doing wrong things again."

So this time he set loose the flood and drowned them. But just before the flood he told his helper to build two boats and to get the seeds of all the people and the animals, so that he could rebuild the world again. So he put all the seeds in one boat, and himself in the other. Once again Coyote begged to come, and once again the Old Man gave in and brought him. This piece of earth was left barren.

When they landed here, Coyote jumped off first and said, "What are we going to eat? There is nothing here, it's just a rock pile."

The Old Man had already fixed another place on the other side, and had put people there on the other side of the great waters. He said to Coyote, "You go over there and teach the people the right way of living. If you don't, if you teach them the same way that you taught them before, I'll have to destroy it. And you will be destroyed, too."

And that's why we are still here. What they did wrong was exactly what they are doing today. Building things that you don't need, building automobiles that are killing you. The things you're making today are making the people sick and killing them. Even the food that you eat. And you're forgetting to pray, to do ceremonies. Every nation, every tribe, every band of people all over the world has certain things to do to honor the Old Man, but they all forgot, and so they are the lost people. Only those who remember are not lost. He told them, "Whatever those people do to you, I will not destroy you, because you cannot help what they do."

And that's the whole trouble with this world today; they have forgotten. They are doing the same things now that they did in the other world. They've gotten to the place now where they say, We can go to the moon, we can go to the stars—we can go all over the universe—we don't need Old Man anymore.

It takes all night to tell this whole story. I'd tell a little bit and you'd get sleepy, and when you woke up, you would catch another bit of the story.

It continues, how they planted the people in different parts of the world. They were told that when the people came back to this place they would be known by what they eat with. The first one got up and grabbed a spoon and ate with it. And the Old Man said, You belong on that little island across the ocean. The next one got up and he ate with a fork. He told him he belonged on the big island on the other side of the ocean. The next one got up and ate with a knife, and the Old Man said, You belong on the middle of that big island. And the next one got up and ate with sticks, and he said, You belong on the other end of that big island. The next one got up and ate with shells, and he said, You belong on that other big island below that other island. And then the rest of them all ate with their fingers, and the Old Man told them they belonged right here.

They were all different colors, and they were each given a special way to pray. Each was given a certain piece of land, and was told that if they took care of the land, the land would take care of them. But, he said, don't you go and bother other people. And what did they do, they started bothering other people. Packing up their so-called religions, taking them from one place to another, and using them as weapons. Trying to change people. And they succeeded some. But not quite, because there are people all over the world who have not forgotten. A little band here and a little one over there who have never forgotten. They are a poor people, you might say, among worldly riches, but they are rich in other ways.

The Indians didn't make war with the people who came with their religions. You go bother a yellow jacket's nest, he is going to sting you. If you leave it alone, it won't bother you. Anything will fight, if you go and bother him, even a mouse. A mouse will fight a bear. He won't win, but he'll fight him.

A lot of these ceremonies now are not of the old way. But the Hoopas over on the coast, their Brush Dance and their Deer Skin Dance, they're doing those in the right manner, the old way. Their prayer time was once a year, mostly in the spring, or in the summertime, when people could travel. Everybody had a different way. Our people from this part of the country prayed only in the morning. You got up and washed your face, you prayed, and that was it for the day.

Our people have sweat houses, but they're mostly for cleansing your body and your mind, or sometimes if you feel bad. The sweat lodge was ruined, I think, by mixing the people. It's against the law for men and women to go in together. Women had their own.

Women taught the children, that was their first education, from the time they were little until they were about ten or twelve years old. The men taught them from then on. Women were responsible for the main teachings of the people, not the men. When men made a decision, they would have to go back to the women to get approval. Our people would meet in what was called the big sweat house. All the older men would go in and talk things over and take care of whatever wrongs had been done to other people. They talked about it, and if it was worth following up, they'd take it to the spiritual doctors. If you went and killed somebody's husband, say, and you were convicted of it, they would go back to the wife and ask what she wanted done with you. She had a choice, she could put you to work to feed her children, or she could have you killed. Any crime was always referred back to the person who was hurt; they were the ones to decide the punishment. They never outright killed the criminal themselves, they used the doctors for that, the spiritual doctors. Child molesters were sent away, and since no other tribe would pick them up, they usually died. Come wintertime, they couldn't make it by themselves.

We all use tobacco in one way or another, but mostly it's the doctors who use the pipe, not ordinary people. Ordinary people only smoked once in a while, very seldom. My father, my grandfather, and my great-grandfather were all doctors. I am more or less a teacher and an adviser.

Bigfoot is a spirit that creates his own body to show people that he is here. His flesh isn't ordinary flesh, and his hair is different. He doesn't walk like an ordinary person. Most of the time he hops on one foot. He can walk out into the middle of a field and his tracks will disappear, there will be nothing left. He was put here to watch people, to see what people do. He is a go-between, between earth and the Old Man. Same as the Little People, those spirits are a go-between, too. They watch to see how you treat the horse and the other animals. It's all reported to the Old Man, and people will always pay for what they do.

Even a tree will watch. There used to be one little tree; my wife, Mildred, always saw it. I never did. Whenever we would go to Big Bend that tree would wave at her. "That tree waved at me again," she'd say. I looked and looked for it, and I never did see it. Those are the things that remind you there is always something watching you.

Bigfoot only shows himself to certain people. Most of the people that he shows himself to are people who respect him. Sometimes he comes as an animal, sometimes a bird, but there is always something that looks different about him. He behaves differently, too; he doesn't react with fright, like a bird or an animal might. Some people know him and will talk about seeing him. Then he might disappear for a while and come back again to see if he can fool you.

At Fall River, before those falls were there, the salmon used to run clear out to Alturas. Coyote had relatives all up and down the river, but he didn't like to travel.

"I know what I'll do," he said. "I'll put a dam there, and falls, and then when all the Alturas people come down to catch fish, all I have to do is go to the falls, and I can visit all my relatives."

So he put the falls there.

There's a slide there on that canyon, too. Coyote was quite a womanizer. He was always chasing women. So the Quan was going to teach him a lesson. He made himself sound like a whole bunch of young women, laughing and giggling across the way, and old Coyote perked up his ears and took off after them. It was getting foggy across the canyon, and to Coyote it looked like water. It was night, he was running and running, and you could hear him almost catching up.

"I'll run and jump across. If I don't quite make it, I'll swim the rest of the way," he said.

So he jumped into the fog and hit the side of the bank. That slide that's there now is right where he hit the side of the mountain. So if you ever go out to Fall River and look over the pit, you'll see it and know that's where Coyote did himself in chasing women.

I used to have dreams when I was little. One time when I was sick and laying in bed, my mother told me, "Go get your brother about four or five o'clock and do your chores because we won't be home until late."

My brother was helping somebody dig potatoes. So I got up, and I gathered all of that sickness up, like a pile of wood, an armful of wood. I picked it all up and went after my brother. As I crawled under the gate, I dug a hole with my hands and put all that stuff in it and buried it. It was a kind of fear that I buried and I wasn't sick anymore. And it's still buried.

My mother was a doctor at one time, before she started going to church. One time my eye was cut with barbed wire, and all this stuff came out, this gooey stuff, and my eye was all shrunk up. I came in the house, and my mother cried when she saw it. She put a patch over my eye and put me to bed. Then she went into the other room. All of a sudden a big cloud came down. It felt heavy when it hit me, then it went back up and disappeared. My mother came back in the room and took the patch off my eye, and my eye was all healed.

Another little child, he must have been about two years old, I guess. He fell off a four-foot-high porch and hit his head on a sharp rock. It knocked a big hole in his skull. His mother grabbed him and took him over to my mother's, and she did the same thing to him. She took him in the bedroom and put something on his head. He was all cold, kind of dead, we thought. She told the child's mother to go on home and do her housework and come back in a couple of hours. When she came back he was completely healed; there wasn't even a scar.

But once my mother started going to church, she lost it. She couldn't heal anymore. People had been begging her to go to church, just like they do now. Preachers are always begging you to go to their church. To them we were heathens, doing our simple things, but those simple things were helping people. Afterward, she couldn't help people anymore.

There aren't any doctors like that anymore. There are some who claim to be, but I know better. If somebody claims to be a doctor, and you want to find out, offer him some tobacco. Or a smoke. It doesn't matter what kind of tobacco it is. Just offer it to him, see what he does with it. If he takes it and smokes more than three puffs, he's no doctor. A real doctor would inhale it once, twice, and then he'd blow it out and give it back to you. Then you are supposed to take a puff of it, and he'd tell you what was wrong. You wouldn't have to tell him. You might have to sit there for a few minutes, but he'd tell you. And he'd tell you if he could help you or not.

If you want to give him something, give it to him, but he wouldn't ask, and he wouldn't expect it. And if he tells you he left his stuff at home, you may as well forget about him. Their power doesn't come in a sack. That goes for any doctor, no matter which tribe.

Real doctors were always doing something out of the ordinary. If you were visiting them, they would always do something for you without asking. Maybe a kind of trick, like my uncle did to me one time. He told me to go in the house and get him a match. He had a cigarette, but he didn't have any matches. So I went in the house to get some, but I didn't find any. When I came back out and told him, he said, "Well, I don't need them anyway," and he took his finger and looked at it a minute. Then he put his finger on the end of the cigarette and pretty quick it was lit, and he was smoking.

Another time we were driving up at Hat Creek one dark night, and suddenly our headlights went out. I was driving. I stopped because I couldn't see the road. My uncle sat there for maybe fifteen minutes, then he said, "Well, what are we waiting for? Let's go."

"We don't have any lights," I said.

He said, "Oh, turn the lights on."

I turned the light switch again, but nothing happened. So my uncle got out and took off the glass cover and took the bulbs out. He broke the bulbs into little pieces and put them back. Then he got back into the car and said, "Now let's go."

I told him we can't, we don't have any lights.

"Turn them on again," he said, "and make sure."

So I did, and sure enough they came on. I couldn't believe it. We drove clear into Bernie, where we stopped for gas and something to eat. I was still wondering how those lights came on, so I got up from the table and told him to wait for me. I was going to look and see if he had played a trick on me and put new bulbs in there. I took the glass cover off, and there were all those little broken pieces of bulbs just lying there.

I don't know how they do those things. You can't call it sleight of hand; it's nothing fake.

We have a story about two snakes, a silver one and a gold one. These two Indians were crossing a lake, and they saw these two tiny little snakes floating on a piece of moss. So they picked them up and took them home and fed them. They said, If we leave them out there, they would drown, poor things. They fed them mosquitoes and flies, anything the little things could eat. When the snakes got big, and they were eating moose and buffalo and elk, they took off by themselves.

The gold snake went to the north, eating everything in his path, and got fatter and fatter. Soon the silver snake went south, eating everything in its path, and it got fatter and fatter. By the time they got to the edge of the land, there was nothing left to eat, so they started eating on themselves. Finally, they destroyed themselves.

And that's exactly what they are doing now. Everybody is living on tax money, and they think they're rich. There's no sense to it. There's only so much money in the world, no matter where you look. And it can't grow. People think it grows; they say a dollar increases three times every time you turn it over. That's stupid. This is the richest country in the world, and it's the poorest country in the world. Your money isn't worth the paper it's written on anymore. There is no backing to it. Why do you think they took the gold coin off the market, out of your pocket. Because if the gold burnt up and melted, you'd still have it. They took the silver off the market because if the silver burnt up, you'd still have it. But if the paper burnt up, it's gone. People think they have money in the bank, but it's all paper. There's nothing to it.

When you pray, don't ask for worldly things—money, riches, or luck—don't ask for that, because the Old Man won't listen. The only thing to ask for when you pray is wisdom, ask to be granted wisdom, then you won't have to worry about the rest. Ask how to live and get by with what you have and to treat the other people like you want to be treated. If you treat other people like you want to be treated, you'll forget about your pocketbook, you'll forget about what you're going to eat tomorrow, you'll forget about what you're going to wear tomorrow, it won't worry you. You'll forget all your worries. That's what life is all about.

When Coyote came across from the other side on his little boat, he landed over there on the east coast, and he looked at the land, and he said, My, this is a pretty place. And he said, I'm going to have it, it's going to be mine. And he thought, There must be people here. He looked and he found them, but he couldn't reach them, because they lived on a higher plane than he did. But he thought, I'm a good talker, I'm a good liar, I'll get them.

So he hollered up to them, "Hey! If you give me one of your children to eat, then I'll be on my way. I'm following the sun. I want to see where it goes. But I'm hungry now. If you'll just give me one of them to eat, I won't bother you anymore. But if you don't, I'll come up there and kill all of you right now."

So the people talked it over and said, Yes, we guess we can give him one. So they did, and away he went.

Quite a while afterward he came back, and said, "I couldn't get across to the other side because I didn't have my boat, so I'm going home. But I'm hungry. Give me another one of your children to eat and I'll be on my way, and I won't bother you again." It was the same story, "If you don't, then I'll kill all of you."

So they gave him another one and thought they were rid of him. Pretty quick he came back and said, "I forgot where I left my boat. I'm still hungry, and my mind ain't working right, but if you give me another one to eat, my mind will be strong again, and I'll remember where I left my boat."

But they wouldn't give him one more, they said no.

So that's where we are today. Coyote is still here, and he has eaten out the center of our people. And he's still trying to get that third one.

# SHOSHONE

*From the Rhoadeses, Craig, Sharon, and I drove south to Susanville, California, near the Nevada border, to see Glen Wassen, a Western Shoshone activist, who brought us up to date on the most recent developments on the Danns' land dispute. A court date had been set for March 3, 1993, just a few months after I was there. The story of Clifford Dann's arrest was tragic. On November 19, 1992, he was arrested for attempting to stop Bureau of Land Management (BLM) agents from removing branded Dann ranch horses and livestock they had illegally captured. He stood on the bed of his truck, doused himself with gasoline, and threatened to set himself on fire if the BLM agents did not release the horses.*

*We were eager to talk to the Dann sisters, Carrie and Mary, and to Chief Frank Temoke. Glen phoned ahead to find out if the roads had been cleared from the last blizzard, and he urged us to leave right away before the next one.*

*We headed across the high desert of Nevada to Ruby Valley, southeast of Elko, to Chief Frank Temoke's. The valley floor was clear of snow and covered with giant silvery sagebrush and brown stubby grass. Craig pointed out the red stems of the willows used for* kinickinick, *the tobacco used by the northern Plains Indians.*

*The Temokes' trailer was set at the base of a mountain overlooking Ruby Valley. We were greeted by Frank's wife, Theresa, and ushered into the living room where the old chief sat. Craig was glad to see the plaster of paris cast of Bigfoot, made in 1958, that he had sent to Chief Temoke by special messenger twenty years before.*

*"This is the footprint that introduced Bigfoot to the modern world," Craig said.*

*We gave Chief Temoke the two-pound bag of piñon nuts I had bought in a supermarket on the way.*

*"Piñons," he murmured, holding the mesh bag, turning it in his hands. "Haven't seen these in a while. What did you pay for them?"*

*"Two dollars, I think," I answered, not sure I hadn't paid three.*

*"They charge that much? We used to pick ten times this many in fifteen minutes."*

# FRANK TEMOKE: RUBY VALLEY

As the Hereditary Chief of the Western Shoshone, I wish to pass along testimony of how I remember things as they happened during my lifetime. It is important to understand that when I was born in 1903, many of the old ways remained. We lived in Ruby Valley and were called the Wat-a-duca, because we used the seeds from a weed called *wat,* which turns red in late summer and black in the fall. It grows on the flats and islands on the east side of Franklin and Ruby lakes, and we used it to supplement our diet by mixing it with pine nuts and other foods to make wat-a-gravy.

One of the much-told stories among our people includes the first time my grandfather Old Temoke [*temoke* means rope] saw a party of white men. They asked where the water was. Old Temoke and the others with him thought the whites wanted "wat," so they offered some to them, but the white men would not take it.

I think we Wat-a-duca people have been as fair as anyone could possibly be with our white neighbors since that time. During the 1860s, when the Gosiutes to the east and the White Knives and Paiutes to the west were causing problems for the white immigrants, we did our best not to take part in any such warfare. In fact, the leaders here in Ruby did their best to help resolve these conflicts.

On the other hand, we Wat-a-ducas have felt that we have not been treated with honesty and fairness in return. Even before the Ruby Valley Treaty of 1863, our people were told that there would be a place set aside for us to live north of Be-a-o-gitch [Big Creek], or Overland Creek. It was through constant pressure from my father and others that we were able to acquire about 120 acres north of Overland. But this was nothing compared to what we were originally promised.

In 1865, the soldiers gave us five hundred head of cattle and encouraged us to become agriculturists and herdsmen. My people ran the cattle on the mountains in the summer, and then on the east side of the valley near Wat-a-bah, or Medicine Springs, in the winter.

In 1874, soon after the white men created a reservation near Carlin, some white men and White Knife Indians from Carlin came and took all but about fifty head of our cattle away. Old Temoke tried to stop them by threatening to get the soldiers, but to no avail. The government agents met with Chief Temoke and tried to get him to move to Duck Valley to another reservation, which was located outside of Shoshone country. But Old Temoke said,

"No, this is where we get our reservation, six miles square. This is my country. The deer for our food are on these mountains; we have ducks on the lakes for food. On the other side of the valley and in those hills are antelope and the pine nuts we need for winter."

When we made agreements with the white man, we didn't know that over time more and more would be taken away from us. We understood that there would be mines, railroads, towns, and ranches, but we never knew we would not be able to hunt where and when we wanted. We never agreed to having to get a license to hunt. We never gave up our rights to harvest what wood we needed, or the pine nuts or other foods that we needed. We never agreed to the establishment of the Forest Service, or the BLM, or the designation of wilderness areas. Nor did we understand that the reservations would actually be controlled and owned by the U.S. government.

We thought the reservations were supposed to be ours to do with as we see fit for our people. We didn't know we couldn't run livestock on open lands as time went on. As more and more time goes by, we have less and less. We are still waiting for the six-mile-square parcel to be granted to us.

When I was a boy, the Wat-a-duca would winter in the piñon and juniper country between Ruby Valley and Ely at Duck Creek. The older Indians showed me where the white soldiers from Fort Ruby had killed many Indian men, women, and children. The Shoshone men serving as scouts at Fort Ruby were able to get word to Duck Creek that the soldiers were coming, but only the Mose and Knight families heeded the warning, leaving camp just hours before the massacre. Many of the bones of the people were still there at the time I was shown the spot.

During the hard winter of 1888 and '89, my family lost most of the remaining cattle the government had given us. But someone in my family has always run cattle or horses on the mountain in the summer and on the flats in the winter. Either my sister, myself, or my sons and grandson have run cattle on the mountain each year. My father, Machoch Temoke, ran more horses than cattle. When I was a boy he would run mustangs in the Butte Valley and Long Valley. He would sell all but the best ones, which he then ran on the Ruby Mountains. Sometimes he would run as many as three hundred horses. We did not believe we needed a permit. Now the Forest Service says we need a permit. I say it's the Forest Service that should get the permit from us.

As I've said, we have many concerns. First of all, we never agreed to let go of any of our use of this land not used for ranching and farming. Secondly, where we run our cattle, by agreement, was supposed to be part of the six-mile-square reservation we never received. We understood that we didn't need a permit, that we had a traditional right to run our livestock on the Rubys, and now they are telling us we can't run our cattle there anymore. And thirdly, the government encouraged us to run livestock and become agriculturists in the first place.

We Indians have kept our part of the agreements, but the white men have not kept theirs. Like my father said, "This is my country. If you pick this country up and move it over there, then I will go with it. But if you can't move our country, then we stay here."

# CARRIE DANN: WESTERN SHOSHONE

*Carrie and Mary Dann are sisters who live with their brother, Clifford, and Carrie's children on a ranch near Crescent Valley, Nevada. In 1973, Mary Dann was herding cattle on their ranch when a BLM agent stopped her and demanded to see a grazing permit. Mary told the agent that she didn't need a permit since she wasn't on U.S. land; she was on Shoshone land, the land her grandmother had ranched on. The Danns were charged with trespassing. This began a twenty-year fight in and out of the courts, and resulted in the tragic arrest of their brother, Cliff.*

*Of the two sisters, Carrie is the most outspoken. A tall rancher with strong features, Mary is the quieter of the two, preferring to remain in the background. Both are determined in their struggle to free their brother and regain sovereignty of their land. On November 26, 1993, Clifford was released, having served his nine-month sentence. He still faces a two-year probation and a $5,000 fine.*

*On December 8, 1993, in Stockholm, Carrie and Mary Dann were among five women from around the world presented with the Right Livelihood Award for their courage and perseverance in asserting the rights of indigenous peoples to their land. The text of their award stated, in part, that "for over twenty years the Dann sisters have been at the forefront of their people's struggle against the attempted expropriation of their land by the United States government and its degradation by mining and nuclear testing."*

*The Awards, often referred to as "the alternative Nobel Prize," were presented again in the Swedish Parliament on December 9, the day before the Nobel Prize presentations.*

I was born in Crescent Valley in a birthing hut in December of 1934. I'm a member of the Western Shoshone nation. We're real survivors. That's the way it was when I was growing up. My mother raised a garden, and we gathered the seasonal native foods and dried them. Deer was our red meat. We were poor as far as money goes, but we always managed to have plenty to eat and our family was very close.

My sisters and I didn't go to the Indian school [an inferior school operated by the BIA]; we went to the public schools instead. My older brother and my cousins had to go to Indian school, and then they were drafted into the service during World War II. When they came back, they could no longer speak our language. I was just a kid then, and English was

a foreign language to me. I really blame the Indian schools for contributing to the loss of our traditions and the practice of our religious beliefs.

We always had ceremonies, especially in the fall and spring of the year. They were private family gatherings to give blessings and thanks. Since the time I can remember we would go to pick pine nuts and conduct our ceremonies in the way that our grandmother taught us. In the 1980s, the BLM allowed chaincutting on our lands—one million acres of piñon pines—and our ceremonial trees were chopped down. I went there once and haven't been back since because of the desecration. Chaincutting is so brutal—they stretch a chain between two bulldozers and tear down twenty-five acres per hour.

My dad was originally from Grass Gully. Whenever he and his uncles would try to develop a field to raise potatoes and grain, the white people there would run cows over the fields and destroy the crops. In the fall, when the grain was ripe, the white people would set it afire. Finally, my dad's family had to move on. I guess he was determined not to let that happen again, so when he married my mom they moved to Crescent Valley. This was according to our traditional ways in which the man moved to the hometown of the bride's family.

My dad looked around and saw the waters coming down and saw that it was good land. He made up his mind that nobody was going to push him off. I don't know how he made it, how he struggled through. He heard from his friends that there were some ranchers in the valley who were determined to run him off his land, but he wasn't going to be run off. Some way or another we're still here. I don't know how he ever managed it, but my dad eventually bought a section of six hundred and forty acres, what is known as railroad land. We didn't know we'd still have to fight.

In 1973, the BLM charged my sister, Mary, with trespassing because she was grazing her livestock on public land without a permit. She informed them that she was in the sovereign Western Shoshone Treaty Land, and therefore couldn't be trespassing against herself or her nation. That summer we had a running correspondence with the BLM asking them for proof otherwise, because if it wasn't Western Shoshone land, we'd like to know who did own it and the names of the people who were paid for it, because we hadn't been. They responded by saying we should move to another reservation.

My grandmother used to tell us about all the injustices that would be coming to us, and that people—like lawyers—would lie to us. Now I realize everything she told us was right. In 1974, they brought a lawsuit against us, which eventually went to the U.S. Supreme Court. We argued that we were within the sovereignty of the Western Shoshone country, which was recognized by the United States in the 1863 Treaty of Ruby Valley.

In 1979, Cecil Andrus, the U.S. Secretary of the Interior at the time, accepted a Land Claims judgment award of twenty-six million dollars from the Supreme Court on behalf of the Western Shoshone nation. But this award was not accepted by the Indian people; we had nothing to do with it. The Supreme Court based their ruling on an Indian Claims Commission claim that the Western Shoshones' land title was extinguished in 1872, so the twenty-six million dollars was some sort of compensation for encroaching upon our land.

I disagree with the use of the words "taken" or "encroachment," and that's the reason we're still out here fighting. Of course, the monetary award was based on the price of land in 1872, which amounted to a dollar an acre. Today, it's around two hundred dollars an acre. I also don't think the U.S. Constitution says anything about allowing the government to "take" or "encroach" upon lands of a sovereign indigenous people.

I look at it like this. During World War II, they said Hitler was one of the worst dictators in history. I look at that, and then consider the history of the U.S., and what they did to the indigenous people of this country. Very few indigenous peoples ceded their lands to the U.S. because they didn't know what the word meant. It must be remembered that we didn't

know how to read, let alone speak, the English language. The interpreters could have said one thing and written down another.

Two months later the district court ruled against our jurisdiction claim because we had supposedly been compensated for our lands. But basically, it was never for sale. I'm saying that my land has never been for sale. This land is my mother. I cannot and will not sell her. My first law is to follow the Creator, and I will not break that. But I will break the laws of man if I have to.

The BLM came here in February of 1992 to start gathering up the horses and to steal our livestock. It was the first time the U.S. government had ever been in this part of our country. They still don't have jurisdiction here. They came in and chased our horses with their helicopters. They ran them through wire fences, and at least four of them died. The year before we gathered about a thousand head of horses without a single injury.

Later that fall, the BLM returned and removed around two hundred horses, all nationalized Western Shoshone livestock. They claimed they were allowed to sell them under the Wild Horse and Burro Act—but they also had some of our branded horses and livestock. They came in with the Eureka County Sheriff Department to block off the roads to prevent us from going in to protest. That's when my brother Cliff took matters into his own hands.

I arrived to find my fifty-nine-year-old brother threatening to blow himself up if the sheriff didn't let him go in to identify our livestock. Now Cliff is a quiet, hardworking man. He's never been involved in any political activity. He calmly asked the sheriff if he'd ever seen anybody blow themselves up. The sheriff said he had, in Vietnam. I was surprised and horrified at what I was witnessing.

Now to me, dying by fire is a horrible death. Earlier, I had told the sheriff and BLM people that what they were doing was absolutely wrong. That, in fact, they were stealing livestock that belonged to the Western Shoshone. That they were out of their jurisdiction.

Cliff pulled this gallon of gasoline out of his pickup and told the sheriff that he would gladly let any emergency vehicles pass, but that the livestock was not going through. He told them, "Somebody has to die." I know he was talking about himself and his ties to the land. To us when your land is gone, you are walking towards a slow spiritual death. We have come to the point that death is better than living without your spirituality.

When he moved to let the vehicles pass, they sprayed something in his face and knocked him down to the ground. It seemed like six guys were suddenly on top of him. They had knocked off his glasses, and he had blood running down the middle of his face. His arm was twisted in an ugly knot behind him. Then they arrested him and took him off to jail.

We got him a court-appointed attorney, but we weren't allowed to call or visit him while he was in jail. We hadn't even talked to him by the time he had his first hearing. I was there, and I know that if they hadn't assaulted him, he would have walked over to the livestock truck and seen that they only had horses, none of our cows. It was never his intent to hurt anybody, he just wanted answers. After a while, you can't believe anybody because so many people are pushing you around.

He pleaded "not guilty" to charges of impeding the duty of a federal officer and assault at the hearing, and we appointed another attorney to represent him who had been helping us with our jurisdiction matters. We also conducted our own hearing for Cliff within the Western Shoshone court system. What he had done was not a crime in our country. It's not a crime to defend your land or even to set yourself on fire. In fact, that was considered very patriotic. Our court ruled that no crime had been committed by Cliff, but one had been committed by the U.S. by bringing BLM agents and the Sheriff's Department into an area outside of their jurisdiction.

When Cliff finally went to trial in federal court, we decided not to contest the "attempted assault" charge. Instead, we argued that this case was outside of U.S. jurisdiction. The judge got really upset and told our attorney, who was from out of state, that he couldn't represent us in his court of law. But I requested his presence as a witness, and the judge allowed that.

As my witness, the lawyer responded to cross-examination by talking about jurisdictional issues. The judge finally asked him how long his answer was going to take, and he said, "All day, if I'm going to do a good job." The judge gave him five minutes. Our lawyer told him again that the U.S. had no jurisdiction over the Western Shoshone nation.

To this day I still believe it was wrong for the U.S. to come in and throw their federal laws at us. It's obvious that the court system doesn't work for indigenous people, no matter how right you are.

Cliff's still in jail [as of October 1993]. He has so much time on his hands right now, I wonder what he's thinking. He's been so busy all his life working on the ranch. He was the handyman and irrigator. He took care of all our equipment. Never in my life did I see Cliff raise a hand against anyone. He yelled a lot at his machinery and at me because I'm his sister, but that's natural. Family's like that, you know.

I ask him how he feels about all this, and he says simply, "We have to go through it. I'm willing to sit in jail for three years for what I believe." That's what he told me. He said, "If we can finally get a jurisdictional argument in front of the courts, I'm willing to sit here."

We all feel so strongly about our spiritual ways. Cliff is not a person that has lost his mind. He's just a person that feels like death is better than living this way at this time.

# CREE

## VERNON HARPER: EIGHTH FIRE

*The Cree nation, with an estimated 30,000 registered and as many as 180,000 unregistered members, is scattered all across Canada and North America. It is divided into bands—Plains, Woodland, Stony, Eastern, French—each with it's own culture.*

*Vernon Harper, a Northern Cree, is the fifth-generation grandson of Mistowa-sis, "Big Child," a hereditary war chief; and he is the sixth-generation grandson of Big Bear, who fought the last battle between the Cree and the Canadian government at Batoche in May 1885.*

*Vern has fought his own twentieth-century Indian battle against alcohol and drugs, which landed him in a straightjacket in a padded cell in a mental institution in 1968.*

*He won that battle and is now a highly respected medicine man and spiritual leader. He is one of the few medicine men permitted into Canadian prisons to run sweat lodge ceremonies and do counseling.*

*His message is simple but powerful, like all the Cree teachings: Clean up the pollution in our own bodies first, then clean up the environment.*

In the Cree teachings, "The Listening" means more than anything else to us. The Cree Indian people learn how to listen to the environment, to the wind, to the rocks. We learn how to listen to everything. Some of the elders are saying that our young people need help to get back to "The Listening," and that's the reason I wanted to talk. I felt your book could help guide them back to this way of being. This is everything in the Cree teachings. Our young people have forgotten. White people forgot how a long time ago. They all need to

come back and learn how to do this. There can be no real respect unless we learn how to listen to each other, not to hear what we want to hear, but to hear the truth.

The Cree philosophy and teaching is the key to understanding that life is about the sobriety of the mind, body, and spirit. That's why Indian people are so lost today, because we've gotten away from that. The Indian people were once the freest people of all humankind. Now I see the Native alcoholic and drug addict in torment because we're the opposite of what our ancestors were. We've now become slaves. Indian people hate slavery, but when they're into alcoholism, they're slaves. Our duty, our responsibility is to be free. To free people—mentally, physically, and spiritually.

The purpose of our simple teachings is to be the caretakers of Mother Earth. We are the environment and the environment is us. Western man has gone too far the other way. We deal with the trees and all of nature as if they're all alive. When we go to the mountain, we go into the mountain. We become the mountain—never trying to overcome it, but always being a part of its energies.

We think of the animals, too. The buffalo means everything to us. The eagle is also very important, but the buffalo and bear are very important to the Cree. Bear is the medicine of the north. He's spiritually strong. When they killed off the grizzly bear in the plains, it affected us deeply.

Some people say that animals are ignorant, but in many ways they're really smarter than us. You don't see a dog trying to be an eagle. You don't see a squirrel trying to be a wolf. The same with the plants. In our language, there is no word for "weed." This word implies something useless, and all of the plants have been given specific instructions from the Creator on what to do. Plants and animals follow their instructions. It's the human beings who don't follow theirs.

The Cree's magic number is four, which represents the four directions, the four seasons, the four colors, and the four races that make up our Sacred Hoop. If a child does not know who they are by the time they are four years old, they might have to spend a lifetime discovering who they are. Their parents are supposed to protect them so they can develop in the right way. We believe that a child is born innocent. When they're four, they take on their own karma. Up until then, their parents are responsible.

My mother was alive until I was four years old. I remember her holding both myself and my twin brother in her arms when she died. At that time we were living in Regent Park, Toronto, which was a ghetto. This was during the Depression in the thirties, and my father was working for the railroad. One of the most powerful things my mother gave to me was right before she died. The last thing—and I remember it clearly—was that she breathed on us. She gave us her last breath. We had to be taken from her arms, and then we were sent to foster homes. But we had the gift of her last breath on us. I've talked to my twin about this, and although we went separate ways as men, each time in our lives when we were in very serious trouble, like when we were almost ready to give up—we both became drug addicts and alcoholics—each time that breath would come to us. I've had that experience a number of times, and just when I was ready to pack it in, I felt my mother's breath.

I finally made it through my addictions. I made it through the sixties, and I told my auntie, "I've made it through. I'm not going to drink again, and my life is going to change, but what a waste."

But she said, "Vernon, it's like this—life is like a garden, and for anything to be worthwhile and grow or bloom, or be productive or beautiful, it takes a lot of shit and a lot of manure." And that's what I went through. She said, "Now it's up to you. You can stay in that manure, and you can feel sorry for yourself, or you can grow and bloom into something very beautiful and very productive—it's up to you."

Right away I realized she was saying that it wasn't all wasted time. That my own healing was the training for the work I do now. That was what I call my "Crow Dog Universe." Leonard Crow Dog and I went to the same school, we call it "The University of the Universe," where everything in life is connected. This was the necessary training for the healing work that I do now. Now when I'm with people, I don't say to them, "I know what you're going through," because I wouldn't insult them that way. But I can say, "I have an idea. I have a feeling about this because I have gone through a similar experience." Then they listen to me because they see that I'm living a good life, that I'm doing things with my life, and that "I walk my talk."

That's when I really started to learn about the Cree philosophy—that talk is cheap—and that the doing is the learning and the blessing. It's like coming around full circle, which is what we believe in, too. Humor is also a very important part of Cree healing. The Cree love to tease a lot, and some of the other nations and tribes don't like it too much. But it's part of our way of coping and surviving. Humor is very important, and although most of the other Red nations might disagree with us, we think that we have "hands-on humor." The other tribes and nations are pretty dry, but ours is more like a kind of craziness. What we call "devil crazy." That's when we tease each other, and if someone can't take it, everyone goes after that person. So sometimes it can be kind of merciless.

Cree instructions are very simple. We are taught that a woman is a complete being and a man is not. Women are complete because they have the fire of life in them, but men have to find that fire to complete themselves. Our instructions are simply to have children and grandchildren in order to keep passing down this knowledge. In some cultures, the male is superior, but we see the woman as the superior one. Historically and traditionally, we have always followed the woman. The woman is what we call "the Caller," the fire, and the life.

This is what I tell the young women who are scared to come into the sweat lodge. I say, "Don't be scared, because it's going to be easier for you than for the men." I've been running lodges for close to eighteen years now, and in all those years there have only been two times that the men were more together psychologically than the women.

Basically, women don't need men. Men need women. We are not complete, and that's the reason we find partners. Our teachings say, "Be a good man and a good woman will pick you." We don't have the sensitivity, the feeling that women do. So the teaching is for a man to focus on being a good man. There's an old Cheyenne saying, "If the women's hearts are on the ground, it's finished for everyone." No matter if the warriors are there with the most sophisticated weapons and are the strongest warriors, if the women's hearts are on the ground, it's finished for everyone.

Our people have also always considered the unborn generation in their decision making. We ask ourselves, "How is something going to affect our children?" So when my great-grandfather was forced to sign a treaty, he was thinking about how it would affect me and what consequences I would suffer if he didn't sign it. So each generation has to be conscious of what they are doing. We consider ourselves like farmers in a sense, not of growing crops but in dealing with the future of our children and the environment.

I believe we have made positive gains for the things that are now coming to be. In the Cree teachings, we're now in the period called the "Eighth Fire." The great changes that are taking place in this generation are part of a larger purification that began in the "Seventh Fire," which was considered the awakening. I believe the 1960s was about the Seventh Fire, when all the changes were taking place in society.

A hundred years before the Europeans came, a Cree prophecy said a time would come when the Rainbow People and the People of Color would appear and be like children. The prophecy talked about how the people would be very innocent and childlike, and that would be one of the signs for the great changes to come. This time would be known as the "Seventh Fire." I've talked to many of my uncles and aunts, and we believe the hippie movement was part of the prophecy. Maybe that's why a lot of Indians identified with the hippie movement in the sixties.

Now we believe that we're into the Eighth Fire, and we don't see this as foretelling doom and gloom. We see it as Mother Earth rebalancing herself and us. That's why it's important that we are physically and spiritually strong. We need to get ourselves together because the Eighth Fire will be about completion. We believe that Mother Earth will cleanse herself from all the poison. The Indian people have survived because we've been very flexible, we adapt, we know how to keep the values of our ancestors and take things from other cultures and make use of them. Since we're now into the Eighth Fire, we need to put everything together spiritually, physically, and mentally. You cannot do this if you're distracted by drugs or alcohol. You need to be sober-minded for the hard times ahead of us. This is part of the purification.

We're going to heal Mother Earth. According to the Cree teachings, how you live your life now is part of your spiritual journey. So if you are remorseful and bitter and angry, that's how your journey is going to be. That's why we see life as sacred. Every day should be a good day with good thoughts and good feelings, because you never know when you are going to leave. I've faced death many times, but I'm a slow learner. I've finally learned to appreciate life, because it is sacred. Now if someone says to me, "I'm not spiritual," I'll say, "You breathe, don't you?" Well, that's spiritual. Spirituality is breath, and you take it from there.

My religion is about the spirituality of the earth. When you go into a sweat lodge, it is a religious act. You have to take that in context with all the other things you do. I asked myself one time, "Why do Indians do ceremonies?" It clearly came to me that the reason was to remind us that life is a ceremony. *Life is a ceremony.* The Cree teachings are very strong about this. So that when you wake up in the morning, that's a ceremony of life, coming out of the dream-world. When you go into sleep, you're in the dream-world, and you're in a different state of being. Waking up is the ceremony. We believe in the birds, who follow their instructions. There's a time in the morning when you don't hear them chirping and our belief is the birds are silent because it's our turn to pray. And if you listen, you can hear that, too. When the birds are silent, then it's our time to pray. That's because everything is connected; everything is related.

Everyone has a responsibility to find out what they're here for. There's only one way you can do that—with a sober mind, through meditation and prayer. There's no other way that I've found, and it's taken me four decades to find this out. Traditionally, Cree men were not allowed to do community work, or speak on behalf of anyone, until we were over fifty. Because up until that point, our teachings instructed us to learn and listen. And when we reached fifty years of age, we would be able to say something. But things have changed because of the need to teach others.

Elders are basically historians. They teach the faith, the old history of life, and as they become older they become more useful, because then the young ones can come and learn from them. I've started being recognized as an elder before I was fifty, and I believe that our destiny is set for us. All my life I've tried to find out what I was here for.

There are some people who are born here who have been given great tasks, and others who are given very simple things to accomplish. And mine is very simple. In the Cree teachings, we believe in reincarnation and always have. And so you get flashes of the Indians here before us, the old souls and new souls. With the Eighth Fire, we believe that people are coming back faster than ever before and that everything is speeding up.

The Cree don't believe in suicide, but we are losing a lot of our young people this way. The reason most people commit suicide is from a sense of loss. They've lost their loved one, or they've lost their self respect, or they've lost their dignity. Mostly, it is a great loss you can't handle. We now have the highest suicide rate among our youth, and I believe it's because of the loss of our culture. A loss of identity and spirituality. But we believe that things never end. We're spirit form. We never die, but we come here for a purpose and for the lessons of life.

That's how we use the sweat lodge. All my life I suffered, but I always did it selfishly. But when I use the lodge, I do it unselfishly. I crawl in there, and I think about my brothers and sisters. I think about the environment, and I suffer and pray in there. Our life here is part of a journey to the spirit world, and preparation means everything. That's why I keep my teachings simple. When I teach the children, I tell them to make life a good journey and then they will be prepared. Take only the stuff you need. We must all prepare ourselves so when our time comes our spirit journey is a good one. I'm here to teach the children, and that sounds very simple, but it's not. I think it's a most beautiful time to be alive.

## ROSE AUGER: BUFFALO ROBE MEDICINE LODGE

*Rose is a Woodland Cree from the area near Edmonton, Alberta, Canada. Her medicine comes from Grandmother Spider, who has been a part of her life since she was a child. She knew spiders and played with them, and even today, when she is in a meeting they will gather.*

*There is a story about a fierce woman warrior, a Cree, who fought in the battle of Little Big Horn and killed many cavalry soldiers. After the battle, the government wanted to find her and punish her, but she escaped to Montana where she lived, protected by her people, to a ripe old age.*

*Rose, a medicine woman, has also been in the front lines, fighting for the rights of her family, and for her people. She has six children, Fred, Ann Marie, Dale, Laura, George, and Michael—all of whom follow the ways. For this, Rose says, she gives thanks.*

*In her Buffalo Robe Medicine Lodge, which is now part of her house, she has healed people from all across Canada and the United States. She hopes to build a separate, larger lodge.*

My name is Osoka Bousko, "Woman Who Stands Strong." I am of the Woodland Cree nation in northern Alberta, Canada. My mother, also a Woodland Cree, bore sixteen children, but only twelve of us survived. Not too much history is written about my ancestors because they were a nomadic people.

My grandfather was a trapper. One time he got very sick, and my father had to go on horseback a long ways to get a medicine man to come do a healing. I remember the room was darkened, and there was singing. I don't know how old I was—three or four—but I remember the ceremony clearly. The medicine man took a bloodsucker out of my grandfather's arm. I was so scared, I remember grabbing my mother and putting my head under her apron.

When the ceremony was well under way, I peeked out and saw the spirits. I saw birds fly in, and they were glowing. I saw them work on my grandfather. After a while he sat up. He wasn't dying anymore. I didn't tell anyone what I had seen because I was afraid that if I told these things, they wouldn't happen again.

As I got older and I began to know things, I began to see how unhappy people were. Especially my mother, who knew nothing of the old ways because she was raised in the mission school and was a very devoted Catholic. When we were in the mountains, in the bush, I began to see the spirits again. I thought that they were just young people who came to play with me. I'd go back and tell my mother, and she would try to suppress me by telling me to stop imagining these things.

After a while, I stopped talking about it. But I'd go to the river and the beavers would come and swim around me. Birds would land on my head, and I would walk around with them on my head or on my shoulder. And the bears—there were hundreds of them. One day we were out picking berries with my father and the bears came. There were loggers who were trying to kill them, but my father said, "You don't need to kill them, just tell them to go away, and they'll leave." Then he walked up real close to the bears and told them to leave, and they did. They just took off. After that I had no fear of any animals because I understood we were a part of them.

My other grandfather was a medicine man, and I remember he had to hide in the hills to heal people. There was a great TB epidemic that was rampant everywhere on the reserves. Our traditional people saw this coming in their dreams. But even knowing was not enough. Some of the medicine people, like my grandfather, knew that they could help and did. But they had to go and hide in the hills to cure people because they weren't allowed to practice what they knew.

There are people alive today that my grandfather cured. In those days, the law would come after the people who were carriers, so after my grandfather cured them, he would tell them to get an X ray to prove there was nothing there. That just baffled the doctors and everybody else. After a while, they tried to get my grandfather to teach them—to tell them what he did—but he wouldn't.

As a small child, I had the power to take people's pains away by rubbing my hands over them. But then I would carry that pain, and I cried too much because of it. So the elders did a ceremony asking the Creator and the spirit people to hold off these gifts until I got older.

It was my grandmother who told me that the Creator would make sure I would see and understand myself, because no one else was practicing these ways at that time. I would always go and visit her at the senior citizens home to learn and study our ways.

My grandmother told me many stories of our relatives, and of the gifts and powers that they had, and that they all knew about mine. This was the first time my gifts were acknowledged. But I would never have the kind of gifts I do today if I had not pursued this learning, or how to practice self-sacrifice and live exactly as I am told. If I was told to go and fast for so many days in the mountains, that's exactly what I did. If I was told to go work with people, I did exactly that. I lived as holy as I could because I carried a great gift, and I was taken care of. No matter how hard things were, I always had these stories that were told to me about my people, like the grandmothers who could bring rain when it was so dry and so unhealthy. How they could bring the thunderbeing and the rainmaker spirits by rubbing their hair. They had those kinds of powers.

Even now, if I have any problems, there's always help. I have such great faith, I'll go anywhere without fear. It is so fulfilling to live by the motivation of your spirit. That's what people lack today, and that's what has to be established. To begin listening to their own inner selves, their own spirit, or for us, our guardian spirit. That's why this traditional life is not hard, because if you listen, you'll know how to have a full life. That's what all peoples need to develop, because all peoples know subconsciously what is right and what is wrong.

When you choose to make your life good, it will be good. If you want to make it for self gain, then that's how it's going to be. But there's a price to pay when you get old, because then you will be very lonely. No one will love you, and no one will take care of you. If you've lived your life serving and loving, then you will always be taken care of. I talk about that fear, because the places that they have the old people are terrible. Those old people die of loneliness. I am trying to instill the old ways into everyone to take care of our elders. Everybody is responsible for them, not just family.

I also pray that I can take care of myself until the day I go, because I see so many elders being badly abused by their families. This is a loss of culture, a loss of identity, and a loss of tradition. One of the things that I find is that people will fall back on how they were raised and what happened to them, saying, Well, my father was a cruel man, and I have low self-esteem, and I can't comprehend what you are teaching me about love and kindness and giving. And I say, Do not fall back on that kind of garbage. The Creator gave you a sound mind and an incredible spirit and a way of being so that you can do anything right now! You can change that attitude same as you wake up in the morning and it's a new day. Your mind and everything else can be new. I've lived through hardships and horror, and I'm a loving, caring, and giving person because I choose to be that way. I choose to listen to the other side to guide me. We all have the ability with our spirit to change things right now.

And you must also think of the next generation, whether you have children or not. The goodness we were born with is what we have to leave behind. That truth always prevails, no matter how many years it may take. So when a person lives in honesty and truth, you never have any real hardships, because truth is like a medicine, and it's always going to take care of you. No matter how much you get persecuted. Even today, I'm being persecuted. My own people are so full of fear. They are so terrified of our ceremonies and our ways because of what they learned at the mission schools.

All the things we do are never a failure. You need to ask yourself: Who are you? What are you about? It's like taking a big mirror and looking at yourself. You must look at it all and try to understand yourself.

If you were to tell me that you were getting sick, and asked me, "Grandmother, teach me how to pray," I would ask, "What have you been doing to yourself that is making you sick?" Then I would tell you how to pray in order to understand yourself. I would tell you, for the next eleven days, take a glass of water and something from your own culture to bless it with—for us it's sweet grass, cedar, or sage—then bless the water and pray early in the morning before the sun comes. That way you will make your connection with the Creator at that same time for eleven mornings. If you miss one morning, then you have to start over and keep going until you complete the eleven days. By that time you will be in touch with the Creator and also in touch with your own self—and your own spirit.

We cannot survive anymore off our land and our waters. So we have to pray for help to survive, to feed and clothe our children, to put a roof over our loved ones. We don't pray and say, "Give me a million dollars." We pray and ask for that kind of help in whatever way it comes, because it's meant the right way. A lot of times I pray for help. Sometimes I can't get around because I don't have a vehicle, or I don't have something else, and I pray and it comes. Someone will bring me what I need as an offering. Often I'll see a family who needs something badly, and I'll give it to them as an offering, rather than an outright gift. So that they will treasure and value it, and that it will have meaning. Everything has to be done that way in order for people to understand the part of giving.

And it's such a good way to be because you empower everyone around you. Whether it's in your job, your home, or in the community—everybody benefits. Maybe it's something as simple as being motivated to make a garden. Our people need to be putting up gardens, even if it's in the city and on top of a roof. You can gather medicines. There's a lot of plants you can use in place of coffee and tea. Natural plants that are so good for you. Each season has food and plants and medicines that we all used to take in order to be strong and healthy.

I've tried to establish simple things like that with my people. We go out in little camps and spend the nights out there to pick our medicines and teas. But it's such a slow process. Every time someone comes to my house and I serve them these special teas, they say, "Boy, is that ever good." And I tell them, "Oh, it's the plant that cleanses our blood, that gives strength to our brain. And it just grows out there, all you have to do is pick it." There are some plants you can pick all season that are a hundred times healthier than anything in the market, and you don't have to spend any money. It's just that little bit of knowledge that you can collect for yourself that can make you self-sufficient and independent.

The best thing is that we can become that way in all that has been given to us. It's still there, and if it's not, we can re-establish it one way or another. We all need to work together because no one was meant to be on an island by themselves. To be what? To be lonely? People get very lonely when they are only motivated for self-gain, self-centeredness. They are lonely and empty. But when you're sharing all that you have it will always be fulfilling, because you will always get it back.

Sometimes I have to sell things in order to keep going, but I am never without help, any place, any time. That's how it used to be, and that's how we need to be now. Greed is useless because you can't take nothing with you, and to be truly serving of the Creator and the gift that is yours to help people, you have to be humble.

To be humble is to be giving, and to remember that it isn't you who did the curing, that it's those spirits working with you. You are a vessel, just a vehicle and a human being. That's why it's really very important to live as closely as you can to the life that was here before this society. And yes, it's difficult, but not unreachable. When you establish that great faith, you can go anywhere and communicate and adapt.

But by the same token, to be humble doesn't mean that you allow people to abuse you and step all over you and take you for granted. I am not one to allow that. I'm real strict on how I live my life, and I have the strength to stand up for what I believe in. It doesn't matter who it is, if I find there's some type of prejudice or injustice being done to me or my people, I will stand up to it. And if someone is going to put a bullet into my head, I will say, "Go ahead, but this is what I'm standing for and you're wrong, you have to stop." There were times I wouldn't allow anyone to put me down, or abuse me, and there were times I had to defend myself physically. But each time I won. I'm talking about violence, even from police, and I stood up knowing they couldn't kill my spirit, ever. No one can do that. You can snuff out the body, but you cannot snuff out the spirit, and that's what's so comforting and so wonderful.

But I'm grateful for these kinds of opportunities, because I have my apprentices continuing the grass roots work that I have done for so many years. It's their time—they're young, they're healthy, and they have do to it. And that's so rewarding that sometimes I lay on Mother Earth and give thanks in tears for the changes that are happening, both for our women and men and our young people. But it's such a slow process. To me, it's so small. I want to see the changes in masses, and for all people, not just Indian people. There is too much war, there's too much violence, there's so much abuse of every kind, and it has to stop because we're all going to become extinct.

We can't just say, "Oh, there's nothing I can do." Even people who don't have anything can do something. Young people have a lot of courage today. They have courage to go to the other countries because they don't like what's going on in their country. A lot of them come here and look to the Indian to give them answers. I have had a lot of young people from other countries come to my home. But they are in such a fantasy and dreamland about the Indians that they want the magic. I tell them, "I am sorry, my friend, you cannot have the magic until you look at yourself and see who this person is in you. This is the way we will do it."

So, some stay and some don't. Those who do really get to see what they're about and what their destiny is. But I have a lot of hope in the young people. There's a lot of them running around searching different parts of the world asking, "What is my destiny? What am I here for? I don't buy into what's going on in the world today, so I don't want any part of it." So they go on searching, suffering and sacrificing in the process, and the end result will be that the Creator will pity them and place them where they will be on their path, their journey in this life. There is a great hope in that.

They say during the last stages of purification, the spider will come back to try and correct what has happened. Spider is back, and that's why I have her working with me all the time, around the clock, everywhere I go. When I am going somewhere far to help people, I like to drive fast, and so a lot of times I have to call her to help me. And so somewhere along the way, where there is a policeman, she'll put him to sleep while I fly by.

People know that I work with the spider. The spiders came to the elders council at the Santa Clara Pueblo. Thousands of them came to listen to us and help us. A spider came up and hopped on the lap of this young holy man. He got so scared, he was going to hit it, but the elder next to him said, "No, it's bringing us a message." But this young man was so terrified he was shaking. The spider got right off his lap and went across the room to the speaker. Nobody really knew what to make of the spiders.

I was sick that morning and didn't come until the afternoon. The spider came back and did the same thing. This time the man picked up what the spider was saying and, with the spider in his hand, came right up to me and said, "It's you. You're the one that works with the spider." And I said yes. I asked him if he had gotten a message from spider, and he nodded.

When you work with the spirit you have that gift; they choose to work with you. We see an eagle in the sky, and we immediately pray and hope to get the message. We ask: What is it? What's it bringing? If we see something else, we immediately pray so that we can communicate.

I work with 126 of these spirits. They are my ancestors, my people. I am still very young, so I still have a long way to go to learn who they all are. Each year more come to work with me and tell me that this is who I am, and that this is my duty. There's one grandmother who's been coming to me called Earth Blanket Woman. She's coming here to tell us what we need to do for what's coming. Through this winter, she came and told us that we have to make special medicines and teas so that we can stay healthy because there were going to be flus worse than there had ever been. That a lot of people would end up in the hospital because of something in the atmosphere. It's going to be like that more and more, diseases that aren't here yet but are coming.

Our instructions are that we have to help ourselves spiritually. That we have to cleanse our whole selves mentally, physically, spiritually, and emotionally. We have to change. Otherwise, we aren't going to survive the diseases that are here now and already killing us. You know you have cancer, diabetes, HIV—all these things that were told to us long ago. We knew they were coming. But if we are not in harmony with all living things and not guided by the spirit people, we'll never survive. We'll never know how to free ourselves of these deadly diseases.

It's such an incredible waste today with the HIV. Last fall, I was down in the Seattle area with the tribes, and I met a lot of beautiful young people who were HIV positive. They were going around to all the schools, wherever people would hear them, telling their story. Telling them what it was like knowing how little time they had left.

A young, nineteen-year-old woman with two children came to talk to me. The man who gave it to her had already died, and she was in a pretty fatal stage herself. I focused on talking about the spirit world, hoping that I could take away all the fear of dying by telling her the stories of what happens when you die and how life only continues and doesn't end. I have been able to prepare a lot of people on their journey to the spirit world. It's very, very hard for them in the beginning, but after they understand—after I put them in ceremonies—then they are at peace. And so are the families.

This is something that no one does—prepare them. They are terrified, and yet it's a part of life. Every culture has a tradition and rituals that deal with death. I'm real grateful for my people. When my father died in 1984, we had been living our traditional life as much as we knew how. I had been a spiritual leader for many years in my area. Although people persecuted me when I started, as time went along that changed. So when my father was passing on of cancer, we had, for the first time ever, a burial without a church, without undertakers, without anything. We did it ourselves.

Everybody was terrified. They said, "You can't do that!" And I said, "Yes, we can. This was our father; this was his request." He never was part of any church and never wanted priests, because he knew what they did to him and all our people. I was only honoring what he asked us to do, and that was to bury him this way.

He died in August on a beautiful, beautiful day. The eagles came. We had a two-day wake with feasts and ceremonies. My oldest son and I led the procession on horses. There were eleven of us riders in front with the sacred staff stick, our young warriors, my mother, and my sisters in one wagon, and my brothers walking. There were the pallbearers and the people with their wagons and horses.

We had to cross the highway, and we had the police hold off traffic until we all crossed. So even the police were a part of our procession. It was just incredible. No one had ever seen this before, no one. So there were a lot of wonderful feelings and amazement that we dared to do this because we had been so suppressed about our culture. And I thought, For my father, I loved him so much; he was a man of the land—I will honor everything he asked me. He once said, "Don't ever take me into the church. I was never a part of it. The sky is our roof and Mother Earth is our floor, our ground, and the Creator is everywhere. You can pray everywhere, you can be a part of the sacred ways anywhere you are; that's how we were created and that's how I want to go."

I am proud to have brought this movement back to our people. We had it for my mother, and the other elders started saying they wanted it the same way, too. They made their kids promise, too, and it's still carrying on. It just keeps getting better and better every time. I am a great survivor, and so are my people, even today, with all our rights being lost and not being able to be self-sufficient like we used to be before the white man came.

There's a new awakening for our people, and it's growing fast. I find comfort each and every day that all that I do is going to bring changes and hope and new visions. Not only for my own people, but for people of the world, because people of the world are also suffering. You know, they are their own victims. So they are looking for answers with us, because we know how to be with life, all life-forces upon Mother Earth.

I think one of the big revolutions for people is that they know and see it but are still afraid to acknowledge our healing. Like myself, I am able to heal cancers with the ceremonies and the medicines. I have been very blessed. The medical profession has seen this because I send their patients back to them after they've been cured. They know, but they never say anything. I don't know when they're really going to acknowledge me and say, Let's work together. Because if we did, it would be so powerful.

At this time I wish to build another healing lodge, a bigger one where my people, myself, and my apprentices can work on a big scale. I frequently get terminally ill cancer people, and it's hard to take care of them in a small house. It's hard, especially for them, because they are in a lot of pain. In this lodge they could have their own special place. I wish to build it with logs, because we still have logs and need to have that kind of energy. I live in a beautiful log house right now, and the energy is just so beautiful, and it stays sacred. You can keep it sacred, unlike modern houses where it's so noisy.

This lodge will have to be a place where we can be in unity with all life-forces and have the freedom to just go out and be with Mother Earth and the birds and every living thing. This will also be a complex place where, not only will there be healing, but there will also be a place of teaching. We want to teach people. We want to take in young people who are in trouble with the law and have them work and learn all of this. This is a lodge that I am going to build, but I have to find the help for it.

Buffalo Robe Medicine Lodge will be the name, and it will be the thing that I leave behind when I journey on to the spirit world. And I know that there will be others who will follow the lodge and the work. Modern medicine cannot heal the things we can. I know that's a big statement to make, but it's true. We don't just focus on the physical being, we focus on the whole human being, that's the mind, physical, spiritual, and emotional.

Every part of a human being must be addressed in order to heal. And it does not stop there, it involves the whole family, and then the family involves the community. There's a lot of questions that I still have. But like I say, I used to have millions of questions, but a lot of them have been answered because of my work and my life. I'm grateful for that, but there are still questions and answers that I need at times such as this. So it has to be the will of the Creator. I tell people, I will do the best I can, I will do anything to help you, I will give of myself. That's how I put it to the Creator, I do the best I can. I do the ceremony, whatever it is that I need to do. And the rest is totally up to the Creator.

# WARM SPRINGS

## Verbena Greene: medicine singing

*The large woman with sloe-black eyes and huge smile who greets me at the door tells me people call her "Beans." I can see why. Age and size aside, this elder has the playful spirit of a child.*

*We enter the large house through the kitchen where last minute preparations are under way for the four-day Medicine Singing, a traditional healing ceremony and prayer, that will begin the next evening. Every available surface in both the kitchen and the dining room has been turned into a sewing table for the ribbon dresses and shirts her daughters are making for the ceremony. Puppies and grandchildren streak through the house while a tape deck beats out Lakota ceremonial music.*

*We go into the bedroom, another workroom, and Beans clears away a place on the bed for me to sit. As we talk she sorts through blankets, pot holders, purses made from scraps of fabric, tablecloths, all for the give-away that is part of every ceremony among the Northwest tribes.*

*The Warm Springs Indian Reservation lies on the eastern side of the Cascade Mountain Range, one hundred miles south of Portland. It is a confederacy of three tribes, Paiute, Wasco, and Warm Springs. Beans is the keeper of the longhouse that is just outside her house, a long rectangular structure consisting of a large meeting room, a dining hall, and a kitchen.*

*The next evening, after a meal, the ceremony begins. Over the next four days and nights the longhouse is filled with as many as two hundred people, including children asleep on their mothers' laps and babies in cradles. Observers and participants sit on benches arranged like bleachers,*

*except for the elders who had brought their own lightweight folding chairs. Walking sticks were passed among the people—some had brought their personal sticks, carved in the shapes of animal heads—used for drumming on planks that run along under each of the benches. Dan and I, there by special invitation from Beans, quickly caught up in the singing, begin to drum vigorously.*

*Beans and her family sit at the far end of the room, beneath rafters hung with dozens of folded blankets. Beans's sister opens the ceremony with a speech given in hypnotic sing-song. The singing and drumming continue throughout the next four days and nights, and in between, the dances. Some dances are only for the children, others are for healings or thanksgivings.*

*On the last day, Beans's nephew Gary, a marine, arrives home from the Gulf War. His return is celebrated by a procession in which he wears white buckskin with a beaded vest decorated with feathers. On the back of the vest is an American flag. To the music of "Soldier Boy," a war bonnet is placed on Gary's head, and a procession follows during which elders wrap blanket after blanket around his shoulders.*

*Beans sings a tearful prayer of thanksgiving for the safe return of her nephew, as the sounds of the drums, faster now, and louder, fill the longhouse.*

My mother used to cut up pieces of cloth and say to me, "Give them to the animals, it will help them. The birds will make their nests. The ants will drag them around, maybe they'll use it for bedding. The frogs will use them, they always like to make clothing." So I would always go and scatter them, especially in the wind. I still carry that on, and I'll be sixty-four years old in a few days. When I am making things for the Medicine Singing, I keep all the scraps to share with the animals.

I like to do this, because a long time ago the old people used to say, "When you share, even with the animals of the land, they will be good to you. They'll show you where the best roots are. They'll show you where there is a waterfall. All the birds will sing, and they'll be happy, and they'll keep you company if you are all alone somewhere." If you listen to the birds you can actually hear them talk.

Many times when I go out into the hills, whether it's for digging roots or getting medicine, there are some birds that I just get a kick out of. I invent my own little words for and with them. There's a bird we have here that has a song very much like the one we have that tells the babies to go to sleep. I call this bird the babysitting bird. There's another bird that we have that talks a lot. You hear it all the time when you are going someplace, because they get real excited. I try and listen to those birds and tell the children that the birds are happy that we are here. I'll say, "Listen to them now. They are saying my Indian name. They are declaring that I have arrived now."

There is another bird that is always around, that I call the "storyteller," because they like to gossip. Gee, do those birds like to gossip. Something could be told here one day, and the next day it could be clear across the country. Because they tell it from the treetops, and the wind comes along and takes it to the next treetop, and then another bird picks it up and tells everyone, and it goes on and on. Ever since I was young, I have paid attention to the birds in that manner.

The old people have taught me many of the legends and told me how to tell the stories. They used to tell me, "You will learn from the animals. They will know what kind of person you are. And they will share with you." Our old people also used to say, "When we have taken care of our animals like we're supposed to, our land shall be intact. We have to always listen to them."

Like the swallows every spring, who used to come along the Columbia River. This was a sign that the salmon were going to start running up the Columbia River. Everyone would be so happy, they'd start getting their drying sheds together. Thousands upon thousands of salmon traveled up the river. It is so sad that today there are not that many that travel up the river anymore.

The salmon also had a song that they used to sing as they traveled along in schools. We would sing this song to children who caught their first salmon, or trout, or whatever kind of little fishes. That's a real pretty song.

This is what I try to teach children who will listen. Two of my little grandchildren here pretty much understand. So when I go to talk to the schoolchildren, I like to take one of my grandchildren with me, so that the students can see how something like this can be passed down from grandmother to grandson or granddaughter. This is the way it's supposed to be. Long ago, our old people educated the young people that way. The grandparents were not just the babysitters, because they worked with the children. They didn't just let them play and get into all sorts of mischief. If they were doing a little something, they would always have the children take part in helping them. Whether they were digging roots, barbecuing a bear, or picking berries. The grandmother would take her grandchildren with her, and she would show them the best way to pick and how they could fill their baskets up really fast.

They always told us to hurry, because when you learn how to do something fast, your hands will be fast. And when you learn to use your hands really fast, then you will also learn fast. You will catch on quickly to what people are telling you. You will learn how to remember things and never forget them because you have learned them in that manner.

When I was young, the first thing in the morning when I woke up, I would hear the old people singing the prayer songs. They were singing the worship songs, and they would tell me, "Get up, time to go swim." Rain, snow, or shine, we would swim. They used to say, "When you go and take part in helping to do something, the first thing you do is wash your body." The morning bathing was a teaching, so that you could learn to be strong and to withstand any kind of bad news, stress, or depression.

They told us to do this, and we'd never weaken. We used to use a big pond near our house that my father dug out, and the water was very cold. And as we grew up, we never got sick. Now I'm an old lady, and every time the wind blows a little bit, I catch a cold. But when we were young, getting sick was something that very seldom happened in our family. Because we also used the sweathouse lodge.

We were taught how to sweat at a very young age, around three years old. I took my youngest grandson to the sweathouse. I had a ceremony for the kids because some had never done a sweat before. It was quite an event, but it was freezing cold outside. If you poured water on yourself, icicles would form on your hair, that's how cold it was. But the children went, and now I only hear one of them coughing.

Our diet in the old days was a lot better than it is now. We ate only the Indian foods, very seldom something from the store. The old folks went to town maybe once a month to get the needs of the family. Other than that, we were children who never knew what it was like to live in the white world. For us children, it was a real treat to be able to go to the store. A lot of times, the weather was bad, and our road was bad, but we went anyway.

My father also used to ranch. We planted grain and hay for our horses and cattle. The ranch was over three hundred acres. Just before the snow came he would plow the ground so that the moisture could go into the ground. Of course, in those old days, he used to plow with a walking plow. We used to help him. When he came in for lunch he would always tell us, "Don't bother the horses, just give them water." But we would ride them around all the while he was eating lunch—just gallop around. He would come back and pick up where he left off, and then we would help him put the hay up.

We always had a big garden where we planted every kind of vegetable and some fruit. My mother would put up the fruit and can the vegetables. Most of them were dried. We also had a little wheat bin where the melons, squashes, and corn would go.

They always kept well; it was like a refrigerator or a cooler. My father would tie string to them, and then put it into the bin. At Thanksgiving time, everybody would bring out their good foods for all the people to eat. We never went hungry; we always had plenty of food. We were never in need. I never could understand why the white man came and called us poverty cases.

We were happy with our own foods and our own way of life because we lived so close to nature, which was the beginning of the way of our people. Everything that Mother Earth gave to us, the people did something in return to take good care of the earth. When they built a fire, they would cover up the ashes before they left, so that it would return to the ground and become dust. Our people never left their trash anywhere because they didn't have any. The hunters or people who went fishing took just enough lunch that they would need, roots, fish, or dry meat. That was all they took, and it was just enough to keep them going until they got home.

Nowadays, if we go outdoors to do anything, you'll see people picking up snacks of all kinds, and pop, and big boxes of food. I always get a kick out of that because I am guilty of that, too. I like to go out sometimes and eat my little lunch.

Our people always took good care of their water and their water holes. They never let their animals out who would abuse our water sources like they do today. They used to put a little rock fence around their little water holes to protect them.

This is how we grew up before we went to school. We talked Indian at home and did everything the old way. When we came home from school, we would have to talk Indian. There would be two or three old people staying with us, and we were taught to wait on them. We were taught to stand back and let the old folks sit down first to eat. Today, when you go to places, the young ones just about knock you over so that they can get to the food first. It's so sad that the children have lost so much respect for our old people.

I didn't know too much English when I was growing up because I never really cared about it. My sisters and my brother went to school, and they learned a lot of things. When they came home, they'd bring a book to me. And yet, I never really cared to learn all of that, but I had to when I finally went to school.

We have five longhouses. Two big ones are here in Warm Springs, one in Agency, and then another one in Simnasho. There's another one near Highway 26, going toward Portland. It's the place where we gather in the fall for the huckleberry season. We also have our own private longhouse; I am the keeper of this one. My husband wanted to build it long before he even sang. He believed in it, and because he was around when my father and my brother sang, he helped them build it. Then when my husband got really sick and almost lost his life, he was shown how to sing.

Healings have happened during these singings. The white people were against the Medicine Singing. That was way back in the early 1800s when a lot of them were coming into our area. Some white people who came were very respectful in the beginning. It wasn't until the army-type came and tried to change our ways. They never thought for a minute that we had lived like this for thousands and thousands of years. They wanted to "civilize" us to be like them.

Medicine Singing is related to Indian doctoring. The government didn't like the Indian doctor, who was the shaman doing his duties to his people. If they found out that you were singing, the police would arrest us. It was not allowed. But the people never gave up; they wouldn't let them take this away. It takes some people forty years of singing before they can become an Indian doctor. It wasn't my intent to become an Indian doctor; I sang because it would make me a better keeper of my children.

If you truly are a spiritual person, the spirits will come to you. Many of the spiritual songs that people sing are different, because there are many spirits that are very challenging. There are songs that will help you in times when another spirit is trying to do you in or cause you to get sick. Those kinds of songs can help you to fight that spirit out there.

There are songs that are only for children. They call on the spirits who take care of little children. There are spiritual songs that many people sing that will only take care of adults. Some come easy, and so very gentle. And then there are some spiritual songs that just slap you. I have had that happen to me, where the spirits just hit you and almost knock you over. Many of them make you sick, and you can be sick for many days. But they are not there to harm you, they are just coming into your life.

There was a song that came to me and, honest to goodness, it almost killed me. I was so sick, all I could do was crawl into the restroom. These are the kinds of things that will happen to you sometimes. You have to go through them because it's like a trial. You have to ask yourself, "Are you ready for it? Are you fit?" It's like this song is entwined around you and feeling you out to see whether you are a fit person for this song or not. There are many songs that will do that to you. There are many songs that will just come and bother you, until finally you sing it. Some of the songs come in dreams.

When people ask me about Spiritual Singing, I tell them that I always wanted to become a spiritual singer. There are many rituals that you have to go through first. You have to cleanse and purify your body through the sweathouse during the course of a year or two, sweating once a week, or two or three days in a row. Or, you could sweat every day, once a day, until you feel you have changed. It's like a total changing in your life. You have to let a lot of things go, like anger, meanness, being rough and tough, and maybe you have to start watching your mouth and what you say.

The Medicine Singing is inherited from generation to generation. There are very few who find their own vision quests to do this. We are supposed to sing in our own language; we can express ourselves better than we could in a borrowed language.

I can go quite a ways back in our ancestry, at least five generations of Medicine Singers. They believed and respected everyone's religion. No one ever told me, "Don't believe in that," and they didn't force us to learn the ways of the Longhouse. They told us that it may help someday, and when we grew up we could pick a religion of our own to learn about the Creator. We all believe in him who is the Creator of all things.

Medicine Singing goes back to the beginning of time with our people. They sang for survival; they sang when times were hard. We are where we are today because of all the Medicine People that went before us. They learned singing through the vision quest.

In our culture, when we lose someone, we give everything away. We don't keep anything. At the time my husband died we had ten davenports in our Singing House. When we lost him, we took everything out of there until it was bare. And also out of the longhouse. You give away the keepsakes of your family in appreciation to the people who have helped you through the funeral, and maybe through the time of illness. It is a time of sharing.

Our people never knew about Christmas because they had give-aways all the time. They didn't have to sit around and wait for someone to say, "Merry Christmas." Many people gave things away in active appreciation. They never said, "Thank-you." Instead they would say, "I am very happy from my heart for what you have done."

We also had no word for "good-bye." People never believed in telling each other good-bye. They shook hands instead, and said, "I'm going now, and I'll see you again."

I used to joke a lot before I lost my husband four years ago. After that I couldn't even tell a joke or laugh. My in-laws gave me mourning clothes, and they put a handkerchief around me so I could shut my eyes. That's how I was for a year and a half. It was hard for me to get used to it. I just withdrew and refrained from everything and everybody. I didn't talk for a long time, and then I got really sick and couldn't walk. After two months, I came out of it and thought, "Why in the world am I doing this? Why am I submitting to this illness?" But it was really myself. I thought, "When I'm good and ready, then I will come out of whatever is bothering me." Sure enough, one day I started practicing walking around again, and I had many falls. That was the most difficult hardship that I had to deal with in my life. Death can really do a lot of things to you.

My husband's name was Perry Greene. He was born and raised here. We raised our children by teaching them to respect all of their heritage, because I'm a Warm Springs Indian, with a little Paiute in my background. Perry's mother was Warm Springs and Wasco, and his father was a Nez Perce. So we taught our children the culture from each of these tribes. That was so they could eventually pick a tribe to be represented by if they wanted. My children were very proud of their Nez Perce heritage and never forgot it.

My husband loved his Wasco ways. Their culture is a little different than the ways of the Warm Springs. And their language is different. The Wasco also have Medicine Singing.

There was a lot of strictness in the Medicine Singing for the children. Little children were not allowed to come, but the older children could come and participate on children's night.

I grew up right here in this valley, which is called Dry Creek in English. But in our language the old people called it Toukse. *Toukse* is a plant that was used by our people. It made the strongest ropes and nets. Many people would come to our home, people that were in need of prayer and maybe having a little hard luck. They would come and stay with us until they got back on their feet. It was a place where we gathered together. And when you are a small child, you are so innocent and pure, you can see and hear many things.

We had a creek where we used to play and talk to the frogs and the water bugs. One time I ran home and told my mother, "Get some food together, the people are starving."

And my mother said, "Well, we had better help them." She went outside and said, "Where are they? I don't see any horses and wagons."

So I ran clear down near the creek, and I turned a rock over. The frog hid when my mother came. But there were little ones there under that rock, and I told my mother, "See, look, they're starving."

She said, "Oh, I thought you meant people."

But that's what they were to me, so I told her, "Don't say anything because they can hear you and understand you." I believed that then, and I believe it to this day.

# THREE SISTERS

*Sylvia Walulatuma, 76; Nettie Queahpama, 91; and Matilda Mitchell, 87, live in the small hamlet of Simnasho, on the Warm Springs reservation. Like the Three Sisters Mountains where once their people lived, Sylvia, Nettie, and Matilda live in houses side by side. They are quiet-spoken but firm upholders of the tradition in which they were raised by their father, a chief. Matilda, confined to a wheelchair by a recent stroke, teaches children the ceremonial songs and chants in the ancient Sahaptin language. When her husband died in 1972, Matilda was the only person left who knew the sacred prophet songs. Sylvia still travels to speak about their culture and to attend meetings with elders from other reservations.*

*I was struck by their warmth and humor, and their gentleness.*

My name is Sylvia Walulatuma. I was born December 10, 1917, here in Simnasho. My sisters, Nettie Queahpama and Matilda, and I are Warm Springs Indians.

We used to live in a two-room little house made out of boards with a wood stove. It had a lot of cracks in it, as did a lot of houses that were built around here. My father built ours when he was a young man, and this is where a lot of us were born. There were people scattered all over, a house here and another house there. Some you couldn't get to because the mud got so bad in the wintertime. Not too many live out here anymore.

Now the government put us in these little communities where we have to live close together. Back then there were a lot of farms, and everybody planted wheat and rye and vegetables, like corn, carrots, potatoes, watermelons, squash. We raised just about every kind of vegetable because the seasons were long. It's changed a lot since then; we can't have gardens like we used to because sometimes we hardly have a summer, and then it gets cold. In the springtime it freezes a lot, and there isn't enough time to plant anything.

When our houses were still scattered, people would leave their houses open, so if somebody came to visit and we weren't home, they could come in and make themselves at home. You can't do that anymore because people will come in and steal everything you have.

Then people were always helpful, like during thrashing season, when people moved from place to place because we had a thrashing machine that was owned by all the people. When we needed the machine after someone else had finished with it, my two brothers would take wood and water over there real quick and ask them to move it to our house. It was a steam engine, so they had to feed it wood. When they moved the machine over to our place everybody would come and help, and we would get it done quickly. After they left our house, my brothers and my father would move with the machine and help someone else.

Sometimes my sisters would go over if they needed help setting tables or cooking. It was really nice in those days. The old ladies used to want me to play stick games with them, and it was really fun because I liked to listen to them sing. They had some really funny songs with funny words in them.

My father, Frank Queahpama, Sr., was the chief, or the head of the whole reservation, which included three tribes. During that time they only had one chief for the whole reservation, but now we have three chiefs: one in Warm Springs, one in Wasco, and one in Paiute.

There's a little shack where the longhouse used to be. It had a dirt floor, and there were three fires burning in there during the wintertime, it was so cold. Around December, the people would all come and move into the longhouse, starting on what we call the Indian New Year, on the twenty-first, which is the shortest day of the year. Everyone would sleep there and celebrate from that time on through Christmas to New Year. They had worship services in the evening.

I remember as a little girl they would have different social dances during the afternoon. They used to have the children dance then because they didn't want us to get in the way when the big people had their dances. They would let us dance in the afternoon, and then they would put us to bed. Our mother used to fix us a little swing on the wall, put in a blanket, and then she would put us in there so we could watch the dances from there. And then whenever we got tired we would fall asleep.

The dancers didn't wear real fancy things. The women wore dresses and the men wore their regalia and feathers. They had one big drum, and the men would sit on their knees at the drum. Some elderly women would stand in the back and sing with the drum. They didn't have a lot of drums like they do now, just the one big drum that took up a lot of room.

The old people told us stories and Indian legends in the winter months. I don't remember too many stories; I just know parts because it has been so long. But what was nice about those times is that my mother would bring out some of the goodies, some of the things we don't have anymore. Sometimes I just think about it and wish that we still did.

We used to have a lot of what we call the Simnasho berries. There are some shrubs out here in the meadow and they have long thorns. The berries are in seedy clusters and are sweet. You couldn't eat too many of them when they were fresh because they would make you sick. When we picked them, my mother would take wooden bowls and a long, smooth, pounding rock and ground them all day, until the seeds were all pounded up. Then she would make little round, flat patties and dry them in the sun. When they were dry they were really sweet. She did the same with the service berries [a kind of blackberry]. Then in the wintertime she would mix them up with different kinds of roots like *howsh*, which you could cook or eat the way they were.

Then there was *camas*, which is barbecued in the ground and put in jars while it's still hot. They are like little onions that grow in the meadows. They have purple flowers, and a lot of people grow them in their flower gardens. People barbecue them in different ways, but my mother used to dig a round pit, and then she would build the fire in there first to get it real warm. You would have some rocks to put right in the middle, and then put all your leaves in there. It has to be different kinds of leaves, and the one that I remember is skunk cabbage. We put them in last and poured the camas right next to them, which made it real sweet. So after you got it all covered and put a stick in the middle, you poured water into it, and covered it with burlap, and then dirt. Then you kept the fire going for three days and three nights to cook it. We would be so anxious for it to be ready.

There were lots of things my parents taught us. But I remember they always stressed that we were never to take our own lives. Even though there were very few people at that time that ever committed suicide. It was just one of the teachings.

I think they told us this in case we ever felt that way. They said if you did take your own life, you would never see the beautiful land that's promised to us. And you would never have any peace, even after death, because it would be worse than when you were alive on this earth. You would be wandering all alone, with no one to help you.

I don't remember anybody taking their life in those days, but you know it was just a warning to us. I don't know how they knew about this, maybe the spirits told them. Because even in the old days they talked about the things that are happening now. There weren't hard times for our children like there are now. Now they take drugs, drink alcohol, commit suicide, and murder one another. There was prophecy that these things were going to happen, but at that time we didn't understand because there weren't things going on like that. The prophecy said these things were coming and to watch out for them. So now we are finding out that they really knew what was going to happen.

Our old people had songs that they used to sing before the white man came. My sisters know these songs, but I don't. They used to talk about what these white people would look like, and what they were going to bring. They would talk about the wood stoves, that they would bring something made of steel that would make fire inside to keep the house warm. These were some of the songs. They would also sing about them bringing saws. They must have been talking about the chainsaws or even the hand saws that were going to knock the trees down. They also sang about the fact that some of our people would be flying and going to the big chief. I think what they meant was that the people will be flying to Washington, D.C., for meetings. These are things they sang about before the white man came.

We never used anything when we prayed, we just prayed—like you do in church, just pray. The best time to pray is when you wake up, and the sun is coming up. Our songs tell us that this is the beautiful time, when your mind and everything else is fresh. Then you pray for yourself, and you pray for your people. And before you go to bed at night, when you see that beautiful painting in the sky, late in the evening, that is when the Creator is speaking to us, speaking to our hearts. If we listen with our hearts, we will do the right thing when he speaks to us, and we will know what he is telling us. Many people don't listen to this, and that's why there are so many problems in this world. They don't listen when he speaks, because he is leading and guiding us and telling us how to live our lives if we'd only listen. My parents taught me how to listen for this.

We also have our ceremonies, like the root feast, which is like a Thanksgiving. We are giving thanks to our Creator for the different kinds of roots and the salmon. And especially the water, because the water gives us life and gives the plants and animals life.

We also give thanks for the mountains, which are very precious to us. He put us here right next to the mountains, and the moisture comes from the mountains to grow things, and gives us our roots. We believe that Creator gave us these mountains to also protect us from the winds, so we don't have those tornadoes. And he gave us all the salmon and the deer and the different kinds of animals.

We are thankful to the earth, which gives us our plants, gives us our trees, and all the things we need for life. We should protect our Mother Earth because that's what our Creator has made our bodies from, and when we die we go back to our Mother Earth.

Our songs do not teach us about reincarnation, although we have many beautiful songs that we sing to teach us about what's coming, how to take care of our bodies, and how to live.

Some of the prophecies say that the earth is going to turn, and I imagine what that means is that it's going to turn very quickly. And so when we bury our people, we make sure that their heads are facing the west. A lot of people bury their people with their head to the east. When that time comes, the earth will be turning real fast. When the earth turns, the Great Spirit is supposed to come and our spirits will rise up to him and go.

I believe we call Jesus our brother; we don't say Jesus, we say our brother. And God is our father, or our Creator. We don't have to take it from the Bible; if we are really listening to him, he speaks right to our hearts. Sometimes, if he wants us to give messages, he'll speak right through us, speak to the people. I think this is really wonderful.

I went to Germany last summer, and I had to speak to some people there about this. I was telling them the same thing, how the Creator speaks to our hearts, and if we listen, we'll do the right thing. This is the same thing that he gave to all the people on this earth, but some do not listen. That's why he gave you the Bible, so you could read it, because you don't listen to your hearts. Many go ahead and make things the way they want them to be, without ever listening.

There is a place called Anola Hill, on the other side of Mount Hood, that we've been fighting to save, because they want to cut down all the trees. That's one of the places where we used to take the children to stay for five days. A spirit animal would come and become a part of that child and live with them throughout their life. That child might one day become a medicine person and heal with that spirit.

That was the only healing that our people knew. Today, it's not that way anymore because we have all the white doctors, and we depend on them. But there are still a few that seek the old way. But I don't think they all do it with all their hearts. There are some we call the "make-believers" because they don't really heal anybody.

Today, they still do Medicine Singing, but it's not their own. They are just copying the songs of the people who have passed them on. The songs were given to them by the spirits, and those songs are very powerful for them. But now there's no power to these songs anymore because it's not their own. That's why we believe that unless people today really seek that spiritual power, there won't be anything for them. In my feeling, I don't think it will ever go back to the same way that we were raised, because there's too much white influence upon our children. Many of our children don't want to go back to the old Indian ways. Too many of them want to live like the white people. There are very few that want to live the traditional life. So I don't believe it's ever going to go back.

We try to teach the children who come to our longhouse, and we do the best we can to teach them what our songs taught us. But there are very few that listen because there are all these things, like drugs and alcohol and even sports, like basketball and baseball, that attract the young people. Sports are all right, but all these things just worry us because we're hoping that these are our future leaders who will bring a change. We want them to do the right thing so that they will always have something here on this reservation, and that they can keep it like it is today.

## NETTIE QUEAHPAMA

I'm Sylvia's sister, and my Indian name is Tunastanmi. In school they gave me the name Nettie Queahpama. My married last name is Showaway, and I was born in 1902. My other sister, Matilda, was born on the fourth of July in 1906.

I was born in Warm Springs the night my mother ran out of matches and baking powder. She was big with me when she went out on horseback to the store. She had just finished some gloves and was going to trade them for what she needed. But she got sick right in the store, and that's where I was born. She wrapped me up with her torn-up dresses, and brought me home the next day to my big sister and my father.

The house then was made of tule poles, which grow in the marshy places near the Dechutes River. They were placed all around just like a tipi, with a fire right in the middle. It was warm, but I remember we couldn't play inside. We made our own dolls with rags, and sometimes we snitched Mother's quilt pieces to make them. Oh, we'd get a whipping if we were caught! We were there about twelve years, and then my father built the house Sylvia talked about.

My grandfather was a chief, and he had five wives. This is how it was a long time ago. If somebody lost her husband, he would take her in. All five women helped him. It was nothing for them to dry fish and make food. We ate everything. His big old house had one kitchen and one big old room, and that's where we slept. There was an upstairs, too, where some of the young boys would sleep.

I went to school until the schoolhouse burned down. We all cried when it did, because we did not want to see it burn. Then I went to a boarding school. This was during the first World War, and at that time everybody got sick with some kind of flu, and we had to stay there through the holidays.

The happy times I remember were when we used to go out to pick hops. We would go horseback, and I would just gallop. I followed my aunt, who was just like a mother to us. Oh, that was the happiest time! I would just whip the horse and gallop behind her. We earned money by picking hops in a great big basket. We got twenty-five cents if we filled it, and if we filled four of them, we got a dollar, which was a lot of money in those days. All the people from the reservation would do that. They would all go to earn a little money, picking hops, berries, and cherries.

When we had two longhouses, we had Indian dances for one whole month. The only dance I knew was the Indian dance. When we went to school I tried to white dance, too, what they call the turkey trot and fox trot. I tried, even though I did not know how to dance.

But when I got married, I really loved to dance. My first husband was William McCartle, and he loved dances. That's when I learned how to dance. He was half Wasco and half Warm Springs. But he got tired of me and got a better woman. So I was alone for seven years. I was sad and cried, but I couldn't do anything. I just let him go. But then I found another one, a better one who was such a good man. He spoiled me rotten. His name was Elby Showaway, and he was really good to me.

My first marriage was a big one, a big exchange with beaded bags, wampum beads, and real pretty blankets. But the second one was not too big, even though we still exchanged things. The parents do the wedding ceremony, as well as all the relatives that want to take part. The bride's side makes the bags, the beads, and all things like that. They also trade roots on the woman's side. They would have these great big cornhusk bags filled up with the dried roots. On the man's side they traded beautiful blankets and a suitcase, made with rawhide, into which they would put the blanket, the shawl, and other materials. Then they traded that for the roots.

My parents gave me some advice about marriage. They told me not to pout or to giggle too much. They also told me to be sure to get up early and cook breakfast, and never to be lazy, and to be sure to take care of my mother-in-law. And I did that the whole time I was married.

My sister Matilda remembers the old stories, but I have to interpret them for her because she doesn't speak much English. She tells us the story of how our people were moved here from Shearsbridge, where our ancestors originally lived in the Tygh Valley area. The soldiers threatened our people, and it was the soldiers that drove our people here to this reservation. She also told us that our great-grandfather, our father's grandfather was the chief at Shearsbridge of all the people. They told us it was supposed to be a big reservation. We were supposed to have a lot of the mountains on our reservation, all the way over to Three Sisters, northwest of Bend and John Bay. The Three Sisters are the Blue Mountains. They took a lot of it away from us later on, and they kept making our reservation smaller and smaller.

The first time they moved our people, they all decided to settle down there where Kah-nee-ta [a resort] is and on down to the mouth of the Columbia River. People lived all up and down that river, because it was warm in the wintertime. They lived there for many years. Later on, the government moved the Wasco people from the Columbia River, and our people said that it was all right to live by Warm Springs. That's where the Wascos settled. And it was later that the Paiutes were turned loose from concentration camps over in Fort Simcoe, in the Yakima Reservation, and then they drove them over here.

And so one night the Paiutes camped across from where our grandfather used to live, because they were on their way back to where they came from, which was Fort Hall, Idaho. Our grandfather was a kind man, and he felt really sorry for them because they had walked all the way here, and their feet were worn out. They had even worn out their saddles that were made out of sage. He felt sorry for them even though they had been our enemies, and had done awful things to our people. Still, I think because of his belief in the Creator's ways, he said their people could stay. So they moved them to the southern part of the reservation where they live today. Many people nowadays still think that it was wrong to let them stay, that they should have been sent back to their own place, but I guess it was all right, because they are people, too, just like our grandfather said.

My grandfather had a longhouse, and they used to worship every Sunday. They had seven drums, and they would dance every Sunday at their worship. The Wasco people had all become Christians and were baptized either Catholic or Presbyterian. We had to be baptized when we went to boarding school. The Christians didn't like what our grandfather was doing; they said that he was worshiping the devil. They didn't like him to have these services.

One Sunday, while they were worshiping in the longhouse, some of the Wasco police-men came in and grabbed all seven drums and cut them all up. Then they got my grand-father and cut off one of his braids, and they tied his hands and legs and dragged him behind a horse all the way to Warm Springs in Kah-nee-ta. His skin was all skinned off, right to the bone. Then they threw him into this jail, which was really a big cellar with rattlesnakes and black widow spiders. They put him in there without treating his wounds. But he was such a religious man that he just prayed and sang the whole night. The next day they came and let him out and told him to leave this reservation, that they did not want him here anymore.

Our father used to tell us and our cousins this story, and we would feel so bad. My grandfather left and took three wives. He left two to take care of the longhouse while he was gone. So he went to a place that was called Priest Rapids on the Columbia River, and he spent three years with the people there, who were also very religious. While he was there he met a Catholic priest who told him that he would go back to the reservation with him and protect him. So my grandfather came back and had another longhouse, and the Catholic priest made a longhouse of his own right next to it. And so in the morning they would pray in the Catholic longhouse, and they would have lunch. And that was their protection.

## MATILDA MITCHELL

When I was being raised, there was always the whip-man. He was chosen by the parents to come to weekly gatherings. Our parents would tell him if we had done bad things during the week, but he would never tell us our parents had told him, he'd say a bird had come. Our parents never hit us, they were always very loving, and we loved and respected them. The whip-man didn't really hurt us. He used a soft willow branch and would whip us on our legs through our clothes. He would say, "If you're going to steal, tell lies, drink—no, no, you're not going to do that." All these ugly things they would name. So I said no. I tried to be good all my life. I never drank; I never smoked. But I liked boys, just like any girl.

My father and mother were against me marrying a Wasco. They wanted to keep me away from other nationalities. I wanted to marry a Wasco, but my mother wouldn't let me. So I minded, even if it hurt me. I tried to mind everything. My father would have me cash his check and told me to come right back. But there was a big event happening over by Warm Springs. So my sister and I would go down and cash his check, even if we wanted to stay and have a good time. I was a big woman then, I was nineteen years old, and I still had to mind him. It's hard to mind folks, I think it's really hard. If kids can mind their father and mother, the world would be a different place. Like my sister's grandchildren. It's nice for them to go to church, but they go with these shoes and shorts on, and I don't like that. They go with all white clothes on.

We're not against the churches, as long as they're sincere in their belief that it will change their lives, then that's good. We want them to change their lives to where they won't take drugs and alcohol. We like that.

I have so many grandchildren and great-grandchildren, even great-great-grandchildren. I would love to tell the children that it's all right when they go to the white churches. It's good for them as long as they believe sincerely. But after they're through, we'd like to see them come to our services. Our longhouse ceremonies go on all day. We believe that they have the same teachings, just like the Bible teaches them at churches. But I would like to see the children come to the longhouse and learn our way also.

## BERTHA GROVE: NATIVE AMERICAN CHURCH

*I first met Bertha Grove at a Native American Church meeting on the Southern Ute Indian Reservation in Ignacio, Colorado. The Native American Church uses peyote in its prayer and healing ceremonies, and though the stories I had heard about the drug intrigued me, I was still a bit nervous. I was with a psychiatrist friend and his wife, who was part Indian and seeking a healing. She and I jokingly assured each other on the way up that if we "freaked out," we had a shrink to put us right. As it turned out, most of the stories I had been hearing can best be described as science fiction.*

*The peyote religion was introduced to the American Indian in the mid-1800s from south of the border—the small cactus plant does not grow north of Texas—where it was widely used by the Huichol and Yaqui Indians. Missionaries outlawed its use because it violated church doctrine, which forbade prophesying. They believed it intoxicated the Indian and kept him from salvation. Many American Indians today are opposed to peyote on the grounds that it is a narcotic and therefore addictive, when in fact members of the Native American Church have had great success using the Sacred Herb to cure alcoholism along with many other diseases, mental and physical. Its medicinal properties have been documented and found to be varied and valuable.*

*The meeting we attended was held on New Year's Eve, an annual ceremony, and like all meetings that occur every Saturday night, lasted from sundown to sunrise. We sat in a circle, perhaps fifty invited guests, around an altar of sand in the shape of a half moon and a fire that was kept burning all night.*

*Empty coffee cans were passed around, and when I asked what we were supposed to do with them, the road chief who guides participants through the ceremony winked and said, "You'll know." I grimaced—we had just eaten a rather greasy meal on the drive up from New Mexico.*

*Many had brought cases or boxes full of paraphernalia, prayer shawls, staffs, bone whistles, prayer feathers, and some had their own water drums.*

*During the night the peyote tea was passed around four times. The staff and gourd were passed from person to person, giving each an opportunity to sing and pray when it came around. The tea was bitter, and I had trouble getting it down. Soon after the first round I found out what the empty coffee cans were for. But in between bouts of nausea, I did experience a contemplative, even transcendental state, produced as much by the hypnotic drums and songs as by the tea itself. I did not hallucinate, and aside from a pleasant tiredness I felt the next day, there were no after-affects. My friend felt she had received a healing.*

*The meeting ended in the morning with talks given by the road chief, fire tenders, cedar chief, and a few of the other elders, followed by breakfast of traditional Indian ceremonial food. I was particularly touched by Bertha's words. She called for unity within the family, for love and understanding among each other, and for respect for all forms of prayer.*

*More than a year later, I went back to visit Bertha in her home in Bayfield, Colorado. She had recently come through a severe illness, a tumor, that had given new meaning to her life. We talked into the night, then Bertha brought me a pillow and a blanket for the couch. I left later that day with a new understanding of "family" and of the Indian's precious tradition of "making a relative." Somehow I felt I had made one.*

Which is real and which is illusion? Seems an experience like the severe illness I had took me through the illusion. Then I woke up and I was in the reality. I see things in a different light now. Things that used to upset me or make me angry, or frustrated, don't anymore. When you've come through the illusion, you look at things with more humor. You take your time and think things through calmly. It seems I know the real meaning of life now. The old people a long time ago said the dream *was* the reality. I'm awake now. I can see what's around me.

When we wake up one of the things we understand is trust. And faith. Every morning I always thank the Creator. We have to show gratitude, that's one of the things I've learned. To thank the Creator for your life. It means a lot to the Creator, to give thanks that we're here.

Sometimes people don't know or can't remember what happened to them. They can't find the reason why they're distraught, especially over things that happened in their childhood. I spent most of my childhood herding sheep, and that's where I did a lot of my meditating. I would always have a couple of dogs with me. It was a lonely time. I did a lot of thinking then on how to prepare for my life. I would listen to the wind and the birds and the animals while watching the sheep. That was my foundation of growing up to be who I am today.

One of the saddest things that ever happened to me was when I was nine years old and my mother died. It made me realize how alone I really was. When she got sick, I was the one who took care of her. I had to saddle up a horse to take her to the hospital where they operated on her. Then I helped my sister clean up the house, because we thought she was going to come home soon, but she didn't. She died after the operation.

That night we had a wake, but the kids weren't allowed to come. When they got her ready, my aunts and uncles came to get all the kids, except me. I watched through the window and saw them lift all the children over the coffin to say good-bye. And there I was, crying, longing to be there. Nobody came to get me. They went to the funeral and left me alone at home. Everybody totally forgot about me, and that bothered me for years and years.

I know that the way I was treated when I was young finally caught up with me and I felt really bad. I felt the same hurt that I had carried for a long time, but I had to forgive it and let it go. There is an Indian way of doing this that not very many people know about. I don't tell very many people about this, but the way to do it is to go out and find a rock, or whatever natural object that you want to represent you. Then you talk about forgiving yourself and forgiving the people that hurt you. You concentrate on everything that's troubling you, and then you release it and give it back to Mother Earth.

Spirituality is what holds the world and mankind together. When it's gone, there is nothing. Like a dead person when their spirit leaves them. It takes years to learn to be the type of person you have to be. It's not like going to school where you graduate from four years of college and then you know everything. Spirituality is not like that. To be a healer or a pipe carrier you have to be humble. The way of my teachings is that the creation came into being, all the trees, animals, insects, then at the end was mankind. We were supposed to be his most wonderful creation, and yet they always tell us that we have to be more humble than the insects, the lowest, crawling creature.

I grew up in a tipi. We grew up with horses and wagons. When I was born the government was building those two-bedroom adobe houses. That was in 1923 around the depression time. I didn't realize that we were very, very poor. That's the way everybody was. I was one of those children whose parents were too poor to keep their children, so they gave one to an aunt or uncle or to the grandparents to raise. There were eight of us children. I was the one who was given to my grandparents to raise.

My grandmother made our tipi herself, and they didn't have canvas then. She used to make them out of those big flour sacks. She would double them, and it kept out the rain. I don't know how she did it; there may have been four layers. The south side was my "room," my space. And the west side, the bigger space, was my grandfather's, the north side my grandmother's. The fireplace was in the middle. All the groceries or dishes were in that space between my grandmother and the door. On my side was the wood and the water. Whatever we had, we kept in feed bags. My grandfather had all his stuff on the back end, which kept the draft out, too.

My grandfather was a shaman, a medicine man. He used to doctor people from Navajo country, Apache country, Utes, who used to ask for help like that. There's a certain etiquette of how you are supposed to live with somebody like that. You wouldn't make noise in the tipi. You would come in from the south side, and you would walk around clockwise, and when you went out, you would keep going the same way.

My grandparents told me a lot of legends, and sang songs to me until I fell asleep. The wintertime is when they would tell stories. Sometimes my grandmother would bake apples for us in the ashes of the fireplace, and sometimes we would have dried fruit and wild berries, which she would make into a pudding. We would eat that with fry bread that she made for us. We didn't have much meat to eat because it was hard to get bullets for guns to hunt with.

Our grandfather talked to us as we all ate together on the ground. That's when he would tell us what life was like. He used to tell us not to smoke, because even way back then they had marijuana, and maybe somebody might give you something to make you go out of your mind. And after you smoke that, it could stay with you for a long time. "Don't smoke, don't drink." I had a lot of respect for my grandfather. I loved him and feared him at the same time.

My grandfather started talking about spiritual things later on. He taught us how sacred the ceremonies were. Once in a while he would open up this big box that had all his ceremonial objects in it. He would let us look at them and maybe let us hold something. And he would explain what the boys can touch and what the girls can't. What a woman can do and what the boys can't. Grandfather would tell us about the eagle feathers and the things used in ceremonies.

We kids would play doctor, in a way. We would have someone lie there as if they were sick, and then we would call a medicine man over, and he would go through all the motions like we saw our grandfather do. We would even go through the things he had said, what he saw. We were really serious in our playacting. That's how we learned.

My grandfather was also a Sun Dance Chief, and I grew up with the Sun Dance way. But when I married into the Native American Church most of my family disowned me. I don't think the peyote medicine was illegal then. When I started, the ceremonies weren't held on the reservation because too many important families, like Chief Buckskin Charlie's,

were members of the Native American Church. He was the one who first started it here in the late 1800s, and he died in 1936.

During the meeting you would take four whole dried pieces. At that time they didn't grind it or make tea out of the peyote, it was whole. They didn't have the smoke either; they just prayed with the cedar. It was the Cheyenne who introduced the peyote smoke. I had all kinds of visions during meetings. I always had this inner side. Even when I was a little girl, I would have nightmares about these dried round strings that were chasing me. It was like someone was trying to put it around my neck, and I was deathly afraid of it. I had this dream repeatedly. Then when I married into this family, I saw the peyote all strung up and realized then that this was the string I was dreaming about. It had been trying to catch me since my childhood. Now I don't have those dreams anymore because I finally came upon what it was.

I began to make friends through the Native American Church. That's where I finally began to feel that I was needed, wanted, and liked. I wasn't lonely anymore. When I married into the Church, my two younger sisters and my brother were the only ones that stuck by me. At that time many people thought that the Church was like devil worship. But my other family disowned me, and when I would pass them on the street they would walk past me like they didn't even know me. It's still like that today, and I've been a member for sixty-four years.

It's true that you make a lot of relations through the Native American Church because it's the medicine itself that brings people together. The medicine is like an instrument for helping people. The same thing is true with the water and cedar we use to purify. We call the medicine "Grandfather," and the fire "Grandfather Fire," and we make yearly pilgrimages into fields in Texas to get the medicine. But even that has changed. When I started there were no fences and no oil fields. You could go out and stay in the field overnight and make a fire and take a smoke. First, each person finds a spot, has a smoke, and then goes to find some more of the peyote. If you eat them, it's easier to find them. You could be standing on them and wouldn't know it, that's how they are. But when you eat one, then you see them.

So we make our prayers like that. We leave our tobacco as an offering, and we leave another gift, maybe a scarf or a feather, as well. Then we ask the medicine if we can take it back to help our people.

I remember one time when I was praying with my eyes closed, I felt somebody behind me. When I opened my eyes I saw this person behind me, shifting his weight from side to side. He was dressed in a ceremonial blanket and moccasins, and for a moment I thought it was my son Junior, because when we go we usually put on moccasins and a shawl like we are going to a meeting.

I wondered why I didn't hear him come up. Finally, I turned around and said, "Share the smoke with me." But nobody was there, and I saw that Junior was further down the hill.

I started praying and I saw him again. And I realized it was the spirit of medicine itself. So now I know that it's a spirit, just like you and me.

A year ago I got very sick. The doctors took X rays and told me I had a tumor in my stomach, and they wanted to operate right away. The weekend before I was supposed to check into the hospital, my son and husband put up a tipi ceremony for me in our Native American Church.

Many people came from all over to pray with and for me. They put me in the southwest corner of the tipi and started giving me whole dipperfuls of the medicine. After the second round I went into a kind of trance. It was past midnight, time to drink some more of the water, and my husband kneeled in front of me and told me to wake up. I came to, like I'd been sleeping, and drank the water. The next ritual started, but I was nauseated and wanted to go outside.

My sister, brother, and husband went with me and held a big tin pan in front of me in case I got sick. I didn't know if I was going to throw up or go to the bathroom. Finally, I started to throw up and something the size of a turkey gizzard came out. It was so hard it made a thumping sound when it hit the pan. My husband tried to cut it open to see what it was, but it was too hard.

Monday morning I went back to the clinic and had another X ray and nothing showed up. The tumor was gone. The doctors couldn't understand it. I didn't tell them what had happened; I just went home. Now I think I could have done this a long time ago, but maybe it wasn't time then.

I have learned how to have patience. There was a time when my faith went out the window, but that was one of those times when you hit bottom and have to find the strength to get up again. Then we're that much stronger, because every time Grandfather knocks us down we learn a little more. It seems the more we suffer, the more we understand.

# SEMINOLE

## Sonny Billie: miccosukee medicine man

*Medicine man Sonny Billie is descended from Josie and Ingraham Billie, the two most famous traditional Seminole medicine men of the twentieth century. Powerfully built, six-foot-two, 250 pounds, his healing practices have been shrouded in secrecy. But on this day in May of 1993, a small group of people gathered at Sonny's campground in the Florida Everglades to launch "The Sonny Billie Foundation for Native Cultural Studies." His goal is to establish a nursery as a continuing source of herbs that are becoming more and more difficult to find in the now pollution-ridden Everglades.*

*In the early 1500s, the Creek nation was made up of two language groups, the Muskogee and the Hitchiti-speaking group, which later adopted the name of "Mikasuki" (Miccosukee). Present-day Miccosukee Indians once lived in what is now the Carolinas and Georgia. Later, they settled in north Florida in the town of Miccosukee, which is between Tallahassee, Florida, and Thomasville, Georgia. The Muskogees named these renegades, who also included outlaws and slaves seeking shelter in the thick forests of northern Florida, "Si-min-oli," which meant runaways. During the Seminole wars of the 1800s, the Miccosukees produced fierce leaders, including the feared Osceola. By the end of the wars only about three hundred were left. They fled into the remote swamps and everglades of southern Florida. There they remained, isolated from the rest of the world, until the twentieth century. Today, there are almost two thousand Seminole Indians, most living on or near the tribe's five Florida reservations.*

*Sonny Billie is pictured with his mother, Edie Buster Billie, born in 1889.*

I was brought up with Miccosukee medicine people. I was born and raised in the medicine, beginning from the time that I came out of my momma's womb. But I didn't realize it at first. I knew things, but I just wanted to be a normal person.

But then my first wife passed away when our baby was eighteen months old, from a heart disease I never knew she had. Her family never treated her for her illness. That shocked me. I went and spoke to my mom and Ingraham Billie and Josie Billie, and they woke me up. I made up my mind then I would study herb medicine.

Josie Billie was a famous medicine man. His herb tea was under study by researchers of the Upjohn Pharmaceutical House. For years his tea had been curing Indians of "brain sickness," but Josie claimed the medicine was not as strong when it's made without the songs and fasting of the medicine man. He used to say the spirit of the medicine comes from inside the man who has the power.

Another of my uncles was also a well-known herb doctor; his name was Jimmy Tommie. When he came to visit, he would sit down with my sisters and brothers and talk to us and teach us things. He taught us that medicine knowledge came in different parts, like the seasons. We had a lot of respect for him. Ingraham Billie, who's considered the most knowledgeable Indian throughout our tribe, also came around a lot and would sit and talk with us.

I once saw Ingraham Billie make a little chickee, or shack, for one of his patients. No one could go around that little chickee but him and his Indian nurse. They prepared all the food and medicine. He told us not to come around, but you know how you are when you're young, so I sneaked in and looked. The patient looked like a jelly-man; he didn't have any control over his body. But in a month's time I saw him leave and walk out with his wife. So I asked my mom, "Why are these sick people coming around?" And my mom told me that my relatives were herb doctors, and that I would have to go through a number of trainings to gain the knowledge I needed to become one myself. She told me if I wanted to, the time would come for me to learn these things.

When I got older I studied with my uncles. Nothing is written down; you have to memorize the teachings. The reason they memorize everything is because we were told the white people were going to be here for a long time. First the French, then the Spanish, and they were just as hungry for what we knew as the white people are today. Our healers felt that they didn't want these people to take everything from us, so they made the information non-readable. You have to memorize it yourself; your head becomes like a book. You memorize the medication on one side of the brain, and the other responsibilities of managing your life and raising a family on the other side. That's how we're taught, to store everything in our brains.

When they first gave me the bundle, I was taught what the guidelines were. They announced that I would be a doctor. They announced it in public, and from then on people would come to me for medicine. You are not supposed to refuse anybody in need for their health. You are supposed to help out. That's what all medicine people should do, no matter what race, they have to help. After they announced it, a lot of people began to come to me.

So, I've been around medicine people all my life. When it comes to training and doing the prayers, I remember one prayer song I used to sing as a kid. It was the song for small burns that would cool them and keep them from blistering. I was never supposed to sing it in public, but I liked the song so much that I just had to. I guess I was given a head-start on this knowledge. I learned it in stages as I got older. And the older I got, the more I got to study. Then I started realizing that non-Indians studied medicine in the same way. I had always thought only the Indians did it this way.

During some of the stages of my teachings, I went to the white man's doctor. I saw that they had guidelines for medicine, too. The difference was that we used herbs. Back in those days it was better because the air and food was clean. Although it seems that life is improving today, our medicine is not. That's what gave me the idea to try to improve this by creating a healing place where we can grow our own medicines.

I have had a lot of patients in my thirty years of practicing medicine. One of them was my second daughter. She had asthma when she was about six years old. I started to study, and I went to different Indian doctors to find out how to help her. I was trying to improve this asthma medicine. I finally broke it down to heart, lung, liver, and kidney treatment, and other systems throughout the body. I studied the parts of the human body, and then I studied the herbs. I learned which particular herb would fit that area of the body, and what I had to do to formulate the medicine and to cure the asthma.

I know that the lungs do not function right for a person with asthma on certain days. Like a moist day or rainy day. On a warm, dry day they function fine. I went ahead and studied hard. Finally, I thought I got it. I talked to my wife about it. Any good husband will always go to the mother of the family or his wife. Especially when you have a lot of responsibilities on your hands, you must sit down with your wife. So I told my wife what I was working on and what I had put together. I told her all the information was in place, and I wanted to treat my daughter. "But since it's your daughter as well," I said, "I cannot take the complete responsibility." I had to have her agreement and understanding, whatever her heart desired on this issue. She asked me if I really knew enough. I couldn't say for sure because there are so many other things still to be learned. She decided that she didn't want me to go through with it. I was kind of upset about it. But we let it go on; we didn't do anything about it.

My little girl had been listening to that conversation, though, and she understood what we were talking about. In later years, my daughter got married and went to live with her husband. She was having a lot of asthma attacks. One day she came to talk to me and said, "Remember when you and Mom were talking about you treating me for asthma, and Mom objected and you two fought over it?"

I said, "Yes."

She said, "Well, I want to take that medicine that you spoke about."

I told her, "Okay, give me a few days. I'll pick up the herb and reformulate it again. But did you talk to your Mom?"

She said, "No, I'm not going to talk to anybody. It's just between you, me, and the medicine."

I told her, "Of course. You're old enough now to make up your own mind. I'm glad you remembered that."

So I formulated that medicine, and I told her how to use it. She used it and had an asthma attack right away. I was afraid it was going to kill her; she had a real hard time breathing. This went on for about twelve hours. But after that she didn't have any more attacks. Once in a while it will act like it's going to begin, but it never gets into a full attack. Since then I've treated a few more people for asthma. That's one area where I have improved a medicine for an ailment.

My next step was to work on the sugar problem with diabetics. I am a stubborn person, I guess. My wife had a sugar problem for a long time. I was using her, with her consent, of course, to test the medicine out.

Today, I see non-Indian doctors working together with us in some areas. If we had worked together from the beginning, maybe there would have been more improvement in the types of medication available. But I don't want to go around and try to confuse anyone, especially non-Indian doctors. Mostly I just cooperate with them and try to help out if I think we can have a relationship.

I sing a prayer song in my language that's about education and befriending all nationalities. You can look at it in many ways. If you have the education, you can do good things for people and help them out. They say if you have a lot of knowledge, you can help people and be happy. But they also say that a lot of people will be jealous of your knowledge and try to hurt you. In our language there is no word to say, "I'm sorry."

That's why a knowledgeable Indian will often not say too much, and some white folks might mistake this for being dumb. But we were taught not to speak too quickly unless we're sure of what we're saying, because words can be like weapons, they can hurt. The white man has lots of words for "I'm sorry."

I remember the priests telling us that we could no longer use our herb medicine. That's what killed so many of us, why there are so few of us left. There are only six of us left in my tribe who know how to practice fixing this medicine, and this is why I'm trying to hang on and continue with this work. I must continue to improve on our life. That's my belief and that's my medicine.

## ANNIE JIMMIE: SEMINOLE LEGENDS

*Annie Jimmie is a respected elder and medicine woman. She learned from her father, medicine man Little Doctor, who also taught her the legends and medicine stories she tells. Annie never learned English, and always dresses in traditional attire. We sat in the shade of a chickee and spoke through an interpreter.*

I was born in Glades County, Florida. I don't know what year because we didn't have calendars or count like non-Indians in those days. We lived in a camp, where we grew a lot of sugarcane and potatoes. People made their own liquor back then from sugarcane. I heard about white people, but didn't have any contact with them until we came down to a tourist attraction place in Miami and stayed there for a while. That's when I first saw non-Indians. That's where I really realized that there was a different race of people other than us Indians.

My parents brought us to see my dad's mother, so she could see us when we were still kids. We went and visited her when she was bedridden. I guess she wanted to see us because she was dying. After she died, they fixed her hair, put beads on her, and dressed her up in her best clothes. I think it was early morning when they took her body to have funeral services in the woods.

Me and my sister Lena stayed at the camp with our baby brother, Joe Doctor. He got thirsty for milk and cried and cried. Finally, they came back and took baths, which was part of the tradition after a funeral, then they fed the baby. We stayed at that camp until four days had passed and then we traveled home. I was very young in those days.

My dad taught me a lot about Indian medicine, but I didn't do medicine until I had children of my own. My husband's mother taught me a lot of medicine songs also. The most recent songs I've learned were from Little Fewell, a medicine man from the Big Cypress Indian Reservation.

I once heard a legend about a snake, in which the snake traveled and traveled until it dis appeared up above, but they didn't know where it was going. They say when the time is right the snake will travel back down from the place it went to.

Another one is about a rabbit that was going to marry a woman. My dad told me about that one. He might have been talking about himself, like a joke.

The story goes that there was a group of elders that the rabbit was around a lot. The rabbit wanted to get married really bad, so he asked the elders to teach him the ways to gain wisdom in order for him to get married. The elders told him that he was to complete some tasks, which included killing a snake, killing an alligator and cutting its tail off, and finally cutting down a tree with only four chops and returning with it. Then they would teach him how to become wise. So he went to fulfill these tasks.

He approached the alligator first because he already knew where one was at. He told the alligator, "Someone needs you to do something for them so come with me." The alligator got out of the water and went with the rabbit. After they had traveled a short distance the rabbit turned into the woods and came out with a limb and started hitting the alligator with it. The alligator didn't know what was going on, so he ran off and slid back into the water.

The rabbit was frustrated, and he didn't know what else to do. He was thinking and walking when he came upon a squirrel. The rabbit asked the squirrel if he could borrow his coat, meaning his fur. The rabbit in turn gave the squirrel his fur, which was a bit too big for the squirrel. He put on the squirrel fur, and it turned out to fit snugly.

Then he climbed up on a willow branch in disguise to look like a squirrel so the alligator didn't realize it was really the rabbit. The fake squirrel kept throwing willow flowers into the water. The alligator finally told him to quit doing that. He told the fake squirrel that he almost got killed that way just a little while ago. The fake squirrel asked him who did it and the alligator told him it had been a rabbit. The fake squirrel then asked him to get out and go with him, so the alligator got out of the water and went with him.

As they were traveling, the squirrel asked the alligator where his death spots were. The alligator told him they were on the back of his head and on his butt, and they continued on.

The squirrel suddenly jumped on the alligator and beat his head and butt until the alligator died. The fake squirrel cut off the alligator's tail, put on his own fur, and returned back to the elders as best a rabbit carrying an alligator's tail could.

The elders asked, "What about the snake?" So the rabbit sharpened a pine wood and left. He found a snake and told him to lay down and straighten his body completely out so he could see how long he was. He told the snake that people said he was short, but he had told them that the snake was very long. The snake stretched out and the rabbit started measuring him, then very quickly, he clubbed the snake on the back of the head. Then he put the snake on his shoulders and carried him back to the elders.

He dropped it on the ground in front of them, and they asked him about the tree. He left and finally returned with the tree. The elders told him he was now very wise. The rabbit had thought they were going to teach him things, not just tell him that he was wise. So he got upset and mad and then ran off into the woods.

There are few young people still trying to learn the ways of the elders. They ask about the legends and some medicine songs. There are some youth who try to keep their tradition alive. Our elders used to tell us of the different changes that will come and I see them now. For instance, there used to be hardly any houses, but just a few camps and plenty of fish and game. They used to say that modern things will be done to the earth, like man-made rivers being dug that will destroy a lot of fish and animals. Then there will be lots of people with nothing but houses popping up everywhere, which I see now. Development in the Everglades, which is also happening now. Yes, changes are everywhere. They said it wouldn't be the same as the old days.

For example, the gardens where the fruit and vegetables were good from each crop will be bad because the earth will get older and contaminated like it is now. They said the fruit wouldn't be the same. Bad crops are the sign of the earth getting old and that's where we are heading now.

# APACHE

## MILDRED CLEGHORN: A PRISONER OF WAR

*Apart from serving as chairperson of the Fort Sill Apache Tribe, Mildred Cleghorn works with the Oklahoma Indian Affairs Commission, as well as being the former director of the North American Women's Association. And for more than fifty years she has been handcrafting cloth rag dolls that illustrate, by their dress, cultural differences among American Indian tribes. They wear replicas of authentic costumes dating from 1900 and earlier. Her dolls have been displayed in museums throughout the country, including the First Folklore Festival at the Smithsonian Institution in Washington, D.C.*

*Mildred was also among a group of distinguished elders asked to participate in the design of the new National Museum of the American Indian in Washington. Her grandfather was George Wratten, a white man who lived on the reservation and spoke Apache better than any white man before him. He rode with Geronimo, the famous warrior, and acted as interpreter. Although Geronimo was frequently taken prisoner, he always escaped. His final surrender in 1887 played a significant part in ending guerrilla warfare in the United States.*

*Mildred's cousin is Alan Houser, the famous sculptor and 1992 winner of the National Medal of the Arts. His sculpture of Geronimo is part of the collection of the National Portrait Gallery of the Smithsonian.*

My name is Mildred Imach Cleghorn. I was born in Fort Sill, Oklahoma, on December 11, 1910, as a prisoner of war. We lived there until 1913. The tribe was taken prisoner along with Geronimo, who surrendered in 1887 at Fort Bowie, Arizona. My father was a small boy then; he was about eight or nine years old.

He remembered being moved to Saint Augustine, Florida, and being on the train. They stayed in Florida for a year, then due to illness, the conditions of the water, and the weather, they died by the dozens.

There were two nuns who saw the conditions there and all the small children suffering. They expressed their concern to Herbert Welch, who was the president of the Indian Rights Association, and got his support. Because of his influence, they were able to go to the War Department and get permission to start a school in the prison and take care of what people they could. The War Department gave them permission to use one of the cells as a classroom. When the classroom was ready, the mothers and fathers went, too. They taught them religion and English. The nuns were also influential in getting us moved. They moved us to Mount Vernon barracks in Alabama, and that's where we stayed until 1894. In 1894, they decided to move us to Lawton, Oklahoma, to Fort Sill, where we lived until 1913. Our people became good farmers.

My grandfather was George Wratten. As a child, he was very interested in Geronimo and the Apache. He went among them when they were in Arizona and learned the language. He became a blood brother of Roger Toclanny, one of Geronimo's people. When they took them prisoners, my grandfather was put in charge of the Apache because he knew the language, and they trusted him. He always knew of the army's plans, and he kept the Apache informed. In Alabama, he fell in love with my grandmother, and they were married. They had two children, my mother and my aunt. Eventually, she left him and married someone else. So my mother and my aunt went to live with their aunt, who didn't have any children. My grandfather paid her for their support.

When they got to Fort Sill, they stayed from 1894 until 1913. Then they were given a choice of going to Mescalero, New Mexico, on the reservation, or getting allotments in Oklahoma. Eighty-two stayed in Oklahoma, and the others went to New Mexico. We moved to the farm.

Alan Houser's father was my uncle. He used to tell us stories about Geronimo in the early days, when he was only twelve or thirteen years old and already a warrior. My uncle's job was to hold the horses when they went on a raiding party. They needed somebody to take care of the horses, and he was one of the young boys that did that. He would tell us stories of Geronimo and the life that they lived, and we would sit at the table and listen by the hour. He took the place of my grandparents, because my grandparents had all died when I was very young.

My parents were teenagers when they were in the prison. But my father went on to Carlisle Boarding School, then later, when they moved to Fort Sill, he and my mom both went to Shelock. They were married in 1907.

Kiowa, Comanche, and Apache were located in that area, and they didn't want us to be close together. I guess they figured that we were going to go on a rampage again. When we wanted to visit our relatives we had to go anywhere from six to twelve miles in a wagon. We went to public schools. Both my parents had gone to boarding schools, and they vowed that they didn't want any of their kids to go to one. There were only five of us Indians at that school, and we were very compatible. Today, it's just the opposite.

I didn't get married until about 1949. I married an Oto, William Cleghorn. He worked in the land division. I went to college, and I got my degree in home economics and became a home demonstration agent. I had been working in Kansas, but then I had a chance to transfer back to Oklahoma.

My husband and I had to go look for a place to live. I went up to this woman's house that was for rent and knocked on the door. Right away she asked, "Are you Indian?" And I said, "Yes." She said, "We don't rent to Indians," and slammed the door in my face. In all my life, I was never treated like that. After working and traveling all around the world, then to come home and have somebody slam the door in my face because I was Indian! I was just burned up, I was fighting mad. I had never confronted racism before, and it shocked me. I became kind of a quiet activist then.

In the late seventies, I got involved in tribal affairs. I felt we needed to help our people. I have always been interested in my tribe and my church.

The Reformed Church of America had come to us in 1895, a year after we were taken to Fort Sill. One of their missionaries was an Indian, Frank Wright, a Choctaw. He was living among the Cheyenne and Arapaho when he heard about the Apaches being held prisoner in Fort Sill. So he went down there in a wagon and saw the conditions, all the children left orphans, and he started working. In 1895, he established an orphanage. From then on we have been the Reformed Church.

It wasn't like being in a regular prison, except that we had to be in a certain area. Geronimo was able to go to local powwows, and Theodore Roosevelt took him to the World's Fair in St. Louis in 1904.

We weren't allowed to do ceremony. Some did anyway, but real quiet. The thing that really touched me is when my mother was coming from Alabama by train to Rush Springs, Oklahoma, which was the end of the line; they had to stay overnight out in the open. They had to wait for the wagons to come from Fort Sill. After dark, they heard the coyotes, and the elderly women in the tribe started crying. This was the first time they had heard coyotes since they were in Arizona, and it made them feel like they had come home again. Later, when I went to our home country around Truth or Consequences [a town in New Mexico], I could see why they felt that Fort Sill was home; the terrain was similar to New Mexico.

In 1976, we organized as the Fort Sill Apache Tribe. We got our constitution, and we had an election. I was elected chairperson, and I've been chairperson ever since. One of the things I do is help kids get loans and grants and help people get housing. In order to get housing, you had to have a land base, so we purchased two and a half acres. In 1980, we got a land grant and built an office, an all-purpose building with a gymnasium, a shelter, and an office.

One of my main concerns for the tribe is health. We have a lot of elders. We lost our emergency room in our hospital. We are the smallest tribe in our area out of seven tribes. We are all given one lump sum of money, and then it's divided out per capita. Well, we only have 350 people, so our quota is very small.

One of the things that really upsets me is that we were promised so many things, and the government has never made good on any of them. They took Geronimo prisoner and said that he'd be back in two years. It turned out that he never did get home; he died a prisoner. And then they said we had a choice to either go to Oklahoma or New Mexico and that we would get 160 acres apiece. Not one soul got 160 acres. Most of us got as little as twenty-five acres. Promises were made and were never fulfilled.

We lived by our word in the early days. We didn't have a lawyer to write up a paper for you to sign your name. When you said you were going to do something, you shook hands or you made a vow, and it was settled. Honesty was one of those things that was a must; it was life or death if you didn't keep your word. The punishment for telling a lie was to cut off the tip of the tongue. And if a woman was unfaithful to her husband, she would be mutilated. I remember seeing a woman with the tip of her nose cut off.

Our spiritual life was nourished by the Reformed Church. It's amazing how the values we live by in our Indian faith, the same ones our old people lived by before the Europeans came, are so very parallel to the Bible. Just like the Holy Spirit came from Christ through fire. For our people, the fire is central. When we dance, we dance around the fire. The fire is the light and the warmth.

All of our families, all of the Apache people, were brought up with the Christian faith after the Reformed Church came around. We still had ceremonies, even though they didn't want us to because they believed they were wicked.

The Puberty Feast is one of our main ceremonies. It lasts for eight days in public, with all the people, and four days alone with the immediate family. A medicine woman takes care of the ceremony; she is just like a godmother. She dresses the girl, does her hair. We use paint, too, and corn pollen, which is our medicine. She is also a teacher, and must teach the girl how to live her life.

During the four-day ceremonial, there is the fire dance and the dance of the mountain spirits. The girls wear buckskin dresses, skirts, and blouses. The men wear the same type of skirts in their dance, with their headpieces. People are given all sorts of gifts.

We still have Indian doctors, men and women, and we have our own medicines. I have seen many healings. I had an uncle that could tame horses. I will never forget when I was visiting them out in Mescalero, New Mexico. That was at White Tail, way out in the reservation. This horse would rear up, and this fellow couldn't get control of him. The horse would just jump up and stomp. So my uncle said, "I want to show you. I'm going to make that horse behave." And sure enough, he came over there and told that fellow, "Let me have those reins." That horse's ears were perked up, and he was looking at him and snorting. My uncle just jerked the reins, talking to him the whole time. Gradually, he worked his way up to the horse. Pretty soon the horse started shaking his whole body. My uncle patted him, talking to him the whole time. He rubbed his back, down his neck, and along his legs. Finally, he led him away. That was a special gift that was given to my uncle.

We had a healing for tuberculosis in the early days. This woman knew exactly what to do and how to do it, according to what the spirits had told her. But the patient has to believe that it is going to help them, that's the way it worked. The power of belief. They also used the pollen and singing and prayer. And they still use it today.

It's too bad that the non-Indians didn't realize that we were really healing people through prayer. And you know another thing, your Bible tells you to share and to love. That's the way our people are. It tells you about the earth and how we are related. "From dust to dust." I remember hearing that at a non-Indian funeral. Well, that's the same thing we believe, the continuous circle. You give and you get, you give and you receive.

# HAIDA

## LAVINA WHITE: HAIDA ROYAL FAMILY

*Canada's westernmost archipelago, the Queen Charlotte Islands off the tip of the Alaska panhandle, is the home of the Haida people, who know the islands as Haida Gwaii. The land and all the creatures that inhabit it represent their history, their culture, their meaning, their very identity. The Haida refer to whales and ravens as their "brothers" and "sisters" and to the fish and trees as the finned and tree people.*

*Because the Haida were never conquered and never signed treaties with Canada, they insist they are a separate, sovereign nation. Lavina White, descendant of the royal family, is an eloquent, elegant speaker for the cause of sovereignty. She is tall and slender, her bearing that of an aristocrat, yet when she speaks of her "causes" she becomes as fierce a warrior as ever defended the rugged coast of her native country.*

*We met in Vancouver where she and her husband, Bill Lightbown, keep an apartment. She would soon be returning to their home in Haida Gwaii to continue her battle.*

My Indian name is Thowhegwelth, and it means literally the sound of many copper shields. But in our way it means that I have many responsibilities, because only those of lineage had copper shields. I was born to Henry and Emily White. My grandfather's name was Charles Edenshaw, which is an anglicized version of Edunsu and means "So Be It." Literally, it means their word is law. He was a great artist and was named the first artist of Canada. His uncle before him was Albert Edward Edenshaw, who was the grandchief or high chief before my grandfather.

The Haida nation has Raven and Eagle clans, but within those are many more. I am under the Ravens and belong to the Yakohanas Clan on my mother's side. On my grandfather's side they have an Eagle. A Raven could not marry a Raven; you had to marry an Eagle and vice versa. This was in the old days. Since then marriage laws have broken down, and so lineages are difficult to keep. Especially when there were only five hundred Haidas left, it became very difficult. We have a long ways to go to make things right again.

There were three different epidemics among the Haida people. I'm seventy-three now, and I remember when I was little hearing the elders speak about them. They remembered the first time that our people were decimated through contact with white people, the diseases killed so many of them. There were once 80,000 Haidas on our island; after the last epidemic there were only 500 left. Today, there are about 6,000, but we're scattered all over. The island is about eighty miles below Alaska and about eighty miles off the mainland. It's called Haida Gwaii, "Island of the Haidas." You know it as the Queen Charlotte Islands, but we're taking our names back, of our homelands, our mountains, and our rivers. I hope that the whole country does this on this, The Year of the Indigenous Peoples.

My principal cause is freedom. I'm old enough to remember what it was like to be free. Free from harassment by police, free from harassment by fisheries. And so it's difficult for me to give up the struggle because I want to be there when we win our freedom. When I speak about freedom, that means that I want the recognition of our sovereignty, as the first people not only of Canada but of the States. I believe that we should be recognized as indigenous people, with the right to make our own decisions and govern ourselves. To once again take control of our lives, our lands, and our resources.

Many young people throughout Canada are committing suicide—something that is very foreign to us as Native people, because life has always been so very precious to us. It's a real concern to us, the trashing of our planet. It's been very painful to hear about all the young people committing suicide because they can no longer see any hope. We are nearing the year 2000, and we are still on the reserves with no economic base, not enough housing, and many areas still with no running water and no sewer systems. I've seen those places. I've been talking to universities, schools of all kinds, and colleges, and I have asked the students to begin questioning the system that's been imposed on us. There is an illusion of democracy, but as Native people we find that the colonial mind-set that runs this country is very exploitive, even to the children.

We're trespassers in our own lands, our own forests. We've been forced to be beggars in our own homelands. We don't own an inch of land; we're on the reserve system. The government says that we are on that land by the grace of the Crown, that it belongs to the Crown, it doesn't belong to us. For instance, on our island of Haida Gwaii, different people have come to write books, but you never see anything in their writings about the Native people. It's as if we're museum pieces.

In 1976, I was the first woman to be elected head of a nation, president of the Haida nation. I have tried to change that term "presidency" to grand chief and chieftainships because that's the way we see ourselves.

But I was a woman who had lost her rights. You could lose your rights in a marriage, even if you were married to an Indian—if they were non-status. You would never ask anyone if they were non-status when we were young, because it wasn't something that anybody knew anything about. And if you married a Native man who lost his rights, then the woman lost her rights as well. It's like losing your identity, since the tribe no longer allows you to live in your homeland or participate as a Native Indian in any way. Yet, if one of our men married a white woman, then she gets Indian rights.

I've been married twice. The first time I was married, I was married to a northerner from the mainland. His parents had signed away their children's rights, or were forced to. That's the way that it was done, even if the parents wanted to give up just their rights and not their children's. The parents lost their rights because he was to become a professor at UBC [the University of British Columbia], the first Native professor. He was a very intelligent man, and in order to be able to work or get an education in white society, you had to give up your rights, so he signed away his family's rights. So when I married Sonny, I wasn't aware that he didn't have any rights, and I lost my rights, too. And my identity, the biggest loss as I found out; I think I minded that more than anything else. The right to live in my homeland, the right to have my identity as a Native person.

Native people in British Columbia are made up of twenty-six different nations, and we all speak different languages. It doesn't mean there are divisions; it means that there are different ways of looking at things.

I think that if the world began to respect each other's identities, there would be a lot less strife in this world. Like down in the States, there seems to be a lot of violence. I think that if we learn to respect each other's differences instead of flaunting a melting pot, we might not have all that violence.

Before white people came we had an educational process and our own way of governing ourselves, depending upon which part of the country you were from. In ours it was the Longhouse. And we don't have divisions, everything is connected, so this whole Western system of education was very difficult to try and fit into. Goodness knows we tried, but we don't fit in where everything is separated.

When we were children we were forced to leave our homeland, off the reserve, and go to school elsewhere. There were nine of us. The government didn't have to get the consent of the parents; they just took us away to boarding school and that was that. Oh, do I remember the first day! Years later, I was asked on a radio interview, "When were you first aware of the aggression by government?" I had to think really hard, and I said, "The day I walked into boarding school." I didn't know that the boarding school had any kind of impact on me until the second I said the day I walked into boarding school, when they took my brother away and I was unable to talk to him again. I had just turned nine, I didn't know a word of English. And it was just the way he looked back at us. I was all right because one of our older sisters was with us. But him, he had to go to the boys' side, and that hallway looked so long and big; it was very hard. I have a lot of healing to do. The day that they asked me that on the radio I started crying. I guess deep down I always felt that they stole my childhood.

Our elders never became senile because they were needed right to the end. Aunts and uncles on the mother's side were the ones who taught you the philosophies and principles that you lived and worked by. We take our lineage through the female in the Haida culture. The parents weren't the teachers because they couldn't be objective about their children, and children can't be objective about their parents. So it was the aunts and uncles who were the teachers about the practical things in life. So that was our educational process.

It's not like sitting down in the classroom; everything is learned by practice. There were very highly specialized skills. One tribe would be canoe makers, another one would be responsible for keeping up the history. You are taught that leadership is not for prestige, it's not for power, it's not for control, it's strictly for responsibility. And we lived by the honor code, because there was no written language. You had to honor one another's word.

The whole idea behind the boarding schools was to alienate the children from their parents. And that was the most disastrous thing that ever happened. I think the saddest thing was that the children never got any nurturing. And so when they became parents they didn't know how to nurture. To this day, we still have a problem with that; we have a lot of healing to be done.

Then after the boarding schools closed, they started apprehending our children and put them up for adoption with white families. That still goes on. I have been working on child care changes. We called for a moratorium on adopting our children, even before legislation comes in, because that's what I insisted on. Children have always been held in the highest regard in our culture; there are never any orphans. If something happened to the parents, there would always be an extended family that took over.

Many years before contact with the white man, the prophecies said that people with light skin, light hair, and light eyes would come and take everything from us, including our lands, our children, and our lives, if need be. But eventually there would be understanding and that we'd each govern ourselves without any interference from the other. I look forward to that day.

Another prophecy that I've been thinking about lately, because it seems to be coming about, is the one that warns when the birds begin to nest on the ground, that will signal the beginning of the end. That doesn't have to mean the end of the world, but maybe the end of one thing and the beginning of something else. I know by the way they are cutting down the forests that the birds will have to nest on the ground because there won't be any trees left for them to nest on.

Our people were very good at building. They built the very first commercial fishing boats on the coast, and they were beautiful. We had the biggest fleet. But then the company they fished for ended up owning them all. Right in court, I said that they stole all our boats, they beached all our men, and blocked them all out of the fishing industry. The Haida were the best fishermen on the coast.

The Haida were always feared along the coast because they were such good warriors. They had to be; they were out on a little island all by themselves, way out in the ocean. They were good warriors, but they were good statesmen, too.

People talk about this country being a free country. They have no idea of freedom. If you ever had the taste of freedom that I have known, you would never give it up, you'd fight for it like I do. It was wonderful. You could go everywhere. We were harvesters, and we would harvest in the summer. The spring, summer, and fall were for harvest time. Winter times were for social gatherings. It was a wonderful life. We knew when it was time to go to the rivers, and we knew where to go. And everybody had their own people that they would go with. Each lineage had their own places that was their domain.

There were no ceremonies by the time I was a child. They were outlawed. The reason that I loved our stories, histories, and our songs so much was, before I went away to boarding school as a very small child, I would sit quietly somewhere when the elders came to visit my dad or my mother. They'd sit and they'd talk about the history that was passed down. Not just one person told the story, it went all around the room, and it was just like watching a play. At a given point, they'd all burst into song and action at the same time, and then the story would go on. That's where I really learned to appreciate our culture.

Our people know their history and the story of the beginning. They even show where first man was supposed to have been enticed out of the clam shell on Rospitas, as you know it—we have another name for it, Nekut—and that's where the first people were enticed out of the clam shell. The Raven is the symbol of the Creator in our culture. Our teachings say, when Raven finished creating the world he found he was lonely. So he went out on the spit and enticed mankind out of the clamshell. I thought it meant both men and women until I heard the further story saying that womankind was enticed out of a mussel shell on the south end of the island.

The reason that I wanted to tell this story is because they keep trying to say that we came across the land bridge. But our people know that we have been here since the beginning of time.

# BELLA BELLA

## Emma Humchitt: the potlatch

*The present-day fishing community of Waglisla (Bella Bella) is descended from several Heiltsuk-speaking tribes that inhabited six thousand square miles on the central Canadian coast now known as British Columbia. The four clans of the Heiltsuk are Raven, Eagle, Killerwhale, and Wolf.*

*Emma Humchitt is the widow of Hereditary Chief Wigvilba Wakas (Leslie Humchitt) and mother of the current chief, Harvey Humchitt, Sr. She is shy and soft-spoken. Connie and Glen Tallio, her daughter and son-in-law, help her with our interview.*

*She talks about the potlatch that she had recently put on in honor of her husband's death two years before. Potlatch celebrations, lasting for days, are held for initiations, births, marriages, mourning, and installing a new chief. The host family gives away blankets, clothing, artifacts, canoes—it takes years of preparation and can cost the family everything they own. However, what they lose in material wealth, they gain in respect.*

*This ceremony was banned by the Canadian government from 1884 until 1951, when it was made legal again. The last big potlatch, in 1922, was raided by Indian agents who confiscated the many relics and treasures and jailed all the participants.*

*The Humchitt potlatch, which also celebrated the initiation of Emma's nineteen-year-old grandson, Harvey, Jr., was attended by chiefs, elders, and their families from all along the coast. Emma is pictured holding her granddaughter, Megan.*

I was twelve when I saw my first potlatch. We were told to sit down and not to interfere or run around, so I just sat beside my mother when there was something going on. The dancers had all kinds of Indian regalia, in different styles and designs, made of button blankets decorated with shell buttons, mother of pearl, abalone, and sequins. We weren't allowed to go and join them unless they asked us, and then we would sit with our parents. We used to sit on a line of two rows of benches in a community hall, and our mother used to bring us bowls, plates, and spoons, and we would bring them back home and wash them. We would eat before the dancing started.

I just wore ordinary clothes. We didn't wear pants in those days, just dresses. My hair was long. We never joined in the dances because they belonged to whoever hosted the potlatch. It could be for the birth of a baby, a death ceremony, a naming ceremony, or for becoming a lady or young man.

When I became a woman, they made me stay in bed for four days without eating, just drinking a cup of tea a day. I would get up really early in the morning and two of my aunts would give me a bath in plain water. I was not allowed out to join any activities for a while, until I got my moontime. My mother would give me something to do, like sewing, embroidering, or knitting. So I love to do that, it's sort of my hobby now and then. You weren't allowed to touch a knife or scissors during those four days.

Our clans are like different families; their crests may be an Eagle, a Whale, a Raven, or Wolf. And then you have different families that belong to these four animals. You're not supposed to marry within your own clan. The people up north will make fun of you if you marry within your own tribe. It's like you're a descendant from the Eagle or the Raven, but it's not like a religion. It's hard to put into words, but I would say that it's more cultural than religious. My Indian name is Ola. I have two other names; this was my dad's name, and the Whale is his crest.

I really didn't get into potlatch seriously until my late husband was to be honored as a chief. So we had to sit through the potlatches until they ended. The ceremony began about four or five o'clock and then went on until really late at night. It was interesting because we learned more and more about our ways and culture by sitting there and watching what was going on, what people offer you and what they do. The potlatch starts with someone giving household things away. The community hall is decorated in cedar boughs or poles, and it looks as though you're in a forest. They start off with a Tanis Dance and the drums and Native singing. They also have whistles, made out of either yellow or red cedar, and some are made to sound like an eagle, raven, or a loon, depending on the occasion.

We had a Settlement, or Tombstone, Feast for my late husband's dad; we didn't have a potlatch. My husband put up this dinner himself when my husband got his ceremonial names. We gave away a lot of things before he got that name, because the more feasts, or dinners, or potlatches, the higher ranking you become as a chief. The chief is like the sole person responsible for his family, so my husband made sure everybody was going to be okay for the winter, foodwise, woodwise, or whatever.

If you are having a Memorial Potlatch, you start off with the mourning songs, because you are respecting and honoring people that have gone on before you. Just the singers sing. Today, they use hollowed-out, red cedar logs for drumming, and the regular round drums are made out of deer skins. They usually have people who are mourning sitting where the carved tombstones are, while the singers sing the mourning songs. These people are usually in mourning for a year or two, and this is to help them dry their tears and get over their grieving stage.

Those that are mourning wear their button blankets. The tombstones are usually covered during the mourning songs, and when the songs are over they're unveiled. Then the chiefs dance the Peace Dance, or Welcome Dance. All the chiefs dance with their headdresses and their eagle down on their head. When they dance all the eagle down flies all over the hall and sometimes covers the floor with eagle down. It's considered a cleansing. Then they say grace for the feast and everyone starts eating.

We have a lot of our Native foods at the feast, like salmon, every which way you can have it—smoked, fried, baked, broiled, stuffed. We also have halibut, crabs, prawns, oysters, potato salad, rice, seaweed, clam fritters, and clam chowder. It's mainly the people who put up the potlatch who will seek out the traditional foods for the first day of the potlatch, but they hire people to do the cooking for the family. We have to feed a lot of people, anywhere from 350 to 500 people. We invite friends from all over to these potlatches.

The next day we have either beef or deer stew, and then sometimes your immediate family or extended family will offer to cook for the day, or for the dinner. We had ours for three days, after my husband died, and we only had to cook for one day, and the hall was packed. The give-away happens on the last night, and all sorts of things are given away— blankets, towels, Indian things. We made a lot of button blankets, vests, and tunics to give away before the potlatch even began. You have pillowcases, towels, dishes, anything you might need in a home. We had to buy some of them. Probably a quarter to almost half of the give-away items are made.

I don't know how the government felt about the potlatch when they banned it. I remember reading about the raid in 1922. I think maybe they were getting tired of the Native people being broke or poor and giving away a lot of their things, because we'd take our fishing money and buy all these things and just give it away. Ceremonial masks and blankets were confiscated, and I've heard in some stories that totem poles were burned down, too.

People were arrested. As to how long they were in prison, I don't know. I thought that was really unfair. After the raid the Native people still danced and sang their songs, but I don't think they traveled around to the potlatch too much. They are still trying to regain these ceremonies. They had to build a cultural center just to keep the artifacts intact.

We are not materialistic. We consider our family to be our riches. During our potlatch we gave away some bowls with apples; that's a tradition with potlatches for the chiefs. The carved feast bowls are like they used to give away years ago, and these are given to chiefs and close friends, or what we call "Umaqs," like a princess or a wife or daughter of the chief. This is where these bowls go, and special friends and families would give them out into the crowd.

Because we were the ones hosting the potlatch when my husband died, we didn't get anything. The family just gives; we never get anything. And it took us about two years to prepare for it. When my husband was really sick, and the doctors only gave him six months to live, I started ordering things to use for when he died. So I had some dry goods put aside that we used when we had our Settlement Feast. Afterward, I started saving again because we had to have a potlatch for my husband since he was so well respected.

We were told what to do, to make black dresses with his design, which was "Eagle and the Whale." The second day we wore them, and the third day we wore vests with his design on it. This is the most important ceremony in our culture. Each chief has a Tanis dancer, that's the wild man of the woods. Harvey, Jr., was always my husband's Tanis, so he was to be initiated to become, spiritually and ritually, a real Tanis. This hadn't been seen in Bella Bella for seventy years. So he had to go out in the forest to be by himself for four nights. He wasn't allowed to have any food, all he had was water to drink.

There were three attendants that would keep a close watch on him, but they were not actually with him. Sometimes they wouldn't even know where he was because he was dressed in a hemlock crown, with hemlock branches around his wrists, ankles, waist, and neck, camouflaged to blend into the forest. There was where he meditated to get in touch with his spiritual self, to find out who he was going to be, and which path he would choose, whether he would come out a good person or a bad person. It all depends on what you have on your mind and your heart when you go into the forest to find your inner self.

Our potlatch started when Harvey's son came in as the Tanis that he had sought through the fasting and meditation he had done in the forest. He was weak and tired, and he had no recollection of entering the community hall or seeing all of the people who were there to witness our Tanis. Watching Harvey, Jr., being initiated was such an emotional and spiritual experience, there was hardly a dry eye in the hall. They made our Tanis dance around the hall four times, then he went into his little shelter made of cedar boughs and decorated with a red cloth.

The Tanis pole of cedar has steps going up it. On the top is a piece of copper that is like a family shield. Lines on the copper mark all the potlatches, a kind of family history. This is like food for the Tanis dancer, who goes up and climbs down, while the drums grow louder and louder, spurring him on to dance again.

This goes on for about three hours. They drum and sing until they get the wildness out of the person and he is returned to normal. It is truly spiritual dancing. Years ago, pictures were never allowed; for Harvey, Jr.'s, dance, only the family was allowed to take photographs.

After the potlatch was over we all chipped in and worked together, helping one another. It took us a little while to get back on our feet, but we managed. My daughter had come up three weeks before, and sent some blankets to be sewn. We had to sew buttons on all the blankets. Her husband and son made masks for the ceremony. A lot of things were burned after the potlatch, such as the Tanis pole, which is the tradition. They must be burned and never seen again. Everyone left the potlatch with a very good feeling; that's how you know you have had it in a proper way.

If you have certain people you wish to honor, then you give special gifts such as carved silver, bracelets, earrings or pendants, or Indian blankets. Some stories I have heard said people would even give away dressers and chairs, canoes, and gas boats. And some people just give away one thing, such as Ooligan grease. We call it an Ooligan Grease Potlatch. Our people use the grease for our smoked fish, or dried herring, or potatoes. You dip it in, and it's very good.

We gave away eighty-four gallon pails of salted herring eggs, which we harvested for the different villages that don't usually get them. Other things we gave away included sea-weed, sugar, and rice, and towels and sheets. On the last night, my husband had a special cousin that he always thought highly of who brought us some food to help us out, like sugar, flour, and rice; so my grandchildren packaged them and we gave them out. My husband always used to get blankets from feasts and bowls with apples and fruits, so we gave them away at the potlatch, too. But not very many of his clothes; I saved them for his grandchildren. Some of his shirts we gave away to his close friends.

We still had lots more when my grandson was sick for a year or so after the potlatch. He had leukemia, which is now in remission. If it doesn't come back in five years, then he's out of danger. He had a bone marrow transplant with his own marrow, and it worked really well for him. So we also had a Settlement Feast, or a welcome home dinner, for him. People were very supportive and generous when he was sick, so that was my way of thanking the people. It was called a celebration, but we had a give-away again. We spent a lot of money then, too. And now we have to start again. Maybe we will do a naming ceremony, because we have new kids to give names to. You can do a naming when they are still in their mamma's tummy.

In our culture it isn't the material things, it's who you have in your family that makes you rich. I think that's what Native people are about anyway; they are so strong in family ties. The other good thing about the potlatch is that the family receives the quality time, which is so important. So when we were growing up, we were always told to help our brothers and sisters, and never put them down if they've done wrong. That's why I feel so good about Bella Bella people, because they are so generous and kind, and if anybody is in trouble, they don't have to be asked, they just come.

# KIOWA

## GUS PALMER: THE BLACK LEGGING SOCIETY

*The Kiowa were among the most warlike of the early Plains tribes, enemies of the Cheyenne and Sioux. At the turn of the seventeenth century, they lived along the upper Yellowstone River near the Black Hills. Then in 1805, they moved south to what is now eastern Colorado and western Oklahoma, where they warred against the Navajo and Ute, as well as the white settlers from the east. Finally, in the 1867 Treaty of Medicine Lodge, at Fort Sill, Oklahoma, they made peace with the U.S. government and were put on a nearby reservation with the Comanche. In 1901, the Federal Allotment Policy, which chopped up reservation lands created in former treaties and distributed them to individual families, was enacted, and today most Kiowa live in western Oklahoma near Anadarko.*

*Gus Palmer is the commander of the Black Legging Society and a priest of the Native American Church. He lives in a handsome house that he took pride in painting himself, inside and out. His family lives nearby in houses he helped build. Gus is a man proud of who he is and what he has accomplished.*

My name is Gus Palmer, Sr., of the Kiowa tribe. I was born right here in Anadarko, Oklahoma, on January 1, 1919. I've lived here for fifty-some odd years. I raised my family here. My father's father was an Irishman, and his mother was a Choctaw—they're from the east of the state of Oklahoma. My father was half-Irish and half-Choctaw, and my mother was a full-blooded Kiowa.

The Kiowa people originated way up in the north around Wyoming. They kept moving south and came down into the western part of Oklahoma and into parts of Kansas, Colorado, and New Mexico. This is where they were living until the government made a treaty with the five tribes, including the Kiowa, Comanche, Apache, Arapaho, and Cheyenne, in 1867. It's called the Medicine Lodge Treaty. The government left them three million acres here in Oklahoma. The three tribes that were placed here had 160 acres allotted; the rest of the land the government sold to the non-Indians. We still live on those 160 acres.

During World War II, I served with the Eighth Air Force overseas and was on a bomber with a crew of nine. I was the Waist Gunner, 96th Bomb Group, on the B-17. It was called a Flying Fortress. We flew twenty-one missions. I received two Air Medals with one cluster ETOs [European Theater of Operations], a World War II Victory Medal, and a Presidential Citation that was given to the unit.

When I was in the war, I made up my mind that I was going to make it back, and that I was going to do something for our tribe. When I got back, I thought we would call a meeting for the Kiowa men that served in the military. We met at Carnegie, Oklahoma, in the VFW Hall. Fifty men attended that meeting. I told them that we needed to get together because the states that we fought for someday won't remember that we have been in the military fighting for this country. So if we organize, we can make them aware. In the fall, on Veterans Day, we'll observe that. At least they will recognize that we did this, and our names will never be lost.

We had always had the Black Legging Society, but the government tried to stop it. It was our warrior society that protected the people. I thought that we should revive the same thing. So for that reason, I announced that we were going to revive the "Black Leggings," the warriors of the Kiowa Tribe.

Now the reason they called themselves the "Black Legging Society" was that they painted their legs black from the knees and arms from the elbows down. Their chest, back, and the rest of their legs were painted yellow. Back then they wore buckskin breech cloths.

Some of us wear a red cape, and the reason why is because of my great-grandfather. He was a captured white boy who was raised by our tribe when he was a baby. When he was a little boy, about three years old, they noticed that when he was angry, his face would turn red. So they named him "Gool-hla-e," which means "turns red" or "red boy." That's the name that he earned.

When young men were growing up then, they wanted to be known as soldiers or warriors. Sometimes they would touch the enemies with their lances, like counting coup. So my great-grandfather would go along with these warriors, and they would go all the way to Mexico.

They would go a long ways, sometimes they'd be gone for months and years. One time, they met the Mexican soldiers, and the officer wore a red cape. My great-grandfather killed that Mexican officer and took his uniform and kept the cape as a war trophy. We are descended from our great-grandfather, so we wear the red cape in honor of him. Only our cousin and my brothers are supposed to wear it as direct descendants.

Ever since we organized the Black Legging Society, we've celebrated the return of the warrior. We get together at least twice a year. We don't dance any other time, just those two times.

There are about two hundred members of the society, and forty of them take part in the special dress. We carry lances. If you have done something outstanding, you also place an eagle feather on it. Mine includes twenty-one eagle feathers representing how many bomb missions I did in enemy territory. White people receive medals, but we have the eagle feathers. Years ago they put scalps on them, and everybody used to decorate their lances however they wanted to.

My Indian name is Mypah. That was given to me by my grandmother's cousin, considered really my grandpa in our relations. She told me that it was given to me after her father, who was a Buffalo Medicine Man, went with the warriors into battle. When they got wounded he would doctor them. "Mypah" means that when you hit an enemy, they jump from the impact of getting hit.

I grew up with the Native American Church. My father was a priest, and they had somebody who assisted him, keeping the fire going all night long. Sometimes I would go with my father when I was young, and he would tell me, "I'm going to go to this meeting for somebody who's sick."

I went to my first meeting when I was nine years old. My father was holding it. I didn't realize then so much of what was going on. I only knew about four songs. But my father told me, "After midnight, you can sing those four songs." The drum and the gourd went around, and they all sang, all night long. Being that young, I didn't realize too much, I just know that everybody was praying and singing these songs. I took the medicine, only about two or three small ones. I didn't fully understand, but I knew that I was just supposed to pray.

I used to see healings when my father and elders were doing meetings. This was all they had to use back then, that was the medicine. They had Indian doctors as well that would doctor people. They would say, "This is the medicine that Creator made. It can cure you if you take it and ask Creator to cure you." They no longer use that too much, now that we have all this modern medicine. But two weeks ago, we did a lodge for a lady with cancer, and she's still going strong, she's not giving up. I gave her a dried peyote and told her, "I'm going to make one for you, pray over it, and give it to you."

When somebody is sick, I have the water bird feathers that my father-in-law had. They call them water turkeys. My wife's father would use them to heal people. I am not a medicine man, but I use these things to help people. This is how they do it. I don't call myself a road man, that's from other tribes; I would say I am like a priest.

I've seen people who have come here be healed. Like a person with ulcers, they take the peyote medicine and it will cure them. If you are too afraid to take it, then you won't be cured. My brother-in-law had ulcers, and he was cured that way. You hardly see people in there for sickness anymore, though. They will have meetings for somebody's birthday or somebody returning from the service.

I have held the fireplace for meetings my in-laws have had. Now and then, for whatever the purpose they are going to hold the Native American Church service, I'll run the meetings.

I was selected to represent this chapter of the church at a subcommittee in Washington, D.C. They were putting out a bill pertaining to the Native American Church, as an amendment to the Religious Freedom Act, that gave us the right to use peyote. A man from the Food and Drug Administration told the subcommittee that there was no problem, as far as peyote being classified as a drug, with Indians using it ceremonially in the Native American Church. There was another man from the northern area who claimed that there are 250,000 members up there.

I didn't do this to protect the church, but to protect the peyote. I call it a sacrament, given to us by Creator. I say that he purposely made the peyote for the Indian, long before Christianity. We use the peyote like the Catholics use the wafer, and you don't see them abusing it. It's the same way with us. Creator made it for us. Creator is in that peyote; he's in everything that we breathe, he's everywhere. I testified that no one knows the use of this peyote, and we want it protected because when we eat it, it's used in ceremony.

Peyote originated in the southwest part of Oklahoma. In the late 1800s, an anthropologist named James Mooney came to live with the Kiowa people. He's the one that incorporated its practice by getting a charter to use it in the church. The government didn't want him to, but he went ahead and chartered it in 1918. In 1944, the Navajo took it up in their religion, and in 1950, the northern tribes started the church.

We are told that women had the first knowledge of the peyote. In the story, a woman and her child were lost. The spirits told her to take the herb that she found and eat it, since it had nourishment and water. They told her that she would then find her people. This is what happened. Once she ate it, it gave her that knowledge.

When you eat the peyote, it makes you feel humble. I don't really recommend curing people who have alcohol problems at these prayer meetings. But when they come in, I tell them, "This is where you are going to learn to pray in your native tongue." These young men get caught up in worldly things. And now I say it's hard to cure, because they get addicted to it, these worldly things. It's hard for them to come in here when they would rather be out there. But if you come in, you are going to hear the people pray to this God. Hear these songs, these beautiful Native songs that were given to the Indian. And you are going to see the outcome, and you're going to feel good.

Now they want me to begin to have language classes. They want me to teach them some of these good things in our tribe, which they need to keep and not lose. The greatest respect for our tribe is not to lose the young ones, because they are assimilated into this other life today. They are losing a lot of their language. Like what to call their relations, and how that comes about, since you don't call them by name. They could respect this far more. It's rather odd for them to call you by your given name. That would be like saying "grandson" and "grandpa" are the same words. We are going to teach them how to greet people. I think a lot of them want to keep that, or learn that, to carry it on.

All of these stories are handed down; they aren't written. So the grandparents tell the grandchildren. And they would tell them one at a time. They tell them about the ten bundles that they have, and where they come from—our creation story.

The short version goes like this: A grandma made a wheel for two boys to play with. "Never throw it up in the air," she told this one boy. Curiosity got this boy, so he threw it up in the air. When it was coming down, he thought he had dodged it, but it was following him. It split him in half and made two of them. They weren't twins, they were called "split boys." They recognized each other as being brothers.

One of them said he was going to go into the lake. And the other one said he would place all of his body parts in these ten bundles. We still have them. Different people have different ones. We used to have one here. It came down through each generation. My father-in-law's brother had it. His brother had it. His wife's grandfather had it before. They were caretakers. They had to take the bundle when they were going somewhere. They can't leave it by itself. Now they keep them in a house, but before it was kept in a tipi. Now that people have cars, they have to take it in a car if they go someplace. As long as a Kiowa exists, the bundles will still be here. It's still here from way, way back then.

These stories help teach children how they are supposed to live, how they are supposed to behave. For something like fifteen, sixteen years, in the summer, I took that on. The little ones are called rabbits, and they are able to walk to my house. I sang for them, and I tell them some of these stories. I tell their mothers and grandmothers to bring their tape recorders and tape them and keep them, so they won't lose them. Someone had a feast for the children, and there was about two, three hundred of them inside the dance arena. One of the songs I sang pertains to those split boys, and I explained what the words meant. They don't know how to speak Kiowa.

Some of the songs are lost. I learned these from my grandmother. For some reason or another, I hung onto them, and I know what they pertain to. Like nursery rhymes, like that buffalo, a little red buffalo. Did you know that buffalo are red when they are small?

There's another one about prairie dogs. There was a man, he was tall. He called everyone *sagee,* nephew. He liked to cheat, lie, and brag. Everything was wrong with him. That's what they say about him, how bad he was. He came up to a group of prairie dogs gathered together. All he wanted to do was get ahold of some of them, cook them, and eat them.

So he told them, "I'm going to do this for you all. I'm going to sing for you all, and you're going to dance. When I sing this prairie dog song, you have to close your eyes and dance. Keep your eyes closed while I sing."

So all that time he had a stick, and he was hitting them in the back of the head, and they didn't know it. He was cheating them, he was killing them. All except one little one who didn't close his eyes. He was looking and seeing that he had killed all of them, except this little one. The little one went in his hole and saved himself. They tell that story to tell why we still have prairie dogs to this day.

I tell the youth before they come out here, have your mothers, grandmothers, dress you up like an elder, a grown person. However you want, painted up. Dress up and come up, and then sit right down in front here where I can see you. Then we'll have prizes for you; we're going to give you something. And your mother or your grandmother is going to see you dancing. They are going to feel proud of you, and they're going to give something away in your honor, like a grown-up. Someday, you're going to become a leader or something in life that is useful. They come with shawls and stuff.

I don't want to be neglected as an elder. We have five great-grandchildren and one is going to be walking soon. I am going to name him after Gool-hla-e, my great-grandfather, "the boy that turns red." Because he looks so light-skinned, and his face turns red.

# YUROK

## GEORGIANA TRULL: A TEACHER

*Georgiana and John Trull's house, on Yurok territory, is twelve miles east of the small town of Hoopa and nineteen miles northwest from the bridge that crosses the Klamath River in northern California. I drove on a narrow, single-lane road that winds along above the bluffs of the river. The land there is steep and thickly forested with oak, maple, and the smooth, red-barked madrone.*

*The Trulls' blue-and-white house sits nestled on a hillside overlooking the river. A large dog and her litter had taken up residence underneath the porch, and various breeds of cats were everywhere. Inside, the low-ceilinged, airy living room was filled with photographs of children and grandchildren.*

*Georgiana's step is quick and agile; she seems younger than her seventy-seven years. There is peacefulness about her; she laughs easily, especially at her husband's stories.*

*We sit on the porch talking, looking up now and then at a hawk circling overhead.*

I am a member of the Yurok nation on the north banks of the Klamath River. We're from the Shregon Village, about a half a mile from here, which used to be a big Indian village. When I was growing up, there were no roads, no cars; we were isolated from everything around us. We would go by boat or horse to the store for groceries, or we would walk. In many ways I think it was a better life because there wasn't much alcohol, and there were no drugs at all. We weren't lonely, because we could go down to the village to be with other

people our age. The only entertainment we had at night was to listen to stories. But then, as village life began to fall apart, there was more drinking.

We Yurok Indian people have never been organized, and yet we have survived and are independent. A lot of us have never really been uncomfortable in our lives; we have worked hard to get what we have. We have never depended on the BIA [Bureau of Indian Affairs] for our needs here. Our young people will survive without having to depend on the BIA for per capita payments or anything like that. Because they know if they want anything, they've got to work for it.

I'm still fluent in my language. Now I teach Yurok to the young people; I just retired this past year. But I taught at the school for about twenty years, part-time. The little kids, from kindergarten up to about third or fourth grade, like to learn the language. But after that, when they get to be teenagers, then they have other things that they want to do. None of their parents have ever learned the language, that's the sad part of it. In this area here, between Wietchpec on down, about a twenty-mile area, I think there are only two of us. There are only eleven of us in the whole Eureka, Klamath, and Wietchpec area that speak the language fluently. I believe that if we know our language, then we know who we are. The basis of our Yurok culture is our language. That's our main thing. Because even in the minor ceremonies, like the Brush Dance, the songs don't sound the same as the old-timers used to sing them. Because when the young people learn their language, they don't get the accent, and it doesn't sound the way it's supposed to. I was just up there last weekend listening to a couple of the girls singing the Brush Dance song. They do the Boat Dance on this part of the river every two years.

I tell my students that all nationalities have their own languages, and they speak them. You go out of town and you hear the Chicanos, the Chinese, the Italians, and they all speak their own language. Except for the Indians. You don't hear Indians talking in their own language. But they say, "We can't learn it. It's too hard."

I've talked to many different people who go to the high country to pray, like the Tolowa, the Hoopa, and the Karuk. The Hoopa go up to Trinity Alps. But I know that the Tolowa and Karuk go up to Chimney Rock; that's where we go, too. And they speak all different languages.

I have three grandchildren, and I wonder what their life is going to be like. Because these young people like my grandchildren and my great-grandchildren, they are going to have to learn to live in two different cultures. For some young people, it's hard to learn their language and to be able to participate in their own ceremonial dances, and to know what it's all about.

The Yurok people don't believe that the women should sweat; that's for men. We never heard of women sweating. When I was growing up my grandmother had arthritis, so my mother took one of those great big aluminum washtubs and put rocks in it. Then she poured water that she had heated in the fireplace over the rocks, and set the tub on the floor with a chair over it. She wrapped a blanket around my grandmother, up to her neck, and let her steam like that. That's the way the women did theirs.

People were real secretive about what they did; they didn't want anybody else to go with them if they were going to go and pray. They didn't want anybody to listen to what they were praying about. It was done in private between them and Creator. Everything was done in private.

When I was growing up, people didn't have as many dresses as they have now for Jump Dancing. Because everything had to be done by hand, and the knowledge of how to make them was passed down from one generation to another. Now, I think they have classes in town for making the regalia. And they have classes in dressmaking, too. They use electric drills now to work with the shells and pine nuts.

When we lived at the village, if we killed a deer, everybody got some of it; they divided it up. Nothing was ever wasted. And they fished until everybody had what they needed for winter, then they would pull the net out and let others fish. They don't do those things anymore. Everything's commercial now. But we never sold the fish, we always gave it to the people, whoever needed it. My mother would never let a child come into her house without feeding them. She never turned a young person away, and she'd always give them a place to stay if they needed one. She treated everyone like family. It didn't matter if they were Indian, white, or who they were. She always made sure that they had something to eat and a place to sleep.

People even treated trees differently. Like when you get wood, you'd get just enough to last you all winter long. You'd know how much to take and not waste anything. I think all this stopped probably because parents don't spend the time with their children to take them out and teach them. My grandmother always took me out and taught me different things, not to destroy other people's stuff, because if you did you always had to pay them back. She also taught me about medicinal things. I was telling my doctor when I was getting a physical a couple of weeks ago. He mentioned my smoking, and I said, "Doctor, my grandmother lived to be a hundred and fifteen, and she smoked all her life." She never went to a doctor in her whole life. She never went to a dentist either, and she still had most of her teeth at a hundred and fifteen. Her teeth had worn down right to the gums. When she laughed it looked like she had buttons pressed up into her gums.

And herbs. They were all the medicine we had, and it worked. Like I told my husband when I went down to go get my physical. I said, "You know there's nothing wrong with me." He said, "There isn't?" I said, "No, my doctor said I'm the healthiest person my age he's ever seen. I'm seventy-seven years old, and there's nothing wrong with me."

Our Indian people didn't believe in being overweight. I was telling my husband, "I wonder what my mother and my aunt would say when they see some of my mother's grand-kids and how heavy they let themselves get." I know that our tribe didn't believe in being fat. It was like committing a sin if you let yourself get fat. It meant you weren't taking care of your body. Because you were never supposed to put anything in your body that was going to harm it. And you never overate. You were to take a mouthful of food and put your spoon down until you swallow it, and then you just sit there and wait a little bit and take another spoonful. That just took too long for me, so they would always preach to us about how the Indians ate.

They used to live off of the woods and the rivers; they didn't have gardens. Until in my mother's generation, they learned how and started planting gardens. But now this younger generation says that everything has to be organic. I never really stopped to realize that now we go and buy all this organic food that I was raised on all along, that's how our food was. Some people still go out and gather acorns and huckleberries, but as the years go by, you forget how.

My grandfather used to tell us prophecies about the river. That it would eventually disappear. He didn't say what would happen to it, just that it would disappear. And now, you can see where they want to build dams in here and take our river out. And that would deplete the fish. The younger generation doesn't realize that by commercializing their fishing, they will soon deplete the fish, and then this will be declared a dead river. Then the dams will go in. Maybe not in my generation, but maybe in the future. . . .

# PUEBLO

## SANTIAGO LEO CORIZ: KIVA CHIEF

*There are twenty pueblos, small villages of adobe houses, throughout the Southwest. The Anasazi are said to be the oldest known inhabitants of the hemisphere. Each pueblo is autonomous and has its own language, and although they share a common religion, their ceremonies vary. According to their creation story, the first Pueblo people emerged from an underworld by way of a lake in the north known as Sipapu. Then, guided by the Great Spirit, their migrations began. During their journey the Great Spirit gave them their original instructions. They were shown the plants that grew in abundance on the land, how to plant, and when to harvest. They were given rituals and prayers for rain and thanksgiving dances for the harvest, which are still held today.*

*They were given instructions on how to live a well-ordered, peaceful life, instructions that have been passed down through the generations. The Great Spirit also warned of the disasters that would befall them if they failed to obey these instructions.*

*Villages are divided into clans, each with their own kiva, a ceremonial chamber entered into by ladders through an opening in the roof. Only men are allowed inside of them.*

*Santo Domingo, south of Santa Fe, lies along the banks of the Rio Grande at the base of the Sandia Mountains, where highly prized turquoise was once found.*

*Unlike many Pueblo people, who are wary of outsiders and guarded in their manner, Leo, who is a kiva chief, is open to strangers. He wants all grandchildren everywhere to know about his people. And like his father and his father's father before him, Leo is a master jeweler whose work is displayed in museums.*

I was born in this house in Santo Domingo Pueblo in June of 1913. I went to a day school here where they taught in Spanish. Then they sent me to a Catholic school in Santa Fe when I was seven or eight years old. I didn't really like it there. They wanted us to forget our Indian ways and learn the Catholic way. They think that is the only true religion.

But the Indian culture was my way of living. I was taught before I went to school, by my grandfather and my great-grandfather, how to live in a respectful, religious way. Today, a lot of our people believe in the Catholic way, but mostly we still carry our own belief. The Zuni, Isleta, all the Indians along the Rio Grande, come here for meetings once a year. This is the main village for keeping the culture and not changing. All the children here are taught the language. That's everyday language here. But in other villages, they don't even teach their kids; they just talk English. Way back when I first went to school, you said one word of Indian and they punished you. But now they are making a law in Oklahoma that they are going to have Indian languages taught in school. I think that's good.

I was at the Indian school in Santa Fe for five years. I never graduated, though. I was expelled in the eighth grade for having a smart mouth. When I was in school, I would come back to Santo Domingo in the summer to work with my uncle on the farm. We raised the main foods which were corn, beans, squash, melons, chile. That's how my people eat. Corn is the main crop in the pueblo. They would take it and trade with the Comanche, Apache, and Navajo.

Then I got a job in Albuquerque and lived in the pueblo and tried to support my parents. My father never went to school, but he took good care of us. He made turquoise and traded with the Hopi and the Navajo. In the 1920s and 1930s, this house was full of rocks, silver, belts.

I got married around 1938 and had four kids from my first wife. After 1940, I was drafted into the navy. I had long hair and had to cut it off. They found out I was a metalsmith, and they made me a federal officer, third class, to patch up planes that were shot down by the Japanese.

When I came home from the service, I started having trouble with my stomach. I wasn't able to keep food down. I went back and forth to the hospital for a year. The doctor said they'd have to cut my stomach, but I said, "You are not going to cut my stomach." So I asked my aunt to get me a medicine man, and I asked him if he would take care of my sickness.

He said, "I will ask my deity, my gods, my spirits to bring me light so I can take care of you. But you have to do what I say and believe in what you ask. I'm not going to be the one to cure you, Spirit is the one to cure. Tomorrow, I am going to come over with some herbs. I will bring a gallon, and you have to drink all of it. And you are going to die for a while. But don't be afraid. You are going to die, but you are going to wake up. When you wake up, you are going to be hungry." And ever since 1952, I had no trouble with my stomach.

When I was a baby, I was sick. So my mother gave me to another person to adopt me in the Indian way, with corn meal. I grew up with them for four or five years. The Indian belief is that maybe other mothers and fathers will have more power with the spirits. So I lived with them, and I got well.

Rabbit hunting is an old traditional thing. We don't go hunting to kill; we hunt to feed the spirit. To ask for another year of good health. Everything we do on the reservation is traditional and ceremonial. We try to find a rabbit or quail. We carry rabbit sticks. When the rabbit jumps, you throw the stick in front of it and hit it on the head. Big game is different. We have to pray—and, of course, we have to have a license now, to kill a deer.

Right now, in August, we are through with our regular ceremonies. But later on we will have the Harvest Dance. Only the men dance. This is the time for good crops. Then we have winter dances, like the Eagle Dance and the Buffalo Dance.

We have all kinds of dances. Some of them are forgotten and never will be danced again, and some we still carry on. A lot are lost. We always have dances at certain times, like Christmas, New Year's, Easter. Our dances are a combination of Spanish, Mexican, and Indian. We have the Matachina dances. I've been dancing the Corn Dance ever since I was able to walk. When I was a boy, maybe thirty people danced, but now there are about two or three hundred to each group in the Corn Dance. For some of the big ceremonies we have to fast for several days.

I'm a kiva chief. I try to take care of our culture. My clan is Fox. My first wife was Corn Clan, so all of her children were Corn. My second wife was Oak, so all my children that she had are Oak. The clan comes from the mother.

In the spring, the men start cleaning the ditches. We have four ditches on each side of us. They go out with shovels and clean them out by hand so we can irrigate our land. Then around April we start planting our corn, blue corn, white corn, chile, melon. By May, we are through planting, and we will have fresh things around August, September, and our harvest, which is around October.

The main problem we have now in the village is the white man's way. Everybody wants it. We can leave the pueblo any time, but we cannot be white. We still have self-government, our war captains, our war chiefs. We had those before the Spanish ever came to this country. The war captains and war chiefs are responsible for everything in the village. The state cannot come in here to give us orders. But the problem is that we don't have anything anymore. All the white people took our land. Rich people are buying up a lot of land around here.

It's the family that helps us keep our culture strong. The oldest one in the family teaches the kids. The village government, or the war chiefs, are responsible if something goes wrong. They tell us how to respect and go back to our tradition. A lot of the kids are what we call "urban Indians"—they go to town and work. But they come back when they are

older. They come back to their tradition and their culture. I think this is a lot better life than going into the city. Here there isn't a belief in violence and all that. Here everybody is people, everybody makes mistakes. They have a way of doing things in the right way, not by force or money, just a respectful way.

All through the Jemez Mountains, there are a lot of ruins where our people used to live. Some white people tried to dig up the stones there, but they couldn't. I think they should leave nature alone. There are a lot of areas where you can get an education, the old way, in pictures, but they've ruined a lot of those ways. We still have generations coming; we want them to know our ways, our life, and they want to know, too. So we have to stop those people from taking the ruins. Most of them are doing it for money.

I tell my kids, "The Creator gives us the corn. You put it in the ground; it grows and you eat. If you don't do these things, then he gives us clay to make pots; he gives us turquoise to make beads. You go and work it and you got something to eat." That's why the Indians don't steal, don't take anything that doesn't belong to them. That's the main thing in our religion, not to take other people's property.

You can go out and make money if you find a job, but what's money? It's not food. Somebody has to grow that food, those tomatoes, chiles, and beans. There are times when you can't find a job. Do it yourself, make your own jewelry, your own turquoise, your own pots. Get some seeds, put them in the ground, and you got food. That's my teaching. That's what I tell my kids. I design my own jewelry, and I teach anybody who wants to learn. If you've got no money, I'll teach for free. I'm not going to take what I know with me. I want to leave what I know in this world so that other people can use it.

The Creator put us here. They say, This is just a borrowed world, and we don't own it; nobody owns it. My grandpa said, "All right, we have all kinds of people in this world. But we came from the same Creator. There's black people, red people, yellow people, white people, all colors, but we are all people. So respect them as people. We are all brothers and sisters. Some day, near the end of the world, everybody will be together." I think he was right. Today, a lot of people are getting married to black, red, yellow people. I have a great-grandson who is a Vietnamese boy. But he looks just like our people here. It's true, what they predicted from way back.

I don't know, but I think it's going to be another thousand or million years before the world ends. Of course, everybody's got their own version. Wherever the rich people go, they dig the ground, spoil the earth, ruin the earth, poison the water. It's all greed. They don't do things to benefit the people in the world, just to benefit themselves. When they die, where are they going to take their money? They might buy more land to ruin, that's all.

We ruin the world ourselves, the world that the Creator gave us to enjoy and to be happy with. He gave us all the beautiful things, trees, mountains, food. Everything is here, even medicine, but we don't know much about medicine anymore. You have to have money to go to the doctor, when everything is free in this world. I don't go to the doctor; I go off to get my own medicine. That's why I'm healthy.

I had two grandpas that were medicine men. They used to go to the mountains every spring and bring back a lot of roots and things and put them out on the porch to dry. Then they would grind it and put it into bags.

They are blaming this new hantavirus [a flu-like virus, sometimes fatal and said to be rodent-borne, that appeared in the Southwest in the summer of 1993] on an animal. You can never blame anything on an animal. He or she was created by the same Creator that created us, who didn't create anything to kill us or make us sick. I think that virus came from the atmosphere or something man-made. The Creator doesn't bring sickness. We are the ones that are causing all the sickness. The Indians were healthy before the white people came.

In Los Alamos, they use all kinds of chemicals. Then the wind comes and takes them and scatters them all over the country, maybe into the water, and makes poison. We are making the world end ourselves, not the Creator. That's what the old people say.

# LAKOTA/ SEMINOLE

**MIKE HANEY: TOMORROW'S ELDER**

*Half Seminole, half Lakota, Mike Haney grew up on the reservation in Seminole County, Oklahoma, where the more than 300,000 American Indians make up thirty-six different tribes. "Every tribe that had declared war against the U.S. ended up in Oklahoma." Mike's fight for Indian rights takes him all over the country. He appeared on the Oprah Winfrey show in 1992 and talked about the use of Indian names as mascots for sports teams. Recently he formed the Coalition Against Racism in Sports and Media. He pointed out that we don't have the Chicago Caucasians, or the New York Negroes, but we do have the Atlanta Braves and the Washington Redskins. In January of 1992, Mike and a group of activists put up a twenty-foot-high tipi outside a gate at the Metrodome in Minneapolis during the Super Bowl and led two thousand demonstrators in protest over the name of the Washington Redskins.*

*He also takes issue with the names of vehicles—such as Cherokee Jeeps, Winnebago RVs, and Dakota trucks—on the grounds that they play off old stereotypes of the dime-store Indian.*

*During the seventy-one-day occupation and siege at Wounded Knee in 1973, Haney came and went, traveling around the country to universities speaking and raising money. He had two FBI agents at his heels, taking notes. "On the road these guys were real nice," he said. "They'd stay at the same hotel, ask where we were going to dinner, when we'd be leaving. We'd almost forget that when we got back to the 'Knee,' they were going to try to kill us."*

*As it turned out, two Indians were killed and many were seriously wounded.*

*Mike's activism is partly inherited. His uncle, Jerry Haney, is the elected chief of the Seminole Tribe of Oklahoma; a cousin, Enoch Kelly Haney, is a famed artist and Oklahoma state senator.*

*Mike, a future elder, is the elected second chief of the Newcomer band in the Seminoles' Alligator Tribe.*

In 1972, I was a member of the first American Indian Movement [AIM] chapter in Oklahoma. It was at a time when many tribes were suffering. My tribe, the Seminole nation, had an operating budget of around twenty thousand dollars, so we met in churches or in the courthouse; we had no facility of our own. We were just a bunch of Indians speaking out about treaty compromises, how wrong it was, how we should have our own court systems, our own schools—things I thought were right on target as far as providing solutions to some of the problems. But the concept of independently vested nations within the jurisdictional boundaries of the United States was outrageous to the Bureau of Indian Affairs [BIA] and the U.S. government.

Being from Oklahoma, my reservation experience was very limited. However, I learned from the elders that these treaties were not just real estate deals, they were sacred documents. Our elders had prayed over them when they signed them.

We were amiss in not understanding that, and in not providing that spiritual instruction to the new generation coming up. Our parents' generation had for the most part turned away from traditional teachings and embraced total assimilation. I know how dangerous that was to us; the elders spoke the truth when they said that we had to have a spiritual rebirth. Become born-again primitives, born-again pagans—like the buttons I see every once in a while.

There's strength in the original instructions. When I fell short of them, I took it very personally, and I turned to alcohol. Then I was given my lesson in spirituality in the form of a life and death experience when I was declared legally dead.

I had accepted a lot of challenges over the years, and I was always somehow able to overcome them. But I met more than I could manage with alcohol and drugs. For three years, I was a drunk. I was in my twenties and one of the youngest leaders in AIM. During that time I was in a self-imposed exile in Oklahoma.

One night I got into a fight at a party at this woman's house. I recognized this guy as being one of the three who had raped my cousin six months earlier. She was young and small, and they busted her jaw and fractured her pelvis. They really hurt her. It was impossible to prosecute them because my cousin was so ashamed she cleaned herself up and destroyed all the physical evidence. They never knew about the fractures because she was too ashamed to tell them. The D.A. said he could arrest the guys, but a good attorney would get them off.

On this night at the party, when I spotted one of the ones who had raped my cousin, I told him to come outside. He didn't know me, but the minute we got outside we started fighting. Then his brother came over. I'm a pretty large fellow—six-foot-five—and I weigh about 245 pounds, so I wasn't having too much trouble handling two twenty-year-olds. But then a third guy came in behind me.

I had seen him earlier; he was shirtless, and he wore fatigue pants and boots with a bayonet strapped to his side. What I didn't realize was that he was their cousin. So when he saw me with those boys, he came in behind me with his bayonet and stabbed me eleven times in the back. One entered my stomach, one went clear through my arm. I knew where the nearest hospital was; I got into the car and a friend drove me to the emergency room.

I had worked as an emergency room technician and specialist when I was in the military, and I knew if I could just get to the emergency room, I wouldn't die. I walked in bleeding—it was about two or three in the morning—the nurse on duty let out a scream. I must have looked pretty scary. I had blood all over me. She called a Code Blue and everybody came running. They took my vital signs; I guess I had lost so much blood they couldn't get a blood pressure. I don't know if they were trying to protect themselves against lawsuits or what, but they reported no blood pressure and vital signs so weak that they declared me dead.

All the time I was saying, I'm not dead. Still, it felt good to close my eyes. They had to cut off my Levis and my shirt. I wasn't embarrassed by my nudity, but then they did something that woke me up. They started to cut my boots off. I was laying there naked, and suddenly I raised myself up and said, "Just a minute!" I really gave them a scare. "It took me four months to get those boots out of lay-away!" They were nice eelskin boots, and I wasn't going to let them get cut. "Wait a minute," I said, and took the boots off myself.

While they were operating on me, I had an out-of-body experience. You know how sometimes when you are dreaming you can look down and see yourself in a scene? Well, that's what I saw, I saw myself lying on the litter. I didn't think I would die. I was positive that I was going to pull through and get stronger than ever.

But at that moment I felt really low-down. I had to be pretty drunk to take on three guys, one of them with a fourteen-inch bayonet. And I had to be pretty drunk to be at someone's house I didn't know at 2:30 in the morning fighting Indians. I swore then I would never lift a hand against another Indian. I realized that Creator was giving me a second chance. Maybe Creator has other things in store for me, there is some other work that I'm meant to do, and it's not my time to go.

After that near-death experience, I had renewed faith in life and of my own purpose. My uncle, Philip Deer, a Muskogee spiritual leader, took me through a series of sweat lodge ceremonies afterward. I vomited and vomited until I was clean. I did that four times. After the third time I had dry heaves, and my stomach and chest muscles ached and hurt, but I still had a lot of poison in my system. My uncle got that sweat lodge so hot I was praying just to survive that ceremony—not to make me a better man or to help make me a good provider for my family. No, just help me to live through this ceremony. I was in such agony and suffering. But that's what I had to experience. I had to sink to the lowest that I could. I couldn't go any lower.

I was lying on the ground naked, with only my friend and teacher there. He suffered in there, too. I wasn't the only one in there who was laying on the ground crying. I tell you, I was crying, I was so overcome with grief, and I was feeling so sorry for myself, but so was he, because he loved me. I know that now. He provided the atmosphere, but I had to provide the willpower to shake off the alcoholism. With alcoholism comes the other "isms," too. I wasn't providing for my family; I was an embarrassment to my mother and father and uncles.

Maybe I had to suffer, maybe I was meant to experience the depths of self-pity and low self-esteem in order to understand that I never want my children to have to go through this. I want to see my children free to pursue happiness, education, and career opportunities. I want them to develop good relationships with people their own age and, of course, with the elders. I succumbed to alcohol because of peer pressure. And this is no reflection on the extraordinary work that the American Indian Movement has done and is continuing to do. I didn't start drinking until I was twenty-four years old. Before that I was in Germany, in the military, with all the beer and wine I could want, and I never tasted a drop.

When I started working with the AIM chapters in Oklahoma, I was organizing press conferences and always speaking out against alcoholism. But I wanted to be one of the boys, part of the clique, so I began drinking and became pretty good at it. I became a good alcoholic. Of course, I had to step aside because drinking really got in the way of doing anything else. I realized that if you wanted to be traditional, then you had to be sober. We were talking about being traditional, but we were doing it in a state of drunkenness. Not only did that have a negative impact on our youth, it reflected badly on our elders. We had taken their message and twisted it. Supposedly, we were role models for the youth.

So yes, I was very unhealthy spiritually and mentally. I'm grateful that I had someone who loved me and took the time with me like Philip Deer did. It must have hurt him terribly to hear stories of me hanging out in bars, not doing anything with my life. I needed someone to treat me and to counsel me. To reach out and take my hand and pull me back onto the red road. I know the white people have that with their twelve-step program, AA,

which is based on their Bible. I just thank the Creator that I was born Indian, and that the Creator gave us these ceremonies to heal ourselves. I want to keep them sacred and holy.

It's my understanding from our legends that the reason we have the four colors is that we were all children of God. Not four races, but one race of four different colors: white clay, red clay, black clay, and yellow clay. And we feel that all people were given original instructions from Creator. Those who have gotten away from them have suffered. I'm told that in Africa, beer was and continues to be, one of the treatments given by their medicine men. But alcohol and sugar were not indigenous to this area, therefore our chemical make-up couldn't metabolize it. Just as diseases ravaged us when they were introduced into our culture because we had no defense mechanism to fight them. The same is true with sugar and alcohol. Our metabolism was affected by it then and still, to this day, continues to be. This can be proven and documented, and it is exactly what our elders have always taught us.

I think that our traditional people are right when they tell us that the Creator gave us everything necessary to survive on this land. There are healing herbs all around us, foods, medicines—it is up to us to learn from our elders. They are charged with the responsibility of keeping the knowledge and passing it on to their own clans and to the young ones coming up. We need to listen more and more to these elders; these legends and stories are not just fairy tales, they're scientific evidence. There is merit to our history.

Lately researchers are getting into what is called microbiology and microarcheology. They're just now finding out with their scientific data what my grandfather told me forty years ago. Everything that was ever done in my ancestors' time is hidden in information in my DNA structure. A close examination of that DNA can tell us about the migrations, the diseases, even what our diet was. It is my hope that this will make the practice of exhuming bodies for these tests outdated. They don't need the whole body now; they can take one tiny bit of hair or bone and do all the testing on a computer.

Philip Deer spoke to the Elders Council after he had just come from Europe and Africa, and he had one of these beaded sacred hoops about ten inches in diameter with the four directions in the middle. He laid it down in front of us—we were sitting in a big circle—and asked, "Can anyone tell me where this came from?"

We passed it around and looked at it. Somebody said, "It looks Arapaho to me because of the peyote stitch here." Another person said, "It looks like a Southern Cheyenne, because these beads come only from a certain period." Everybody had their own ideas about which particular tribe it had come from.

He stunned us all when he said it came from Africa. It had the four colors of mankind on it. Our legends talked about the coming of the white man, the "Kalani," which means blond or yellow. And they told of the African people. Our stories say that we came from a darker people, that the Africans were the original people; you can get white from black by dilution but you can never get black from white. The colors in between were evolutionary phases according to our legends.

More and more I understand how important our traditional teachings are, and how important it is to keep them alive by talking about them in classrooms and over the dinner table at home. The real reason that we are still here five hundred years after Columbus is that we have kept the original instructions sacred and holy as the Creator instructed us to do. We still speak our languages, and we still do the same ceremonies that we have been doing for generations. Our reward is in our youth. I became a grandfather for the first time just last year. That's evidence to me that Creator wants my bloodline to go on, and I feel good about that.

That same year, I was given an award for courageous acts—"outrageous," I called them. We took over a museum in Illinois and held it hostage. The museum has 237 human skeletal remains of Indians on public display, and people pay a price to come in and gawk. They throw cigarette butts and candy wrappers and pennies at them. We tried to work with the government, and we got some legislation. But when we got the proposal, we saw that they had lied to us. They weren't going to do anything, so we ended up seizing the museum. We covered up some of the remains with the earth that was around it, and negotiated with the governor for total and complete amnesty, and then left.

I was given an award by the National Conference of Christians and Jews because I was the architect of that action. When it was presented to me, they asked, "What's the most memorable award that you have received?" I didn't give them the answer they were looking for. My answer was that two weeks earlier the Creator had blessed me with my first grandchild, and that was the memorable award. His name is Ishokpi, named for the Santee Sioux War Chief, who led the people with Chief Little Crow. I have a son, Kungetankalo, my oldest, named for Chief Little Crow. I wanted to keep those names alive, to honor them. My youngest son is named Hin-Han-Ska Hoksila, White Owl Boy. And I also have a daughter, she's the one who gave me the grandson, her name is Akidoi, an old Kiowa name that means Medicine Flower. *Aki* means flower, and that's what we call her. Her mother is Kiowa; the Kiowas have a tradition of never letting a name die.

I didn't want English names for my children. I wanted them to have Indian names and to be proud of them. When a teacher sees the list of students, she knows which ones are Indian. My Indian name is Caske, which means the first-born male or the defender of the village in the Warrior Society. My Seminole name is Kuakagee, Wildcat. There was a great leader named Wildcat. The traditional people I work with and get advice from back home still stand up for Seminole rights. It is their ultimate purpose in life. I bring a lot of the youth back to the grounds for a celebration of the continuation of our traditional lifestyles.

Anywhere on this earth I walk I would have to go through four layers of earth to get through this crust to get to the middle of the earth. That's how long we have been here, how long our people have lived and died here. When I walk here, I walk on the bones of my ancestors. Our other neighbors do not share this relationship with this land, and maybe that's why it is so hard for them to understand the impact of the policies they placed on us. The strip-mining, the discharging of toxic wastes into river systems that eventually poison the soil. And they continually ignore the danger signs that warn that the atmosphere cannot take more air pollutants.

I think about the hippies of twenty years ago. I used to like them. They were always really friendly, and they wore beads—love beads, they called them—and they wore flowers in their hair. And they talked respectfully about the earth. "Hey," I said, "these guys are talking Indian!" We've waited 480 years for them to start talking Indian. And here they are, this generation of young ones. I remember they were always complaining about their relation-ships with their parents, a generation gap they called it. That always puzzled me. The hippies had a slogan, "Question Authority," and I thought that was pretty good—in regards to white authority, but I never considered questioning Indian authority. Still, I liked their sense of freedom and total lack of prejudice.

The name "hippie" always reminded me of Hopi, and the Hopi are one of the most traditional and spiritual people I know. I see some of these hippies twenty years later, and they're either freeze-dried from drugs and alcohol, incarcerated, or working in their dad's corporation.

We survived the "Me" generation, now we have the "Nintendo" generation. I think that they're going to have to overcome even bigger obstacles than we had—teenage pregnan-cies, drug and alcohol abuse, all hard decisions at increasingly earlier ages. There is a lack of spirituality that's epidemic today, too. And I think that has to do with the confused messages that we are sending our youth. To say that life is sacred on one hand and to support execu-tion on the other is a confusing message to the youth. Just like the Christians teaching about loving thy neighbor and treating them like you would like to be treated. The thought is cherished but very rarely applied today.

Our people are not without contradiction either. We have tribal leaders and medicine men who tour the country speaking about environmental concerns. They say that the Indi-ans were the first environmentalists, that Indians are the stewards of the land, and Indians hold the answers to many environmental ills. But drive to our villages and look in our back-yards; we're probably the worst polluters. We talk about spirituality and the sacredness of the eagle feather, and yet you see alcohol sold at powwows and companies like Coors sponsoring contests. I've seen women dressed in traditional regalia, adorned with eagle feathers, wearing endorsements for Coors at these contests.

Many of these people will drive a thousand miles to go to a powwow, but they won't drive twenty-five miles to go to their own ceremonies. That's the sort of contradiction that confuses our children. They are having a hard time separating fact from fiction, what's good in theory but not practical in everyday use. It's a good reason to monitor the television pro-grams your children watch. Not just the X-rated programs, but the negative imagery in movies from the forties and fifties that shows Indians walking around grunting, speaking broken English, and never attacking at night because we were too afraid. We couldn't just "walk" in the woods, we had to "lurk." And all the slogans and racial slurs in those movies that are now being dusted off and colorized for the new generation. We're creating a whole new generation of racists because of this kind of television programming.

My most immediate concern is that my elders and traditional people are taken care of in the tribes in Oklahoma. I head a committee called the Repatriation Committee, which is working to provide legislation and legal protection for our elders and our ancestors. We are also working to add three new amendments to the American Indian Religious Freedom Act. There is a general feeling among my people that a lot of our failures today are a direct result of our not taking care of our ancestors. We must get their remains out of repositories across the nation and off display. The sacred items that are in collections in museums or hidden away in basements must be returned. Tribes need these religious artifacts.

I think that there's a relationship between our spiritual health and the disposition of those ancient items. We've been to many different states, and we've effectively passed legislation in seven of them. But it's a continuing effort. Not only do the museums have repositories, but so does the Department of Defense through the Corps of Engineers, so does the navy through the Suitland, Maryland, collection. Suitland, Maryland, redesigned the collection center, called the Cultural Resource Center, that's going to house all these collections. Not only sacred items but burial items as well. I want them to return those items that came out of burials or in and around burial sites. If they have to have them, let them make replicas, but I would prefer they give them back and forget about what they saw.

The government compares repatriation—the return of these skeletal remains to the tribes for proper reburial—to book burning. But to us it is not destructive, it is part of the natural order of life. Once we pass on, we are put into the earth and the acids and chemicals in the earth work on our remains to decompose and become one with the earth again. These nutrients provide life for plants to grow, and the cycle begins again. I agree that there is valuable information about our life and our history. But that information can be obtained by other methods than digging up our ancestors. Talk to our elders, they're the best source. Those bones will not tell you the songs that we sang when our children were ill. They won't tell you the reason we migrated from one part of the country to another on a seasonal basis, or of the move that resulted in the destruction of an entire group, or the assimilation of several groups into one.

All they can get with their expertise is an educated guess. Often, in the archaeological impact surveys that I go on, I am able to tell them a good deal about what they find in those ancient sites because the way that we bury our traditional people today is very similar, if not the same, as we buried them hundreds of thousands of years ago. They could learn a lot more from asking these elders than they do from desecrating the graves of our ancestors. These historical sites are being looted by grave robbers and pot hunters that aren't licensed. Or, by grave robbers that are—like the archaeologists and the anthropologists from universities that come and dig up our ancestors. It's desecration whether they have a license or not.

We need to get the academic community, medical research community, and spiritual community to understand that we deserve the same right as any other American to rest in peace.

The traditions that were passed on through my clan, the Alligator Clan, are the focus of my life right now. But it was a slow process. At first, I was caught up in the excitement of standing up and being considered a revolutionary and an activist. I enjoyed the recognition given to us at powwows, and being invited to speak at universities and colleges about what it feels like to be an Indian in a white society and how to survive all the pressures to assimilate.

When Vern Bellcourt, an early AIM leader and good friend, called me to come to Rapid City for National Indian Civil Rights Day, I had just come back from Washington, D.C., where we had a minor victory there over the recall of a trial concerning the treaties. It was a caravan of hundreds of Indians from all across the country for The Trail of Broken Treaties, which ended at the BIA building in D.C. Promises of accommodations and food and of meetings with key government figures were broken, and we wound up occupying the BIA building. The FBI called it the BIA takeover. We were given sixty-six thousand dollars in cash to leave town, and we did. We took it and left, and patted ourselves on the back. It was during the 1972 presidential elections, and it made the front pages of all the major newspapers across the country.

They called it civil disobedience. We called it protecting our rights of sovereignty and self-esteem according to treaty provisions. A lot of celebrities and civil rights organizations came through for us. No one was prosecuted after that, and I was feeling pretty invincible. I went back to Oklahoma, where I got the call from Vern to meet him in Rapid City to go to Wounded Knee. I thought he was inviting me to some sort of powwow there.

I arrived on the night of twenty-sixth of November. There were probably between 300 and 350 people. When I woke up the next day, I realized we were surrounded by huge tanks with machine guns and radio-equipped, armored personnel carriers and helicopters with the latest technology. I had just gotten out of the army, and I was familiar with the type of equipment they were using—listening devices so they could kill you and you wouldn't even know where the bullet had come from, devices that allowed them to see us but we couldn't see them.

There I was, surrounded by the same army I had just gotten out of. They opened fire on us, and it continued on for several hours. A lot of the Indians were Vietnam veterans that had just put their lives on the line for this very same country that was now trying to kill us. But we were experts at defense; we dug bunkers and built strategically placed shelters. We had help from Mother Nature, too, and from the spirits of the people who had died a hundred years ago; they were there with us.

It got to fifty and sixty below zero with the windchill factor. If you've ever been to Wounded Knee, you know that there are no trees, and the wind really builds up velocity when it comes swooping off those Black Hills. But that helped us, too, not particularly myself, but those people from that part of that country who are used to suffering and starvation. They cut off our food supply, but that didn't affect the people that were used to starving. So that actually helped us, because even though they were highly trained forces, they weren't trained to handle that kind of weather. They had just come out of the jungle and the tropics, and suddenly they were hit by three blizzards. We could walk right past their outposts when we needed more supplies—medicine, ammunition, food—because they were too cold to come out.

The women and the elders were the real reason for us to be there in Wounded Knee. For years our people had been persecuted by Dick Wilson, a petty dictator who was president of the Pine Ridge Tribal Council and his BIA-supported regime, the "goon squad," that catered to mixed bloods and Christian people, and was against the traditional people.

The elders asked us, "What are you going to do about it? What are you going to do about the poor health care here on the reservation? Our people are dying of alcoholism and diabetes, our children are sickly—what are you going to do about it? We have uninvestigated deaths, murders—what are you going to do about it? Are there none among you that have the fighting blood and spirit of those that have gone on—Crazy Horse, and Gall, and Sitting Bull?" We were challenged by these elders and these women that said, "No other people have helped us, you are our last chance, you boys in the American Indian Movement."

I remember times during the occupation I was afraid, but then I would accept that I could die and the fear would disappear. I would think maybe my role in life was to be there to call attention to the predicament that American Indians are in today. I never carried a weapon inside there. A lot of people did. Pete Catches carried his pipe, that was better than any weapon they had. And it worked.

There was a time when we relied on the help of our ancestors. I remember the first time I came to the realization that these spirits are very real, and they were out there, and they had to be dealt with. It was when Leonard Crow Dog performed a Ghost Dance, the first time in a hundred years or so. He did it to bring up protection, for the spirits to help us, the spirits of those that had been killed or murdered in the first Wounded Knee in 1890. We asked for their help, to help us in that same area almost a hundred years later, and it worked.

Dennis Banks and Russell Means stood trial in St. Paul, Minnesota, for their roles as leaders of the Wounded Knee occupation. It was one of the longest trials in history; the prosecution took nine months, the defense one day. Dennis and Russell were finally acquitted on the grounds of government misconduct. The only other historical precedent for such an acquittal was the trial involving the Pentagon Papers.

I remember through the motions that were filed that the attorneys received volumes of transcripts, radio communications of daily shift reports, from different military units that were out there, including reconnaissance teams. And the transcripts were just filled with signs of mysterious figures riding horses. The army would go to pursue them, and they were nowhere in sight; they heard voices and horses and movements that couldn't be explained, interruptions in radio communications. There was a general fear among the people, particularly those that were out on the perimeter; they were radioing those fears and concerns back to their base units, asking them for additional surveillance. They found nothing. I knew that these ceremonies worked, and I knew that the spirits were out there. Never again will I ever question the teachings of these elders that know so much and show me how little I know.

I really feel fortunate that I have these ceremonies that are available to me and my people, and I wish that other people had ceremonies. I guess they do, the Christian people that truly believe in that way, they have a certain degree of comfort and are at peace. To me, another man's religion is as sacred and holy as those given to my people. I learned that from Pete Catches.

# EPILOGUE: RECLAMATION

My travels were at an end. It had been three years since Pete Catches' face had come to me in what I now understood had been a vision. "Sometimes I appear to people as an eagle," he once told me. I had traveled the four directions, from the reserves in Northeast Canada to the Florida Everglades, from Victoria Island, British Columbia to the Arizona desert.

And now it was Sun Dance time, the time "when the moon is still hanging in the sky when the sun rises, and the chokecherries are ripe." Pete invited me to Pine Ridge to the Sun Dance led by his son, Peter, who is also a medicine man.

The Sun Dance grounds stand high on a hilltop overlooking the beauty of the sage-covered hills and tall cottonwoods under an impossibly blue sky. Not all the dancers are Lakota, some have come from other tribes, some are not even Indian. They have all pledged to dance each year for four years. It is a grueling four days of personal sacrifice, of dancing from sunrise to sundown without food or water under a broiling mid-August sun. On the last day a flesh offering is made to *Wakan Tanka*, a prayer for the life of the people. Some say it is a way of reclaiming some part of one's own spirit that's been lost.

The drums and songs begin, the eaglebone whistles sound, and the dancers, sixteen of them, enter the Sun Dance area. The men are bare-chested and wear long tunics, mostly red; the women wear long dresses. They are barefooted and wear wreaths of sage around their heads, their wrists and ankles. Eagle feathers are tied to their hair worn loose and flowing. The sage is for purification, the colors, medicine bags, and shields the dancers wear are chosen by each dancer, everything is *wakan*, sacred.

They dance slowly, steadily around the Sun Dance Pole, their eyes fixed on the sun. A cottonwood tree, selected and ceremonially cut, is planted in a hole into which the heart of a buffalo has been placed. Offerings of tobacco bundles and ribbons the colors of the four directions have been tied to the pole.

I stand underneath the arbor that encircles the dance grounds with the dancers' friends and family members who have come to support them. The ground vibrates with the sound of the drums as we dance in place, small steps, feeling the heartbeat of the earth itself. It pulses through the soles of our feet and flows through us, becoming one with the beat of our own hearts.

I watch as Pete, also in ceremonial dress, kneels at the altar to fill the dancers' pipes, each time raising the tobacco high to the four directions, and speaking his prayers aloud in Lakota. Then he puts his forehead to the ground in such reverence that tears spring to my eyes.

On the third day his son, Peter, came to where I stood. "Dad wants you to go stand in the doorway." I stared blankly at him. "Now?" "Yes, now. Go."

The doorway, an arch of pine boughs, is where the pipes are passed each time they are filled. Uncertainly, I went and stood there, holding the small eagle feather that had been a gift. Pete came dancing toward me, no longer old, his steps strong and sure, arms outstretched like an eagle's, an eagle-feather fan in his hand.

I looked at his face, at the kind and compassionate eyes that had grown so dear to me, as he began to fan my hair and shoulders with the eagle feathers, all the while singing a blessing song in a voice that resounded in the hills to the Grandfather Spirit above.

In my mind I looked back at the distance I had traveled, not just in miles, but in that other dimension that lies between the heart and the mind. Without knowing it at the time, I was crossing a bridge into a world that was once as invisible to me as it is to the majority of white culture. A bridge to yesterday, to the land where the first people walked. They had welcomed me into their homes, shared their stories with me, and I am forever changed.

I looked back to that single instant in my New York City apartment that set me on my journey, and believed with absolute conviction that other forces had plucked me out of that place, that life to stand here at this moment.

Around my neck was the gift that Sara Smith had given me, a silver chain with a small crystal held in place by a tiny silver turtle, a symbol of her clan. Lower on my chest hung the large beaded medicine shield that "Beans" had given me after the Medicine Singing. And there was another gift, a medicine bag, filled with herbs and healing objects that other elders had placed inside. All of these gifts filaments of the Golden Fleece to bring back to the unseeing world.

And I thought about the illness that had beset me while on the journey, and the dream I had had during the worst of it. A man's voice spoke. He said, "You must get well, you have to build a sweat lodge for George Bush." I woke up laughing and couldn't wait to tell Pete, who always enjoys a good laugh. But he was strangely quiet. Then he said, "But that's what you must do. You must build a sweat lodge for all the George Bushes." Strange orders for a girl from Philadelphia who made her home in New York.

My beliefs had all been turned inside out. "Every time you admire something in nature," Vern Harper told me, "it's a prayer to the Creator." And I'd been shown it's possible to stop time by a medicine man who said I must not mention his name lest our schedule-mad world beat a path to his door. I wouldn't swear to it in a court of law, but I think I did it myself one day on the way to the airport. I had had to turn back to get something I'd forgotten and I was going to miss my flight. There was no way in the world I could possibly make it. No way in this world, anyway. So I focused my attention on the other world where time did not exist, the way I'd been shown, and somehow I made my flight with time to spare. And without a speeding ticket.

The elders taught me to trust, so I have stopped questioning the miracles, or analyzing them. I have witnessed healings; more than that I experienced my own. It is a time of reclamation.

# POSTSCRIPT: A FUNERAL

On the first of December, Dan Budnik came to Santa Fe to take my picture for the book jacket. When the last frame was shot and the intense New Mexico sun had begun to cast its cold evening shadow, we thanked each other for our work and hugged our good-byes. But as I got into my car, Dan remembered something. He reached into the back of his Scout and withdrew a large envelope. In it was a print of the portrait of Pete Catches he'd done for the book, one I hadn't seen before. A wave of sadness swept over me as I gazed at a face bearing the expression of a man weeping for his people. Moved, I thanked Dan and drove off with my treasured gift.

The phone was ringing when I walked into my house. It was a call from Pine Ridge, from Cindy Catches, Pete's daughter-in-law. Maybe it was the tone of her voice when she said my name or the fact that she was calling me in the middle of the afternoon, but I held my breath.

"We've been trying to get you all day," she said, her voice sounding small and far away. "Pete died this morning at 3:37." I listened, numb, as she gave me the details. It was only when she began to talk about the instructions he had given, on the manner in which he wished to be buried, that I broke down. He had requested to be buried in the ceremonial shirt I had made for him the summer before.

I had spoken to Pete ten days earlier, just after he had gotten out of the hospital (he had been in poor health ever since his wife, Amelia, had passed away in October). I told him I planned to get up to see him before the heavy snows set in. "Yes, I would like that," he said. Then he added quietly, "I don't expect to make it through the winter." I learned later that the spirits had told him the exact day on which he would make his journey to the ancestors.

It was night when I arrived in Pine Ridge. People were gathered at the house for the "wake." The women were in the kitchen preparing food—enough for the entire Sioux nation, it seemed. Everyone else was in the large room, seated on benches arranged to face the blanket-draped closed coffin. I went in and placed Pete's photograph, which I had framed, on a table next to it. I stood a moment, unable to imagine Pete lying dead inside that coffin. It felt wrong. Shouldn't he be scaffolded high on a hilltop, wrapped in a buffalo robe, as befits a holy man? I was told that was not legal. Not legal? On an Indian reservation? What about the Freedom of Religion Act? I asked Pat Locke, scholar and human rights activist from the Standing Rock reservation in North Dakota, and a dear friend of Pete's. She explained that since the American Indian Religious Freedom Act was passed in 1978, more than fifty religious freedom cases had been lost by various groups. It seemed Pete was not quite free yet.

All night long people filed in to sit, heads bent, deep in their own thoughts and private memories. Some kept an all-night vigil. Outside, men kept watch over the fire that would burn all four days and nights. I went into the kitchen to help, glad for the busywork and the camaraderie of the women who have become my Indian family.

Brother Simon, from the Red Cloud Mission, came in and sat with the others. After a time he stood and led a prayer. I couldn't help but wonder, Is this OK with you, Grandfather? I decided it probably was. Pete believed the Creator saw all people as the many colors in a garden.

Later Kevin Locke came in and played hauntingly beautiful prayer songs on his flute, while Isaac Dog Eagle and Virgil Taken Alive sang.

Morning dawned clear and startlingly bright. I sat outside Amelia's house in the sun to resume my kitchen duties. Other women joined me, and we sat around large vats peeling potatoes and exchanging Pete stories, laughing on this fourth day, the day that Pete's spirit would complete its journey to the spirit world; it must have been his joy we were feeling—to be released finally, from another punishing winter on the reservation. I had brought snapshots I had of us taken the summer before only a few feet from where we now sat—four white women cutting up a buffalo.

Arvol Looking Horse appeared. He had driven down in a terrible snowstorm from Green Grass, more than four hours away in good weather. He said that he had arrived late the night before, after I had left to spend the night at the Brave Hearts, and was among those who kept the all-night vigil. The sight of him renewed my sorrow. Tears flowed again.

At noon we served lunch, assembly-line style, to at least 300 people. They filed past our makeshift buffet table while we filled their plates with beef, soup, potato, egg, and fruit salads, wild rice, baked ham, roast turkey, fry bread, and *wasna,* the traditional Lakota ceremonial dish made from chokecherries.

The burial site Pete had chosen sat high on a hill overlooking his sacred Sun Dance grounds. At two o'clock the four-mile procession through the silent, snow-covered village began. A horse-drawn wooden wagon that bore the coffin was led by four horsemen from the Blackfeet tribe. Behind, cars and pickups carried as many as could fit. Pete's daughter, Pat, Basil Brave Heart's son, Bob, and I crowded into Basil's sturdy truck, and were among the first to reach the top of the long, winding, ice-encrusted hill. From there we watched the steady stream of cars, headlights on, a giant serpent that stretched as far back as the eye could see, broken only when a car skidded sideways.

The rest of the hill had to be climbed in almost knee-deep snow; pallbearers had to use a rope to help them get the coffin to the top where the grave had been dug. Beside it, underneath an arbor of pine boughs, an altar had been built for the medicine objects to be used during the ceremony. A scaffold held all of Pete's clothes and possessions, wrapped in a star quilt bundle that in accordance with Lakota tradition would be burned.

People from tribes in Montana, Minnesota, and Canada had come—and Cree, Chippewa, Navajo, and Lakota and Dakota people were represented. Several white people were there too, paying homage to a man who was deeply honored by many.

Family and friends stood in a circle around the grave, silent and motionless, eyes fixed on the coffin, until the drums shattered the silence, and then, under an immense and unstained sky, the singers cried out the Sun Dance songs that Pete loved. A Lakota man conducting the rites took out his pipe and filled it to the *canupa* song. Then he sprinkled a painting of a man's head, representing Pete, onto the red felt cloth that covered the coffin. He poured four sips of water into the mouth, adding food for sustenance for the journey Pete was about to make. A man holding a white cloth moved among the family members, wiping tears from their faces.

Two of Pete's daughters, standing at the south, held a large, white cloth that was cut with a knife and then quickly torn, releasing in one swift motion Pete's spirit. A loud, happy trill sang out from the crowd, and the fire under the scaffold was lit.

Then, at the very moment the sun began to sink behind the bluish hills beyond the far, quiet valley, a coffin of the most ordinary sort, and holding the body of a most extraordinary man, was gently lowered into the sacred earth he so cherished.